# Dave Miller's

# HOMEBREWING
# GUIDE

## Everything you need to know
## to make great-tasting beer

## Dave Miller

**A Storey Publishing Book**

STOREY

Storey Communications, Inc.
Schoolhouse Road
Pownal, VT 05261

*The mission of Storey Communications is to serve our customers
by publishing practical information that encourages personal independence
in harmony with the environment.*

Edited by Christine P. Rhodes and Elizabeth McHale
Cover design by Greg Imhoff
Cover photograph by Nicholas Whitman
Text design by Cindy McFarland
Text production by Carlson Design Studio, production assistance by Susan
  Bernier
Drawings on pages 5, 7, 21, 23, 75 (bottom), 79, 114, 158, 160, 166, 206
  (top), 216, 268 by Brigita Fuhrmann. Drawings on pages 12, 20 (top and
  bottom), 22 (top and bottom), 24, 25, 31, 75 (top), 78 (top), 93, 138, 143,
  152 by Kay Holmes Stafford. Drawings on pages 78 (bottom), 80 (top
  and bottom), 144, 163, 206 (bottom), 212, 235, 236, 247, 248, 249 by
  Carl F. Kirkpatrick.
Indexed by Northwind Editorial Services

*Printed in the United States by R.R. Donnelley
First Printing, August 1995*

**Library of Congress Cataloging-in-Publication Data**

Miller, David G., 1945–
    Dave Miller's homebrewing guide  :   Everything you need to know to make
great-tasting beer  /  Dave Miller.
            p.        cm.
        "A Storey Publishing book."
        Includes bibliographical references and index.
        ISBN 0-88266-905-2 (pbk.)
        1. Brewing—Amateurs' manuals. I. Title.
    TP570.M53   1995
    641.8'73—dc20                            95-13385
                                        CIP

# Dedication

*To my children, Steve, Tony, Paul, Bart, and Cathy;*
*and to my wife, Diana,*
*my toughest critic and biggest fan.*
*Without them, there would be*
*nothing to celebrate.*

# Table of Contents

1 — Introduction                                                    1

2 — How Beer Is Made                                                4

3 — Getting Started in Homebrewing                                 10

4 — Malts, Adjuncts, and Sugars                                    28

5 — Water and Water Treatment                                      50

6 — Mash Methods — An Overview                                     68

7 — Equipment for Wort Production                                  73

8 — What Happens in the Mash Tun?                                  84

9 — Mashing and Lautering                                         101

10 — Hops                                                         113

11 — Kettles, Wort Coolers, and Other Equipment                  123

12 — What Happens in the Kettle and Wort Cooler?                  128

13 — Boiling, Trub Separation, and Cooling                       135

14 — Yeast                                                        140

15 — Yeast Propagation and Maintenance                           147

16 — Fermentation Methods                                         155

17 — Fermentation and Lagering Equipment                         162

18 — What Happens during Fermentation?                           168

19 — Wort Aeration and Pitching                                  180

20 — Running the Fermentation 186

21 — Maturation and Lagering 192

22 — Beer Clarification 196

23 — Clarifiers, Filters, and Filtration Equipment 201

24 — Clarification and Filtration Techniques 209

25 — Carbonation 214

26 — Beer Carbonation Methods 221

27 — Bottle- and Cask-Conditioned Beers 228

28 — Draft Beer Equipment 234

29 — Draft System Design and Operation 240

30 — Bottled Beer and Bottling 245

31 — Cleaning and Sanitation 251

32 — Cleaners, Sanitizers, and Cleaning Equipment 255

33 — Cleaning and Sanitizing Procedures 260

34 — Beer Evaluation 267

35 — Troubleshooting 275

36 — Beer Styles 288

37 — Recipe Formulation 298

38 — Recipes 305

Metric Conversions 327

Sources 334

Glossary 338

Annotated Bibliography 347

Index 351

# Acknowledgments

I owe a special debt of gratitude to all the homebrewers who have encouraged me by their questions and compliments and inspired me with their enthusiasm for the craft of brewing; in particular, I would like to single out the Saint Louis Brews, my hometown club and a continuing source of inspiration and good fellowship.

Individually I would like to acknowledge my friends George Fix and Byron Burch, who have done so much to advance homebrewing and my own fund of knowledge; and Charlie Papazian, founder of the American Homebrewers Association, who, besides contributing to the ongoing dialogue of homebrewers, created the forum for it in the first place.

**Note:**

The words that appear in *bold italics* are defined in the glossary.

# Introduction

**A**mid the many changes taking place in America at present, one of the most pleasant is a change in the attitude toward beer. Once regarded as a uniform commodity, whose manufacture was the province of large corporations, beer is increasingly regarded as a beverage of great complexity and variety, worth learning about and cultivating an appreciation for. This development has spurred, and in turn fostered, the growth of a new industry in this country — the microbrewing industry, which has grown at a spectacular rate through the early 1990s and shows no signs of slowing down.

Microbrewers are a throwback to an older culture, where quality was the result of individual efforts and the craftsman or craftswoman gave each product a unique character. In the Old World, hundreds of small local breweries still function this way; in America, it is a tradition that we are just beginning to recover.

But behind the microbrewery movement lies a slightly older one: homebrewing, which was long a discredited relic of the Prohibition era but which re-emerged in the 1970s as an effort by a small number of dedicated beer lovers to supply themselves with the type of beer they had fallen in love with in Europe. To them, domestic beers seemed monotonous and imports old and oxidized. The perishable nature of beer, as much as the price of imports, is what forced these pioneers to try their hand at the ancient art.

The phenomenal growth of homebrewing in the past decade has pushed the hobby into the national consciousness. Homebrewers have appeared on national television and radio programs, and have been interviewed by major newspapers. One major American brewing company has paid the hobby the supreme compliment of denigrating homebrew in a nationally run television ad. Such an attack acknowledges that homebrew is, indeed, an alternative to commercial beer; and if it is a real alternative, it must have reached a certain stature, both in popularity and in quality.

Homebrewing is no longer a cult phenomenon. But there are still many people — probably the majority of beer drinkers — who have never tasted home- or microbrewed beer, and do not yet realize that quality as well as variety is quite achievable for the small-scale brewer.

Quality is what this book is about. You can make beer at home that is as good (by whatever criteria you choose) as any beer you can buy. However, to accomplish this goal, you need a practical understanding of brewing, and some knowledge of the science that lies behind it. I have tried throughout this book to convey those two things. The intent is to provide you with both a guide and a reference source as you explore the craft of making beer.

If you are a beginning brewer, I would suggest that you get, in addition to this book, my earlier book *Brewing the World's Great Beers* (Storey Publishing, 1992). That book takes a somewhat different approach, leading you step-by-step through the various techniques that homebrewers use, gradually introducing more elaborate procedures as you grow in confidence and experience. This book is more comprehensive, describing the steps of the brewing process in detail and outlining both alternative procedures and the science behind them.

The impetus for this book was Storey Publishing's suggestion, in late 1993, that I consider revising *The Complete Handbook of Home Brewing,* which was written in 1986–1987. I accepted their offer gladly. I have enjoyed hearing comments from readers of *The Complete Handbook.* Many people have urged me to write about some of the newer advancements and developments in the field. With this volume, I have addressed these issues.

The result, I hope, is a book that is up to date and easy to use, with each chapter standing as a self-contained treatment of its topic. Chapters 2 and 3 contain a description of the brewing process and basic homebrewing instructions, and almost all the rest are a systematic account of the brewer's craft, arranged according to the major steps of the process — wort production, boiling and cooling, fermentation and aging, post-fermentation treatment, and finally, sensory evaluation and troubleshooting. The last two chapters deal with the brewer's art, introducing recipe formulation and giving sample recipes for a number of beer styles.

In writing this book, I have drawn on the experience of many homebrewers. Some are old friends, some I know only as names at the bottom of a letter; but all of them have helped me to keep abreast of this rapidly growing and changing phenomenon of homebrewing. I thank them all, and I hope that they, and you, dear reader, will find my new book helpful in turn, as you pursue your quest for the perfect beer. May your mash never set, and may the dark shadow of pediococci never fall across your fermenters. May your ales be robust and your lagers smooth, and may you enjoy all the rewards this pursuit can bring to mind and spirit. Cheers!

# How Beer Is Made

**B**eer, like wine, is the product of honest, natural processes. Both beverages are created by yeast working in a mixture of sugar and water. The yeast uses the sugar as food for its own growth and energy, and the chief products of this process (fermentation) are ethyl alcohol and carbon dioxide gas. Wine and beer are both dilute solutions of alcohol, but wines are made from sugars that occur naturally in fruit. Thus, winemaking is simply a matter of introducing yeast into fruit juice and letting nature take its course. Beer, on the other hand, derives its alcohol from grain starch. Starch cannot be fermented; it must be chemically converted to sugar before the yeast can take over to complete the transformation. Thus, brewing is the more complex art.

## Malting

Chemically speaking, brewing is a two-stage process. Practically, it also involves two stages, which are usually carried out by different businesses. The steps are *malting* and *brewing*. Malting is

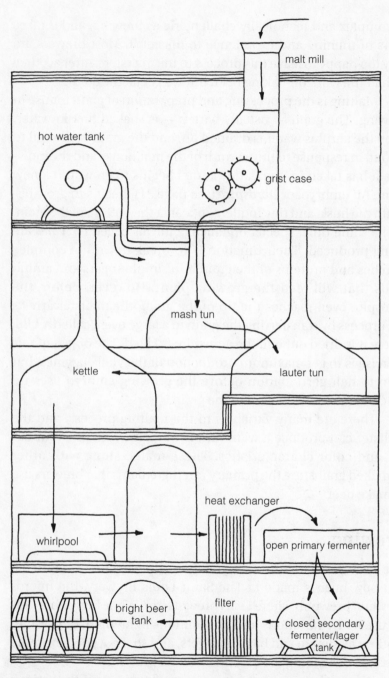

*An illustration of the standard pieces of equipment in a commercial brewery*

as complex and technically challenging as brewing, and it takes years of training and experience to master it. Most brewers are only too happy to leave this process to the maltsters. After all, they do half the work of making beer, but we get all the credit!

Malting is the processing and preparation of grain for use in brewing. The grain — usually barley — is soaked first in water. Then the surplus water is drained off, and the grain is allowed to sprout. In response to the warmth of the malthouse and the moisture it has taken in, the barley kernel begins to grow into a new plant. An embryo, or *acrospire* (see page 31), begins to grow beneath the husk, and tiny rootlets appear at the bottom of the grain. At the same time, special organic chemicals called *enzymes* are being produced. Their function is to break down the complex starches and proteins of the grain into simple sugars and amino acids that will feed the growing plant. However, before the acrospire even reaches the tip of the grain, the maltster arrests the process by transferring the grain to a large oven, called a *kiln,* where it is dried out and the acrospire is killed. The object of this exercise is to get maximum production of the vital enzymes, but then to halt germination before the growing embryo uses up much of the food material in the grain.

There are many variables to the malting process, and the maltster can produce a wide variety of malts, with different flavor and color characteristics. These malts, along with other unmalted grains, are the primary raw ingredients that brewers use to make beer.

## Brewing

The easiest way to introduce you to the brewing process is to tell you how beer is made at The Saint Louis Brewery, the microbrewery/brewpub where I was brewmaster. While bigger breweries use many variations and elaborations in method, our system is about as simple and basic as it gets, and so it is a good example to use in describing the essentials of the process.

We start by weighing out the correct amounts of the various grains for our recipe. Then we mill the malt in a roller mill, which

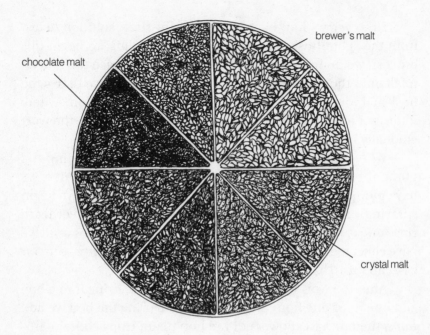

*Brewer's grains can include pale malt, crystal malt, chocolate malt, and flake maize.*

has two large steel rolls driven by a motor. The crushed grain is collected in a large box called a "grist case." There is a valve at the bottom of the grist case which, when opened, allows the grain to flow through a chute into the *mash* tun.

The mash tun is a large stainless steel vessel with a false bottom made of screen material. This screen acts as a large strainer later in the process. To begin the brew session, we start by filling the mash tun with a predetermined amount of hot water. When the screen is covered with water, we open the grain valve and allow the grain and water to mix as they flow into the mash tun. We also stir the mixture — a thin porridge called the *mash* — to assure a uniform consistency and temperature.

If we have set our water temperature correctly, the mash will settle in at about 150°F. We let the mash stand for an hour, during which time the malt enzymes convert all the starches in the grain to sugar. This completes the first chemical transformation.

However, we now have to separate the sugar solution *(wort)* from the spent husks and other remaining solids. To begin this process, we pump wort from the bottom of the mash tun and let it fall onto the surface of the mash. This *recirculation* draws the husk material down against the screen of the false bottom, where it forms a natural filter bed. As recirculation continues, the wort gradually becomes clearer.

When the wort is sufficiently clear, we stop recirculating and pump the wort into the *kettle,* where it will be boiled. After we have pumped as much wort as possible into the kettle, we begin spraying, or *sparging,* the spent grains with hot water, in order to rinse out as much sugar as possible. Sparging continues until we have collected the required amount of wort in the kettle — in our case, about 16 barrels.

After the wort is collected in the kettle, we bring it to a boil and boil it for one hour and 15 minutes. During the boil we add *hops,* the aromatic flowers of the hop plant. Hops contain aromatic oils and bitter resins, and they greatly enhance the aroma of beer while their bitterness balances the sweetness of the finished brew. Hops must be boiled in wort to extract their bitterness.

After the boil is over, we set the wort spinning in a *whirlpool,* which forces all the hops and other solid matter in the wort to form a conical shaped pile on the bottom of the kettle. We are then able to pump the clear wort out. It passes through a cooling device called a *heat exchanger* or *wort chiller* which quickly drops its temperature from near boiling to fermentation temperature (50–70°F).

From the heat exchanger the wort goes to a large tank called a *fermenter,* where yeast is added. The yeast is a pure strain that has been selected for its ability to make good-tasting beer. The yeast ferments the malt sugar in the wort into carbon dioxide and alcohol. This takes from three to seven days. At this point we chill the young beer and allow it to stand from one to three weeks. During this period of cold storage, the beer ferments slowly, most of the yeast falls out of suspension, and, at the same time, carbonation develops and the flavor of the beer matures.

After the period of cold storage, we draw the yeast from the bottom of the fermenter, then pump the beer into *bright beer tanks* (large pressure vessels) from which it may be either kegged or served directly at the bar. Most of our beer is filtered on the way to the bright beer tanks; filtration removes the remaining yeast and yields a bright, clear beer.

# Homebrewing

If you have never brewed beer before, you are probably wondering how it is possible to do it at home. All the references to stainless steel and pressure tanks make it sound like a huge investment is required. Fortunately, that is not necessarily true. While some homebrewers have spent thousands of dollars on their homebreweries, many others have found it possible to make first-rate beer using a far less elaborate setup. Remember that a kettle can be nothing more than a black enamel-coated steel canning kettle; a pressure vessel can be an ordinary beer bottle. A homebrewer does the same things a microbrewer does, but there are many options about how to do them.

Ultimately, it is not the size of your bank account, but your dedication to good beer that will enable you to brew the best. There is no need to settle for mediocre results just because your time and money are limited. Homebrewing has attracted more than its share of adventurous practitioners, and, as a result, tremendous strides have been made in the range of materials and equipment available. If you have the desire, you can get the results.

# 3

# Getting Started in Homebrewing

**The process of brewing** breaks down into a series of steps: wort production, boiling and cooling, fermentation, and finished beer treatment. The first of these steps is the most time-consuming and complex for beginners. Fortunately, it is possible to bypass it by buying prepared *malt extracts*, which are concentrated worts. When working with malt extract, wort production becomes as easy as reconstituting orange juice from frozen concentrate. If you have never brewed before, I recommend starting this way.

Another way to simplify your entry into this hobby is to buy a basic equipment kit from a homebrew supply store. Most large communities now have one or more of these businesses, and many of them also serve the entire country by mail order.

Many equipment kits, especially those available by mail order, offer all the hard-to-find, specialized equipment required. However, some bulky items that are easy to get, such as a boiling kettle, may be omitted for the sake of keeping shipping costs down. A good supplier (local or mail order) will explain exactly what is and is not included, and advise you on obtaining any missing items locally.

Many suppliers also offer kits of ingredients for brewing a number of types of beer. These kits are a far cry from the old "homebrew kits" once offered by malt extract manufacturers, which were nothing more than a can of hopped malt extract syrup and a packet of dry yeast. The suppliers' kits are much more sophisticated, offering a combination of malt extracts, fresh hops, yeast, and sometimes specialty grains, all chosen and tested by experienced brewers to produce a good-tasting and authentic "old world" style of beer. These kits are a viable alternative to the recipes found in this chapter.

If you do not wish to put yourself in the hands of a homebrew supplier, the alternative is to assemble your set of equipment and ingredients yourself. This option may be preferable, especially if you are the intrepid type, and sometimes it is possible to save money by seeking out alternative sources. For those who wish to follow this route, here is a list of equipment needed to begin brewing with malt extract:

| | |
|---|---|
| 1 | 5-gallon enamelware canning pot (boiler) |
| 1 | large stainless steel or wooden spoon |
| 1 | fine nylon mesh bag |
| 1 | 6.5-gallon (or bigger) plastic bucket, preferably with a tight-sealing lid that will accept an airlock (food grade only) |
| 1 | plastic racking tube |
| 1 | plastic racking hose, 5 feet long (fits over racking tube) |
| 1 | 5-gallon glass carboy (a large jug used in water coolers) |
| 1 | plastic airlock and drilled rubber stopper (to fit carboy) |
| 1 | carboy brush |
| 54 | returnable or imported beer bottles, taking pry-off caps |
| 1 | bottle brush |
| 1 | bottle capper |
| 1 | hydrometer and test jar |
| 1 | thermometer with a range from 32°–212°F |
| | Cleaning and sanitizing compounds (homebrew suppliers sell chlorinated trisodium phosphate, an excellent combination cleaner-sanitizer) |

# Basic Homebrewing Equipment

Even this list is not truly complete, because it assumes that you have a standard set of kitchen equipment, including a stove. I have also omitted a few items that may be considered optional. For example, you will need a small scale if you cannot weigh out hops at your local homebrew supply shop.

All the equipment consists of either common household utensils available at hardware and discount stores or specialty items sold at homebrew suppliers. The specialty items are the ones whose names you may not recognize. Their use will be explained in the instructions that follow.

Having assembled your equipment, your next job is to decide upon a recipe, which means choosing a *beer style*. Many readers are familiar with this term from Michael Jackson's books on

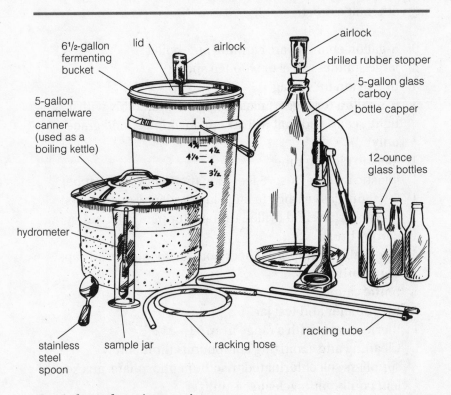

*Basic homebrewing equipment*

the beers of the world. If you are not, the word *style* refers to the combination of characteristics that gives a beer its basic flavor profile. For example, all American lagers have a very light body, have high carbonation but low bitterness, are rather dry, and have a delicate aroma of malt and hops. Brown ales, on the other hand, have a medium body, are rather sweet, are moderately carbonated, and have low-to-moderate bitterness levels.

I recommend British ale styles for beginning brewers. These beers can be brewed successfully from malt extract and fermented with dry yeast. Dry yeasts are easy to work with, and there are several brands available that give good results with these styles of beer. Equally important, these beers ferment at room temperature, eliminating the need for refrigeration. All in all, they are by far the best class of beers to start with, and there are a number of styles from which to choose. One is almost certain to please you.

## Beginners' Recipes

All recipes in this section are formulated for 5-gallon batches.

### Pale Ale

*Pale ale is one of the most popular British beers, and many American microbreweries make examples as well. Pale ale is amber in color, fairly bitter, but balanced by the sweetness of caramel malt.*

| | |
|---|---|
| Malt extract: | 3.3 lbs. British pale, syrup, unhopped; plus 2 lbs. British pale dry, unhopped |
| Specialty malts: | 8 oz. 40 L caramel (crystal) malt |
| Bittering hops: | 1¾ oz. Fuggle or Willamette at 5 percent alpha acid |
| Finishing hops: | 1½ oz. Golding hops at 4 percent alpha acid |
| Yeast: | 2 packets Munton & Fison or Lallemand Windsor or Nottingham, or 1 packet Edme or Whitbread |
| Corn sugar for priming: | ½ cup |

## Brewer's Specifics

Original gravity of the wort: 1.042
Total time of boil: 45 minutes
Add the bittering hops at the beginning of the boil.
Add the finishing hops at the end of the boil.
Terminal gravity at the end of fermentation: 1.007–1.011

# Light Ale

*Light ale is golden to light amber in color, with a milder bitterness and a drier character than pale ale.*

Malt extract: 3.3 lbs. British pale, syrup, unhopped; plus 1 lb. British pale dry, unhopped
Specialty malts: 4 oz. 20 L crystal malt
Bittering hops: 1 oz. Fuggle or Willamette at 5 percent alpha acid
Finishing hops: 1 oz. Golding hops at 4 percent alpha
Yeast: 2 packets Munton & Fison or Lallemand Windsor or Nottingham, or 1 packet Edme or Whitbread
Yeast nutrient: 1 teaspoon
Corn sugar for priming: ½ cup

## Brewer's Specifics

Original gravity: 1.033
Total time of boil: 45 minutes
Add the bittering hops at the beginning of the boil.
Add the finishing hops at the end of the boil.
Terminal gravity: 1.004–1.008

# Brown Ale

*Brown ale is sweet and malty, with a distinct toasty flavor derived from the dark chocolate malt. Bitterness is lower than that of light ale or pale ale.*

| | |
|---|---|
| Malt extract: | 3.3 lbs. British pale, syrup, unhopped; plus 1 lb. British pale dry, unhopped |
| Specialty malts: | 8 oz. 40 L crystal malt, 4 oz. chocolate malt |
| Sugar: | 1 lb. dark brown sugar (add to wort) |
| Bittering hops: | 1 oz. Fuggle or Willamette at 5 percent alpha |
| Finishing hops: | none |
| Yeast: | Two 7-gram packets Munton & Fison or Lallemand Windsor or Nottingham, or 1 packet Edme or Whitbread |
| Yeast nutrient: | 1 teaspoon |
| Corn sugar for priming: | ½ cup |

### Brewer's Specifics
Original gravity: 1.042
Total time of boil: 45 minutes
Add the bittering hops at the beginning of the boil.
Terminal gravity: 1.006—1.010

# Scotch Ale

*Scotch ale is basically a darker, sweeter, heavier version of brown ale. Alcoholic strength is often quite respectable. The use of brown sugar imparts a rum-like flavor.*

| | |
|---|---|
| Malt extract: | 6.6 lbs. British pale, syrup, unhopped |
| Specialty malts: | 1 lb. 40 L crystal malt, 4 oz. chocolate malt |
| Sugar: | 1 lb. dark brown sugar (add to wort) |

Bittering hops:  1½ oz. Fuggle or Willamette at 5
          percent alpha
Finishing hops:  none
      Yeast:  Two 7-gram packets Munton & Fison
          or Lallemand Windsor or
          Nottingham, or 1 packet Edme or
          Whitbread
Corn sugar for priming:  ½ cup

### Brewer's Specifics
Original gravity: 1.055
Total time of boil: 45 minutes
Add the bittering hops at the beginning of the boil.
Terminal gravity: 1.010–1.016

## ——— *Porter* ———

*Porter is a very dark, often almost black brew, with a dry, coffee-like taste derived from the roasted grain that is used. Bitterness is moderate to high.*

Malt extract:  3.3 lbs. British pale, syrup, unhopped;
          plus 2 lbs. British pale dry, unhopped
Specialty malts:  8 oz. roasted barley
Bittering hops:  1¼ oz. Northern Brewer at 8 percent
          alpha
Finishing hops:  none
      Yeast:  2 packets Munton & Fison or
          Lallemand Windsor or Nottingham,
          or 1 packet Edme or Whitbread
Corn sugar for priming:  ½ cup

### Brewer's Specifics
Original gravity: 1.042
Total time of boil: 45 minutes
Add the bittering hops at the beginning of the boil.
Terminal gravity: 1.007–1.011

———————————— *Dry Stout* ————————————

*Stout developed from porter. It is dead black, with a strong, sharp, coffee-like flavor of roasted barley. Dry stout is, as its name suggests, dry in character — the flavor is balanced toward the bitter rather than the sweet side of the scale.*

|  |  |
|---:|:---|
| Malt extract: | 3.3 lbs. British pale, syrup, unhopped; plus 2.5 lbs. British pale dry, unhopped |
| Specialty malts: | 1 lb. roasted barley |
| Bittering hops: | 1½ oz. Northern Brewer at 8 percent alpha |
| Finishing hops: | none |
| Yeast: | Two 7-gram packets Munton & Fison or Lallemand Windsor or Nottingham, or 1 packet Edme or Whitbread |
| Corn sugar for priming: | ½ cup |

### Brewer's Specifics

Original gravity: 1.048
Total time of boil: 45 minutes
Add the bittering hops at the beginning of the boil.
Terminal gravity: 1.010–1.014

———————————— *Sweet Stout* ————————————

*Sweet stout resembles dry stout, although the bitterness level is lower. Some caramel sweetness is often in evidence and this balances the bitterness of the hops and the roasted barley.*

|  |  |
|---:|:---|
| Malt extract: | 3.3 lbs. British pale, syrup, unhopped; plus 2 lbs. British pale dry, unhopped |
| Specialty malts: | 8 oz. 60 L crystal; plus 8 oz. roasted barley |
| Bittering hops: | 1 oz. Northern Brewer at 8 percent alpha |

Finishing hops: none
Yeast: 2 packets Munton & Fison or
Lallemand Windsor or Nottingham,
or 1 packet Edme or Whitbread
Yeast nutrient: 1 teaspoon
Corn sugar for priming: ½ cup

### Brewer's Specifics

Original gravity: 1.045
Total time of boil: 45 minutes
Add the bittering hops at the beginning of the boil.
Terminal gravity: 1.008–1.011

# Notes on the Recipes

All recipes follow the method outlined below. The method is geared to the use of the equipment listed earlier in this chapter. Many other brewing methods are possible, and if you have purchased a set of ingredients and equipment assembled by a homebrew supplier, the instructions provided may differ from these. In general, you will get better results by following the advice of the supplier regarding the use of their own equipment. Also, many steps will be simplified or eliminated, such as the calculation of hop quantities. The one point I urge you not to skimp on is cleaning and sanitation, as this is crucial regardless of what equipment you are using.

Regarding hop quantities: the numbers given in the recipes are based on the use of pelletized hops. Do not substitute whole hops. Most of the recipes call for hops of a certain type and a certain bitterness (alpha acid) specification. You should substitute types only on the advice of an experienced brewer. You will find that the hops you buy in most cases will not match the bitterness specified. This means that you will have to adjust the amount in order to compensate. For example: If your Fuggle hops contain 4 percent alpha acid, whereas the recipe calls for Fuggle hops at 5 percent, you should use more hops than the recipe calls for. In a recipe calling for 2 ounces, you would add 2½ (2 x ⁵⁄₄ = 2.5).

The specifications list an *original gravity* and a **terminal gravity**. These are measurements of the specific gravity of the wort. Water with sugar dissolved in it has a higher specific gravity than plain water. As the yeast ferments that sugar, it converts it to alcohol, which has a lower specific gravity than water. Thus, as the wort ferments into beer, the specific gravity will drop. Original gravity is the specific gravity of the wort just before or after the yeast is pitched; terminal gravity is the specific gravity of the beer when fermentation has ended. Taking gravity readings is not absolutely essential for a beginning brewer, but you should get in the habit of doing it right from the start. The gravity readings will tell you a lot about your fermentations and are an excellent indicator of the health of your yeast. They also make it possible to estimate the alcohol content of your beer if you are interested.

## The Basic Step-by-Step Method

**1** *Preparing the Ingredients.* The night before your brew session, put a couple of gallons of tap water in a large pot and bring to a boil on your kitchen stove. Boil for 15 minutes uncovered. This will remove all chlorine. Turn off the heat, cover the pot tightly, and let the water cool overnight to room temperature. This will become your reserve supply of brewing water for topping up your wort to the final volume.

On brewing day, begin by heating your syrup so it will pour easily. Fill your kitchen sink with hot tap water, preferably 140°F or more, and immerse the can of malt extract syrup in it for an hour or so. Then crush the specialty grain(s) on a hard, flat surface, using a rolling pin or a champagne bottle. Put the crushed grains into a nylon mesh bag. Then draw 3½ gallons of cold tap water into your kettle and set it on the stove. Turn the heat on full and heat the water to about 150°F. Toss in the grain bag and let it steep for 15 minutes. Then resume heating, stirring continuously and checking the temperature often. When the water reaches 170°F, remove the grain bag. Keep the boiler covered and the heat on full until the water comes to a boil; then turn the heat off.

**2** *Making Extract Wort.* To make the wort, transfer about a gallon of the boiling-hot brewing water to a large pot. Open the can of malt extract and empty it into your boiling kettle. Stir thoroughly — make sure there is no lump of thick syrup sitting on the bottom of the kettle. Only when you are sure that the syrup is thoroughly dissolved should you reset the heat under the boiler to maximum. Use some of the hot water you set aside to rinse out the syrup container,

*Making extract wort: add malt extract to hot water in the boiling kettle to make extract wort.*

adding the rinsings to your brew kettle. Use another portion to dissolve the dry extract (if called for), and stir it into the kettle as well.  Note: Make sure there is about a gallon of headspace in your kettle, as the wort will foam up as it comes to a boil. Then cover the kettle, but not completely — leave an opening of about an inch at the front so that you can observe the wort as it comes to a boil.

**3** *Boiling the Wort.* Keep an eye on the wort. It may seem like a watched kettle never boils, but an unwatched kettle always boils over and makes a terrible mess. When the foam wells up, remove the kettle lid and, if necessary, stir the wort or spray with water to keep the foam from flowing over the sides. As soon as your wort has come to a good rolling boil, add the first lot of hops and stir them in.

spoon

*Add hops to the boiling wort as soon as the wort comes to a boil.*

In some cases, the wort may not boil unless it is partially or entirely covered. In this case, the best that can be done is to partially cover the kettle, if that will allow a rolling boil, or stir constantly, if it will not. The agitation provided by the rolling action is important, but you cannot cover the kettle completely.

**4** *Stirring in the Finishing Hops.* Boil the wort with the hops for 45 minutes. At the end of this time shut off the heat, stir in your finishing hops, and cover the kettle. Fill a bathtub or large sink with cold water, and place the kettle in the sink to cool it for 30 minutes. Depending on the quantity and temperature of the water, you will have to change it one or more times as the wort cools. While you wait, clean the fermenting bucket with chlorinated trisodium phosphate and rinse thoroughly. Also clean the lid, and put it over the fermenting bucket.

*Adding the finishing hops*

To read the temperature of the wort in the kettle, clean and sanitize your stirring spoon and thermometer with chlorinated trisodium phosphate, then rinse well. Stir the wort while holding the thermometer in it. You are looking for a temperature of about 70°F. If the wort is still warmer than this, cover the kettle, change the cooling water, and recheck in 10 minutes or so. Remember that each time you check the temperature you must re-sanitize your thermometer and spoon. Also, be sure to keep the kettle covered except during temperature checks.

**5** *Preparing the Yeast.* At the end of wort cooling you should prepare your yeast by rehydrating it. Sanitize a pint measuring cup, rinse thoroughly, and add a cup of warm water. Adjust the water temperature carefully to 95°–105°F by adding hot or cold water as needed. Pour off any excess. Tear open the yeast

## Sanitizing Equipment

*Bottle brush (left) and carboy brush. Note the bend in the bristle section of the carboy brush.*

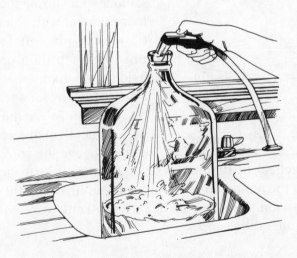

*Rinsing out a carboy in the kitchen sink using a sprayer. Add 2 tablespoons of chlorine bleach to one gallon of water to sanitize your equipment. Utensils and bottles should be immersed in this sanitizing solution for ten minutes. Remember: Unless a surface is clean, it cannot be sanitized.*

packets and add the yeast. Stir with a clean, sanitized spoon, cover, and let the yeast stand for at least 10 minutes before use.

**6** *Allowing Solid Particles to Settle.* Particles settle in the whirl-pool. A stainless steel scrub pad can be used as a screen to keep hops from being drawn off. When the wort is cooled, take the kettle out of its water bath and set it on a table. Give it a quick but vigorous stir with your clean, sanitized spoon. This will set all the solid particles spinning in a whirlpool, and after about 10 minutes they will settle in a mound in the bottom of the kettle. Place the fermenting bucket on the floor beneath the kettle, assemble the racking tube and hose, and set the bottom of the racking tube in the kettle at the rim, away from the mound of solids. Holding the racking tube in place with one hand, place the end of the hose to your mouth and give a quick suck to start the siphon going. Siphon the wort into the fermenter, tipping the kettle at the end to get as much clean wort out as you can.

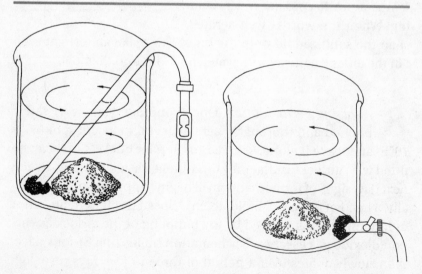

*A quick, vigorous stir of the wort with your clean, sanitized spoon will create the whirlpool, which will allow the solid particles to settle.*

**7** *Aerating the Wort.* Add cooled, boiled water to make up the volume of wort to the required volume of 5 gallons. Then stir in your rehydrated yeast slurry, and continue to stir vigorously for 5 minutes. Repeat this stirring three more times at 10-minute intervals. The idea here is to thoroughly aerate (incorporate air into) the wort. Yeast requires oxygen for growth, so it is very important to give it lots of air in order to get a quick-starting, vigorous fermentation.

During the aeration, you can clean and sanitize your hydrometer and test jar and take a specific gravity reading. Most hydrometers come with good instructions, including a table to show you how to correct for temperature. Record the gravity reading. When the wort is well aerated, snap the sanitized lid onto the bucket to make an airtight seal. Fill the airlock halfway with water, and fit it into the hole.

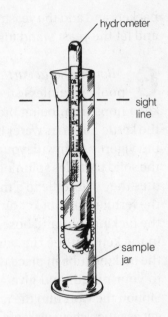

*Reading the specific gravity of the wort. Note the sight line.*

**8** *Allowing Fermentation.* Once you have your wort safely pitched and thoroughly aerated, set it in a cool spot (65°–70°F) and leave it alone. One reason I prefer buckets that can be fitted with airlocks is that they discourage casual peeking. By the next day, signs of fermentation will begin to appear, and, eventually, a head of foam will build up. In a closed fermenter, the onset of fermentation is marked by the bubbling of the airlock as carbon dioxide gas escapes. Fermentation builds to a furious pace, then slowly abates over a period of three to five days (usually). With an airlock, you can judge that fermentation is over when the bubbling is down to once or twice each minute. With an unsealed fermenter, you will have to judge by appearances.

**9** *Racking the Fermented Beer into the Carboy.* Sanitize your equipment (yet again!), and rack the beer off the old decaying yeast. Racking is simply a transfer by siphon that is done slowly and gently, so as not to stir up any of the stuff that has settled on the bottom of your fermenter. Be careful not to splash or introduce air into the beer. If your carboy is not completely full, you may want to top it up with cool, boiled water. Fill or refill and fit

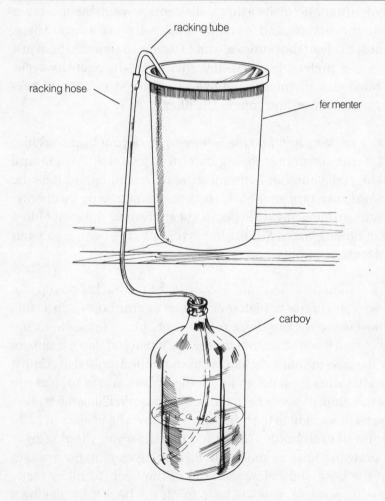

*Racking the fermented beer into the carboy*

the airlock, and let the beer settle out for at least 5 days — longer if fermentation is still apparent. During this secondary fermentation the beer should be kept in a cool spot, ideally around 55°F.

**10** *Sanitizing Your Equipment.* Relax; we are finally coming to the end. While your beer ferments, you should be getting your bottles clean and sanitary. Probably the easiest way to loosen labels and deposits is to soak the bottles for several hours in a large tub or sink of warm water to which you have added a cup of automatic dishwasher detergent. A windshield scraper helps remove labels, and the bottle brush will prove its worth here. It is best to clean the bottles ahead of time and sanitize them just before use, preferably in a dishwasher using the heat-dry cycle. You must also chemically sanitize your fermenter bucket, racking tube and hose, and your bottle filler.

**11** *Racking Beer into the Fermenter.* Rack your beer back into the fermenter, being careful to avoid splashing and bubbles. Take another hydrometer reading and record it as the **terminal gravity** of your beer. Then, make up a syrup by dissolving your priming sugar (the corn sugar given in the recipe) in a pint of boiling water. Stir the hot syrup into the beer, gently but for at least 2 minutes.

**12** *Siphoning Beer into Bottles.* Place the bucket on top of a refrigerator or high shelf and set out the bottles on a table below. Fit the racking hose to the tube, place the tube in the bucket, and if possible cover the bucket. When you start the siphon, have the hose in your right hand with your thumb poised to crimp it about 10 inches from the end. Start the siphon, and as soon as you get a mouthful of beer, crimp the hose and begin filling the bottles. If you fill them right to the brim, you will leave a headspace of 1.5 to 2 inches in each bottle. This is too much, so you should slowly withdraw the hose as the bottle fills, being careful, however, to keep the hose end below the level of the beer. To fill as many bottles as possible, you will have to tilt the bucket by placing a book under the bottom.

**13** *Filling Bottles for Fermentation.* Some headspace is required as a cushion for the gas produced in the bottle during fermentation. However, you want as little air (oxygen) in that headspace as possible. To minimize it, you can set the caps on the bottles and let them sit uncrimped for 15 minutes or so. The corn sugar will begin fermenting as soon as it is added to the beer, and the evolving carbon dioxide will tend to push the air out of the headspace ($CO_2$ is heavier than air). Finally, crimp the bottlecaps, rinse the bottles off, and let them dry while you clean up. Put the cases in a dark spot at room temperature, and let them sit for a few days. Then move the beer to a cooler spot to allow carbonation to develop. The bottle fermentation is very quick, but it takes at least two weeks for the carbonation to dissolve into the beer.

**14** *Decanting Bottled Beer into a Glass.* Homebrew made by this method has a layer of yeast at the bottom of the bottle, so when it is time to try a bottle you will have to decant it carefully into a glass. Select a glass somewhat larger than your bottle size to allow for the head of foam.

If you can wait it out, bottle-carbonated beer usually tastes better after the yeast has dropped to the bottom, leaving clear brew to be decanted. In a few styles of beer, such as wheat beers, a yeasty taste is part of the flavor, but for these mainstream British ale styles clear beer is preferable.

In sampling your first batch of beer, you should not expect it to taste exactly the way you want it to taste. You may find the bitterness is too high or too low, for example. That is the beauty of homebrewing: you are free to make your beer taste just the way you want it. It is better, though, not to make too many changes at one time, because you will never be able to tell what any particular change had on the beer's flavor. Stick with one recipe and fine-tune it until it suits you. Then you will be ready to branch out and eventually work in all your desired adjustments.

# 4

# Malts, Adjuncts, and Sugars

**I**n this chapter I will describe the various materials that the brewer can use to make up the wort. You have already used several of them in the beginners' recipes, and you know what a tremendous variety of colors and flavors they can bring to your beers. Now it is time to delve into how and why they are made, and to get a better understanding of what each of these materials can do for you.

## Pale Malts

The main ingredient in beer is barley malt, which homebrewers often call "grain malt" to distinguish it from malt extract. There are many types and varieties of grain malt, but the most important one, which constitutes the majority of the grain bill in most styles of beer, is pale malt, which American maltsters often call brewers' malt. Even though very few brewers make their own malt, you should know how this most fundamental ingredient is made.

## The Malting Process

In this section I will describe the centuries-old method of malting grain called *floor malting.* This method is nearly obsolete, but it separates the various steps clearly and is easy to follow.

The first step is to soak the grain in a vat, or *cistern,* located at one end of the malthouse. This soaking, or *steeping,* takes two or three days, and during this period the water must be changed several times. This is because the barley husk is covered with bacteria that will begin to ferment some of the grain material, thus souring the steep water and interfering with the subsequent development of the embryo. During the steep, the moisture content of the barley rises from around 12 percent to over 40 percent: the exact figure depends on the type of barley being malted and other factors.

After the desired moisture level is attained, the steep water is drained off for the last time. The barley is allowed to sit for six to ten hours before being removed from the cistern and cast into a heap, or *couch,* on the malting floor adjacent to the cistern. The grains then begin to germinate, and the growth and attendant biochemical changes generate considerable heat. Germination also requires a continuous supply of oxygen; without it, the grain would literally suffocate. For these reasons, the volume or *piece* of germinating barley is spread out on the floor and then turned periodically with wooden shovels. Turning aerates the grain and permits heat to escape. Traditionally malthouses are kept cool, around 55°F, yet even so the temperature of the piece may quickly rise to 65° or 70°F as germination proceeds. It is usually necessary to spread out, or thin the piece during turning, in order to control the buildup of heat.

As the piece is repeatedly turned and thinned, it is moved along the malting floor toward the other end of the malthouse, where the kiln is located. The journey, which is the germination phase of malting, may take six to ten days. The final step in making malt is to load the wet green malt into the kiln for drying. At first, the temperature of the kiln is kept very low. Later, when the grain is almost dry, the enzymes are able to withstand more heat, and the temperature is raised for *curing,* which develops the flavor and color.

As you can see, traditional floor malting takes a long time. For economic reasons, maltsters have worked hard over the last century to automate and speed up the process. Clearly, the less labor and time are required, the lower the cost of the malt. Several totally automated malting systems have been invented. Most malting is now done in revolving drums, which eliminates the hand labor of turning the piece. Variations have also been introduced in the steeping process to aerate the grain while it is absorbing water; this hastens the onset of germination. Other innovations include the use of higher temperatures and hormones (the most popular is *gibberellic acid)* to accelerate germination. This sprouting process is what causes the production of enzymes and the accompanying changes in the grain that are called *modification.*

## Modification

During germination, the embryonic barley plant, or *acrospire,* begins to grow. It pushes its way from the bottom of the grain along the dorsal side (the side opposite the crease) just beneath the husk. At the same time, tiny rootlets appear and grow out of the bottom of the grain. From the brewer's standpoint, the most important changes take place within the *endosperm* — the non-living part of the grain where food for the embryonic plant is stored. The endosperm is mostly starch, but prior to germination it is very hard and is appropriately described as *steely.* As the acrospire grows, complicated chemical changes are triggered that result in the production of numerous enzymes that are organic catalysts. Enzymes are capable of altering molecules by forming or breaking chemical bonds. The changes in malting are mostly breakdowns, and the end result is that the starches and proteins in the endosperm are reduced in size and complexity. These changes are termed modification. When malt is well modified, the steely endosperm becomes soft and friable. Maltsters test for this by biting the grain to see if it yields easily. If the grain is easy to chew, it is termed *mealy,* and what brewers want is a mealy, fully modified malt. Modification proceeds from the bottom (rounded end) of the grain up toward the pointed tip, and steely tips are the sign of a malt that is not fully modified.

In general, modification of the endosperm correlates with growth of the acrospire, and one traditional measure of modification is the length of the barley embryo inside the kernel. It is usually considered desirable for the acrospire to have grown to between ¾ and the full length of the grain. However, this test is not reliable. Differences in the strain of barley being malted and the malting method employed can greatly influence the degree of growth that is needed before the endosperm is fully modified. Thus the steely/mealy chewing test is still the most reliable one.

Modification is important for several reasons. First, it determines whether the grain can be crushed properly. Second, soft friable malt starch is easily broken down to sugars by the enzymes

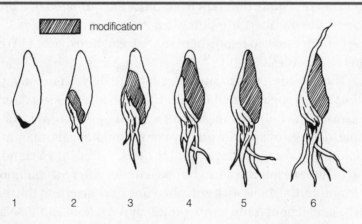

*Modification and growth of acrospire and rootlets during malting. 1) No modification. 2) Rootlets first appear and acrospire begins to grow; modification commences at bottom of grain. 3) Acrospire about half the length of the kernel; modification continues upward and outward. 4) Acrospire about ¾ length of the kernel; modifiation almost complete. Only tip remains hard and "steely." 5) Acrospire fully grown: full modification. 6) Acrospire overgrown: germination has gone too far.*

*(amylases)* formed during germination. That is why brewers want fully modified malt. They also want a high quota of enzymes, and that also correlates with modification to some extent. However, other factors, including the type of barley used and the final kilning temperature, are even more important to the enzyme content of the malt. The higher the temperature at which the malt is kilned, the more of its enzymes will be destroyed.

## Malt Specifications

Many tests have been developed to measure the various properties of malt and thus aid the brewer in using it to the best advantage. Most of these numbers are derived by making a *standard mash* — that is, grinding a specified weight of malt in a specified way, then mixing it with a specified amount of distilled water and holding it at certain temperatures for a standard time. The mash conditions are quite different from those encountered in a brewery, and the numbers are purely for comparison. Brewers learn by experience how to relate them to what can be expected in their own mash kettles.

The most important numbers have to do with *extract,* that is, the yield of sugar from the malt. This can be expressed directly, in terms of the units of measurement used by the brewer (for example, degrees of specific gravity per pound per gallon) or as an absolute percentage of dry weight to be extracted into a standard mash. This measurement can be taken under different conditions; for example, the malt can be crushed fine or coarse, and the mash can be cold (about room temperature) or hot (about 150°F). Naturally, these conditions give very different results. Finally, comparisons can be made, for example, the difference between the yield of a fine- versus a coarse-grind hot-water mash. Fine-grind mashes always yield more sugar, but the less the difference is, the better modified the malt. Similarly, hot-water mashes always yield more sugar than the cold-water varieties, but the closer the numbers are, the better the modification. (Cold-water mashing essentially measures the amount of sugar formed during malting, and the more there is of this, the greater modification and cold-water extract will be.) However, if you are just looking for an indication of how much sugar the malt will yield in your mash kettle, the only number you need to look at is the coarse-grind, hot-water extract. These are the conditions under which real mashing takes place.

Another important specification of malt is the *diastatic power,* which is a measurement of its enzyme content. *Diastase* is a collective name for all the enzymes involved in the conversion of starch to sugar during the mash. Malts with high diastatic power will convert faster and are also capable of converting additional starch besides that contained in the malt itself. This is an extremely useful characteristic, as it allows the use of unmalted cereal grains, such as rice or corn, in the mash tun. Diastatic power is usually measured in degrees Lintner.

Another important set of numbers deals with the *nitrogen* or *protein content* of the grain. Protein contains nitrogen, and starch does not; chemically, it is simpler to measure the percentage by weight of nitrogen in the malt rather than the total amount of the many proteins. By convention, the total protein content is assumed to be 6.25 times the total nitrogen content. Soluble nitrogen is often measured separately; this refers to the amount of nitrogen that exists in soluble form, meaning amino acids and very small protein molecules. The greater the modification of the malt, the higher will be the proportion of soluble nitrogen. Protein is also important because it is largely responsible for the hazes in finished beer. Other things being equal, the lower the total protein or nitrogen content, the less you have to worry about haze; likewise, the better the protein modification (as expressed by a high percentage of soluble nitrogen), the less haze there should be.

Another specification of considerable interest is color. This reflects the degree of curing given in the kiln. Curing affects both color and flavor, but there is no way of quantifying the latter, and so the color specification is perhaps our only clue to how the malt was cured and, therefore, what type of beer it is suited for. In America, color is measured in degrees Lovibond; the rest of the world uses European Brewing Convention (EBC) units. Both of these scales compare the standard wort (which is made by

| *Typical Malt Analysis* | Assortment | | | H$_2$O | Color | Protein | | |
|---|---|---|---|---|---|---|---|---|
| | 7/64 | 6/64 | 5/64 | % | ASBC | Sol | Tot | S/T |
| | +/-5 | +/-5 | +/-3 | +/-0.3 | Deg.Lov. | +/-0.2 | +/-0.5 | +/-2 |

## Schreier

(Sheboygan, WI)

| | | | | | | | | |
|---|---|---|---|---|---|---|---|---|
| SMC 2-Row Pale | 70 | 20 | 10 | 4.0 | 1.4– 2.0 | 5.4 | 12.5 | 43.0 |
| SMC 6-Row Pale | 45 | 40 | 15 | 4.0 | 1.5 – 2.1 | 5.6 | 13.0 | 43.0 |
| SMC Caramel 10 | 40 | 40 | 20 | 5.5 | 8 – 12 | 5.6 | 13.0 | 43.0 |
| SMC Caramel 20 | 40 | 40 | 20 | 3.5 | 17 – 23 | 5.6 | 13.0 | 43.0 |
| SMC Caramel 30 | 35 | 40 | 20 | 3.0 | 26 – 34 | 5.6 | 13.0 | 43.0 |
| SMC Caramel 60 | 40 | 40 | 20 | 3.0 | 55 – 65 | 5.6 | 13.0 | 43.0 |

## De Wolf-Cosyns

(Imported from Belgium)

| | | | | | | | | |
|---|---|---|---|---|---|---|---|---|
| DWC Pale Ale | 79 | 19 | 2 | 3.6 | 2.7 – 3.8 | 4.7 | 11.0 | 43.1 |
| DWC Pilsen | 77 | 19 | 4 | 3.0 | 1.4 – 1.8 | 4.9 | 10.0 | 48.6 |
| DWC Wheat | | | | 3.6 | 1.6 – 2.0 | 4.5 | 11.3 | 40.3 |
| DWC Munich | 75 | 23 | 22 | 3.0 | 5 – 7 | 4.8 | 11.7 | 41.3 |
| DWC Aromatic | 61 | 34 | 5 | 2.6 | 17 – 21 | 4.7 | 11.3 | 41.1 |
| DWC Caramel Pils | 40 | 51 | 9 | 7.3 | 4 – 8 | | 11.5 | |
| DWC Caravienne | 63 | 28 | 8 | 5.6 | 19 – 23 | | 9.6 | |
| DWC Caramunich | 80 | 15 | 4 | 3.6 | 53 – 60 | | 11.2 | |
| DWC Special B | 48 | 37 | 13 | 5.5 | 75 – 150 | | 10.4 | |
| DWC Biscuit | 60 | 34 | 6 | 3.9 | 23 – 26 | | 10.5 | |
| DWC Chocolate | 36 | 54 | 9 | 4.8 | 375 – 450 | | 11.1 | |
| DWC Black Malt | 50 | 44 | 5 | 4.2 | 525 – 600 | | 11.1 | |
| DWC Roasted Barley | 79 | 20 | 0 | 5.6 | 450 – 600 | | 11.4 | |

Used with permission of Schreier Malting Company, Minneapolis, MN.

| D.P. | Extract | | F – C | Alpha | Conversion | Mash | Filtration | Clarity |
|---|---|---|---|---|---|---|---|---|
| Dg. Lint. | FG | CG | | Amylase | Time | Odor | Speed | Degree |
| +/-10 | Dry Min | | Max | +/-5 | Min | | | Visual |
| 1208 | 1.0 | 80.0 | 1.5 | 50 | 5 | Aro | Norm | Clear |
| 150 | 79.0 | 77.5 | 1.5 | 40 | 5 | Aro | Norm | Clear |
| 10 | na | na | na | 5 | 15 – 20 | V Aro | Norm | Clear |
| 0 | na | na | na | 0 | 15 – 20 | V Aro | Norm | Clear |
| 0 | na | na | na | 0 | na | V Aro | Norm | Clear |
| 0 | na | na | na | 0 | na | V Aro | Norm | Clear |
| 60 | 80.8 | 79.3 | 1.5 | 23 | 10 – 15 | Aro | Slow | Sl Hazy |
| 105 | 82.0 | 79.8 | 2.2 | 48 | 10 – 15 | Aro | Norm | Sl Hazy |
| | 83.5 | 82.3 | 1.2 | | 25 – 35 | Norm | Norm | Sl Hazy |
| 50 | 80.9 | 80.0 | 0.9 | 20 | 10 – 15 | Aro | Slow | Clear |
| 30 | 79.3 | 77.8 | 1.5 | 8 | 15 – 25 | V Aro | Slow | Clear |
| | 76.8 | | | | 15 – 20 | V Aro | Slow | Clear |
| | 77.7 | | | | 10 – 15 | V Aro | Slow | Clear |
| | 75.9 | | | | 15 – 20 | Aro | Slow | Dark |
| | 68.9 | | | | 15 – 20 | Aro | Slw | Dark |
| | 79.3 | | | | 15 – 20 | Sl Burnt | Slow | Sl Hazy |
| | 68.1 | | | | na | Burnt | Slow | Dark |
| | 68.2 | | | | na | Burnt | Slow | Dark |
| | 68.8 | | | | na | Burnt | Slow | Dark |

centrifuging the standard mash) with a series of discs of colored glass; both are arranged so that the higher the number, the darker the wort made from a given amount of the malt will be.

## Pale Malt Types

The following malts are all kilned at low temperatures and, if used by themselves, will produce a beer that we Americans would think of as pale — that is, yellow in color. Such malts constitute the majority of the *grist* (the total amount of all grains) in many dark beers as well.

*Six-row brewers' malt* is named after the type of barley from which it is made. The grains grow in six rows on the ear, and if viewed from the end, form an asterisk. Six-row barley has a high protein content and a thick husk that is rich in tannins. Tannins are complex organic substances that have a drying, astringent quality in the mouth: a puckering sensation like tea. Tannins and proteins cause haze in beer. However, 6-row malt is also very high in enzymes. One reason American beers are light in body is that American brewers long ago learned that the best way to use 6-row malt is to make their beer with a substantial amount (25–50 percent) of unmalted grains, chiefly corn and rice. These cereals contain almost no tannin or protein, and so, by using them, brewers can drastically reduce the haze potential of their beer while maintaining its strength. The high enzyme level assures conversion of the cereal starches in the mash kettle.

*Two-row brewers' malt* is similar to 6-row in that it is kilned at low temperatures to preserve enzyme activity and minimize color. However, it is made from 2-row barley, which means, as you would expect, that the grains grow in only two rows on the ear. Two-row barley is somewhat lower in protein than 6-row, but the specification will vary from one strain to another. Also, 2-row malt is often said to have a low enzyme content, but, again, this depends on the barley strain and on the malting method, especially the kilning. American 2-row malt is slightly lower in enzymes than 6-row but is still capable of converting a good percentage of additional starch. Two-row malt has a thinner husk than 6-row, and thus it has a lower tannin content. Beers brewed from it should have less astringency, and most super-premium American beers, which are made with a higher proportion of malt in the recipe, are made from 2-row barley. In Germany, where all-malt beers are the rule, it is the only type employed in making beer.

*Pale ale malt* is the standard British malt, and it is quite different from American brewers' malt. It is very fully modified and undergoes a long kilning. The modification means it has a lower haze potential than American malt, but the kilning means it has fewer enzymes. Another result of the long kilning is that ale malt has very little s-methyl methionine and dimethyl sulfoxide — two chemical compounds that, upon heating, are converted into *dimethyl sulfide,* also referred to as DMS. This is what gives that sweet creamed-corn aroma to a lager mash. Many pale lagers have perceptible amounts of DMS, but it is never noticeable in British ale.

Please remember that throughout this discussion I have referred to British ale. Most American microbreweries use domestic brewers' malt for their ales, and most Belgian and German ales are likewise made from malts that closely resemble our 2-row malt.

## High-Kilned Malts

Pale malts are used for the bulk of the grist in most styles of beer, whether light or dark. However, there are some malts cured at higher temperatures (around 220°F rather than 175°F) that still retain some diastatic power and can be used as the basis of a recipe. They can also be blended with pale malts if desired. They impart a deeper color and a fuller malt flavor and aroma to the finished beer. However, they should not be counted on to convert additional starch.

*Mild ale malt* is kilned at a little higher temperature than pale ale malt and will give a golden- to amber-colored wort. These days, most mild ales are dark and require the addition of special malts. Some experts feel that in such brews the difference in flavor between mild and pale ale malt is not noticeable.

There are several types of high-kilned mild ale malts made in Central Europe. *Vienna malt* has a sweet aroma and gives a golden- to amber-colored brew. *Munich malt* is more aromatic and darker. The difference between the two is that, for Munich malt, curing is begun while the grain is still slightly damp. This causes some starch conversion, and the sugars are then caramelized to give a rich aroma and flavor. Some malting companies produce an even darker grade of high-kilned malt called "aromatic."

Homebrewers need to understand that terms such as *Munich* and *Vienna* are not exact. Color specifications and flavor characteristics vary considerably from one brand to another, and you cannot substitute without altering the finished beer, sometimes drastically. Much more than with brewers' malt, you need to stick with the same malt if you want repeatable results.

## Home Kilning

It is possible to cure pale malt in an oven to make a reasonable approximation of Vienna malt. In fact, a whole range of special malts can be made in this way, which can give your beers literally unique flavors. This topic is beyond the scope of a general book on homebrewing, and I refer interested readers to the sources listed in the bibliography. However, I do have a few hints on making a home-cured version of Vienna malt.

First, you will need some sort of curing frame with a screen bottom to hold the malt. This is easy to make from 1" x 4" wood and standard metal window screening. Second, before you start, calibrate your oven thermostat with a good thermometer. You must find a setting that holds the temperature between 212° and 225°F. If your oven will not go that low, you will have great difficulty holding the temperature in the proper range. Third, set the thermometer on the layer of grain during curing, and monitor the "off-air" temperature (temperature of the air rising through the grain) carefully. Curing begins when it reaches 212°F. After one hour of curing, remove the frame and turn the grain thoroughly with a scoop. Repeat this procedure after another hour of curing. Three hours total at 212° to 225°F should do it, but the time may need adjustment.

After curing your malt, you must let it cool before storing it. You should not use it until it has been stored for at least eight weeks. If you try to use it sooner, it will probably impart a burnt, coarse flavor to your beer.

Home curing of malt is well worth experimenting with, especially if you are interested in duplicating older recipes that call for malt types that are rarely made commercially any more. However, the range of malts available today is sufficient for almost all the styles of beer described in this book, and I suggest you experiment with commercially available malts for a while before setting out to create your own varieties.

# Specialty Malts

The term *specialty malts* can be applied to any malt other than standard brewers' malt. However, I consider specialty malts to be those made by a process fundamentally different from the normal one. Specialty malts have several other features in common. First, they have little or no enzyme activity and, therefore, cannot be used alone in a mash. Second, they are used in relatively small amounts, because their effect upon taste is out of proportion to the amount used. Many of these grains will likewise contribute color. They basically fall into two categories, according to how they are made: crystal and roasted malts.

## Crystal Malts

I use the familiar term crystal malts, although it is something of a misnomer. The maltsters call the method used to produce these grains *stewing*. Briefly, what happens is this: The barley is steeped and germinated as usual. However, when kilning time is at hand, the green malt is loaded into a kiln that is sealed to prevent moisture from escaping. The idea is not to dry the grain; instead, it is raised to mash heat (about 150°F) and the enzymes inside each kernel convert the endosperm starches into sugars. At this point each husk contains a soft, gummy ball of malt sugar. Then, the kiln vents are opened and the heat is raised. The malt sugar caramelizes (darkens and takes on a luscious burnt sugar flavor) and sets into a dry crystalline lump during the high temperature kilning. At the same time, the color of the husks deepens.

The caramelized sugar gives crystal malt its other, more descriptive name of *caramel malt*. These malts impart a rich sweetness to the beer and are a major component in the flavor of many dark and amber beers. The kiln temperature at the end of the process determines the color and flavor of the grain; generally, the higher the kilning, the darker the grain and the more intense its flavor. Crystal malt is made in different grades, rated according to color in degrees Lovibond.

There is one crystal malt that stands apart from all others, both in its manufacture and use. This is *dextrin malt,* also known as cara-crystal or cara-pils malt. It is stewed at a higher temperature than caramel malt, which results in the creation of a large proportion of compounds called "dextrins." Dextrins are carbohydrates that are intermediate in size between starches and fermentable sugars. They are tasteless but impart **mouthfeel (body)** and foam retention to the finished beer. To avoid darkening the color, dextrin malt is kilned at a very low temperature. This makes it useful both in pale and darker beers.

## Roasted Malts

Roasted malts are made by the conventional malting process and are not stewed. They are simply dried to a certain moisture content, which depends on the type of malt to be made, and then roasted at high temperatures in a special closed revolving drum, in order to darken the husks and interiors. Time and temperature determine the color and flavor of the finished product.

*Amber malt* goes by several names, depending on the manufacturer. It is used in a few amber and dark ales, and it has a dry, grainy, biscuit-like flavor.

*Brown malt* is kilned over a hardwood fire, which imparts a smoky flavor. Traditionally, it was used in dark ales, but it is very hard to find and is rarely made commercially anymore. It is possible to smoke malts at home in a smoker, and this technique, in combination with oven kilning, can produce a wide range of smoke-flavored malts.

*Chocolate malt* is drum roasted at high temperatures to a very deep, brownish-black color. It has a smooth flavor and is widely used in brown ales and other amber to dark beers.

*Black malt,* sometimes called "black patent," is roasted at a higher temperature than chocolate malt and has a sharper, burnt flavor. Ounce for ounce it also has a somewhat deeper color, but one usually chooses between the two on the basis of taste.

*Roast barley* is not malted. It is listed here because it is used exactly like chocolate or black malt, as a minor component (by weight) in the grist of dark beers. It is made by roasting raw barley in a sealed drum, just like black patent. The flavor, however, is different: the sharp burnt character is there, but coupled with a dry graininess that is quite unlike the sweet acrid undertone of malt that has been given the same treatment.

## Malts from Other Grains

*Wheat malt* is made like pale brewers' malts, but using wheat. This has important consequences. Wheat is a naked grain — that is, it has virtually no husk, and when it germinates the acrospire is external and unprotected. As you might imagine, this makes wheat difficult to malt, especially if the piece is turned by machines. Wheat malt has a lower diastatic power than pale barley malt. Because it has no husk, its tannin content is low, but the protein content is high. Wheat beers are notoriously unstable in clarity. Even if they are filtered "star bright" they may begin to throw a haze after a few weeks of cold storage. On the other hand, the head on a glass of wheat beer is usually prodigious, with the same component — the high protein content — being responsible for both phenomena.

*Rye malt* is a naked grain and in other ways also resembles wheat malt. It is even more difficult to work with than wheat malt, however, as it has a high content of gummy substances that can readily clog a mash, making it almost impossible to run off the wort. Its flavor is much stronger than wheat's and can be overwhelming if the grain is used in large proportions.

# Using Specialty Malts

Most specialty malts are best used in a mash along with pale and/ or high-kilned brewers' malts. This method assures conversion of any residual starch and, in the case of naked grains, provides some husk material to give porosity to the mash. However, the dark roasted grains and caramel malts (not dextrin malt) can be extracted in hot water to enhance the flavor and color of beers brewed from malt extract.

# Buying and Storing Malt

Usually, you can get a much better price by buying pale brewers' malt in bulk quantities — basically by the 50-pound sack. On the other hand, most specialty malts, including crystal, chocolate malt, and so on, are used in small quantities. As a rule it is not worthwhile for an individual homebrewer to buy these in bulk. However, with imported malts, shortages can occur, and it is wise to buy in advance of need.

Your local retailer may be the person who has the most interest in getting you a good deal on malt. Remember that shipping costs are a large percentage of the price of grain, so the difference in cost between mail order and purchasing locally may be less than it seems. On the other hand, mail order may be more convenient for you, and most firms that do mail order are highly reputable and offer excellent service.

One fact that makes bulk purchasing practical is the long keeping qualities of pale malt. I have stored whole grain in my home for over a year, with no noticeable change in its performance or in the flavor of the finished beer. There are just a few precautions you should observe. First, keep the temperature moderate. Do not store your malt in an unheated garage, attic, or basement. High heat is worse than cold, so attics and garages in the summer are the worst. Second, keep the grain dry. If your basement is damp, do not store your malt there. If you live in a humid climate, as I do, be doubly careful to keep the grain away from moisture-laden air. I used to store opened bags of malt in a 30-gallon galvanized steel trash can lined with two heavy-duty plastic lawn bags. The tops of the bags were kept twisted shut and held with twist ties. This system assured that there was no airspace above the grain from which it could absorb moisture, and the metal can kept out rodents and insects.

## Measuring Malt

An alternative to using a large scale for measuring malt is to carefully measure the volume of 1 pound in a glass pitcher. I have found that both 6-row and 2-row brewers' malts take up about 3⅓ cups per pound. Other malts vary, but in any case you should do the measurements for yourself. A 2-pound coffee can holds 7½ cups of dry grain, so it is easy to figure the weight of a canful. For brewers' malt, one can is about 2¼ pounds. Volumetric measuring is faster than weighing out the grain and has the additional advantage that it does not reflect moisture content. If, despite your precautions, your pale malt picks up a little atmospheric moisture during storage, this will not affect your measurements or results.

## Malt Extracts

Malt extracts are concentrated worts. The manufacturing process resembles conventional brewing, but there are some differences. The first runnings are drawn off separately and sent to the vacuum evaporators. The mash is sparged, but the runoff is used to mix with the grain for the next batch. This is rather wasteful from the standpoint of extraction, but it saves a good deal of energy because the concentration process is shortened.

A vacuum evaporator is a sealed vessel with a vacuum pump. At the low pressures obtained, the wort boils at a very low temperature. Nonetheless, some changes do take place. Even the palest all-malt extracts will not make a wort that can stand a 1½-hour boil without severe darkening and coarsening of the flavor. Boils of this length are acceptable and even routine with comparable worts made from pale grain malt. There is also the limitation that extracts impose on the brewer's choice of recipes and the range of possible flavors. The manufacturer has chosen the malt(s) and mash conditions, which largely fix the character of the finished beer.

On the other hand, malt extracts have improved considerably over the past ten years. If treated with respect to their limitations, the best of the current brands will make a very satisfactory beer within a certain range of styles. In general, the "extract tang" is far less noticeable in darker and stronger-flavored beers. Extracts are also useful for boosting the gravity of worts, as many brewers have a limited mashing capacity.

## Types of Malt Extract

Extract can be bought as either canned or bulk-packaged syrup or as a powder. The dry form is more convenient from several points of view. For one thing, it allows you to use exactly as much as you want. It is also very handy for making up small amounts of wort for yeast starters. Many grain brewers keep dry extract on hand for just this purpose. Nonetheless, syrups are more popular, possibly because they are less trouble to store and handle. Dry extract must be carefully packaged and kept sealed to prevent it from absorbing atmospheric moisture. If this is not done, it will set up like poured concrete. Another factor may be the price, but, in analyzing this, remember that syrups contain about 25 percent water, so that 3 pounds of dry extract is equal to about 4 pounds of liquid.

Extract is often available in a choice of light, amber, and dark. It is usually impossible to determine what combination of special malts was used in making the darker varieties. Some, unfortunately, are still darkened simply by adding dark caramel coloring. In addition, many brands contain a percentage of corn syrup, which will lighten the color but contribute little to the flavor or body of the finished beer. Even so, many "pale extracts" make a beer considerably darker than you would expect.

Thus, you must choose your extracts carefully. If in doubt, talk to your shop manager or other homebrewers. They can help you decide which product is best suited to your needs.

One other warning I would issue concerns hopped extracts. These are not made by boiling wort with hops. Instead, a hop extract is added *before* the syrup is packaged. As your homebrewing advances, you will want to be the one deciding the amount and type of hops to go into your wort.

## Malt Extract Specifications

Microbrewers now have access to some specifications about malt extracts, and gradually it is filtering down to homebrewers as well. However, many key pieces of information are still regarded as trade secrets, forcing brewers to work blindfolded. There is no reason why extracts could not be labeled as to the type or types of malt that were used to make them and, if more than one malt was used, what the proportions (stated as a percentage) were.

Two useful pieces of information are sometimes available. One is an extract figure, which basically states, "One pound of this extract dissolved in water to make one gallon of wort will yield a gravity of x." Similarly, a color specification means, "When this extract is diluted to make a standard laboratory wort, its color will be y degrees Lovibond." These statements are valuable guides to the end user (brewer). However, more information needs to be given.

## Adjuncts

*Adjuncts* are unmalted grains that provide additional starch in the mash tun, which is ultimately converted to sugar for the yeast to ferment. These grains widen the range of flavor profiles available, and they have an important place in modern brewing.

The chief unmalted grains in use today are corn (maize), rice, barley, wheat, oats, and rye. All of these grains consist mostly of tough, unmodified starches and are not mashable in their raw state. They must be cooked so that the starch *gelatinizes* (disperses in water). Until this happens, the starch molecules cannot be reached and broken down by the malt enzymes.

Large American breweries use corn and rice almost exclusively. These adjuncts are usually prepared by cooking the grains in a special brewery kettle with a small proportion of the malt. This method is also used elsewhere in the world, but many British breweries are not equipped with a cereal cooker and buy their adjuncts ready-to-use in the form of flakes. Flakes are made by steaming the whole grain, often under pressure, until the kernels soften and swell. Then the grain is passed between a set of hot rollers, which flatten it and pull the kernels apart. The end product can be mixed with crushed malt and mashed-in without further treatment.

Although it is possible for amateurs to use raw adjuncts, the special brewing flakes are a far better option. They cost more than the raw grain and, indeed, more than malted barley, but they pay for themselves in the work and time saved. Chapter 6 outlines the basic "double mash" system used by American breweries, and it will probably convince you that flakes are well worth the cost. In any case, here is a basic description of the adjuncts and what they can do for your beer.

Corn has a sweet, smooth flavor that is compatible with many styles of beer. It is the most popular adjunct in American breweries. It lowers the protein and tannin content of beers, thus lightening body and reducing haze potential. Rice has these same virtues, but has almost no taste of its own. It gives a light, clean palate and is employed in several premium brands, including Budweiser.

The remaining adjuncts do not lighten a beer, but rather increase its body and flavor. Barley, for example, gives a rich, smooth, "grainy" flavor. It has a high content of protein and beta glucans (a gummy type of starch material), which can increase haze and cause other brewing problems. Thus, the use of barley is strictly a matter of taste. It is essential in dry stout, and also is used in North German pale lagers and different types of ale. Like the other high-protein adjuncts discussed here, it also increases head retention.

Oat flakes are used in making oatmeal stout and a few other styles of beer. They have a large fraction of gums and proteins, and again will build up the body of the beer and enhance its smoothness. In a similar way, wheat flakes and rye flakes will add their distinctive flavors and increase the viscosity of a beer.

Having made some mashes using other forms of raw barley and oats, I have come to appreciate the special brewers' flakes that are available now. They are much easier to work with and cause far less trouble during the *lautering* (runoff and sparge) process.

Flakes are not as stable during storage as are whole grain malts. Because of the pre-cooking they have gotten, they pick up moisture readily. Store flakes in two layers of plastic, and keep them away from humidity. Do not buy more than you can use in one brewing season.

## Sugars

Like rice and corn, sugars diminish the haze potential and body of beer without reducing its strength. Some dark sugars also contribute flavor. Unlike adjuncts, they are totally fermentable and generally do not enhance the smoothness of the finished beer (exceptions will be noted later). Thus a beer made with sugar is usually dryer and thinner than an all-grain brew of similar gravity. Sugars are not common in lager brewing, but they have been part of ale recipes for over 100 years.

In spite of long acceptance, sugar remains a controversial material. Some experts feel that it has no place in the brewhouse. They point out that it creates a wort of abnormal composition, which can lead to fermentation troubles. Personally, I sit firmly on the fence in this dispute. I agree that sugars have no place in lager brewing, but I think they can enhance the flavor of some ales. There are four major types of brewing sugars:

*Corn sugar.* Corn sugar is glucose (also called dextrose), a single sugar which is 100 percent fermentable. It contributes to alcoholic strength, but in large amounts it may lead to a cidery off-flavor, as well as a thin body. It is useful for priming because it ferments quickly in the bottle.

*Cane sugars* (sucrose). Sucrose is very likely to leave a cidery taste in the finished beer. This is due to "spillover" byproducts created during its fermentation. I can see no reason to use plain white table sugar in any beer; if one wishes to lighten body while maintaining strength, grain adjuncts are preferable.

On the other hand, partially refined forms of sucrose, such as light and dark brown sugar, give a rum-like flavor which some people like very much in ales. The strong flavors of these brews seem to mask the cidery note.

British recipes often call for other forms of sucrose that are not available here, such as Demerara sugar or treacle. These are all variations of brown sugar or brown sugar syrups. The main difference between them is how much unrefined black molasses they contain. If you wish to get this rummy flavor while minimizing the cidery off-taste, you can experiment with light-bodied molasses. One and a quarter cups will give about the same flavor as a pound of dark brown sugar. You can then make up the gravity in your recipe with grain or malt extract. However, for the sake of simplicity I use brown sugar in my own recipes.

*Grain sugars.* Some sugar products derived from grain are now available. They are intended as "adjunct equivalents" for extract-based beers. They should be a great help to homebrewers, but I would ask a few questions before buying them. Unmalted starch can be converted to sugar by several processes, using acid, industrial enzymes (derived from bacteria or fungi), or both. The spectrum of sugars can be varied according to the manufacturer's aims. Obviously, what you want is a syrup with a sugar spectrum that approximates that of an all-grain wort. (For the record, this would be 1 percent or less fructose, 8 to 12 percent glucose, 3 to 5 percent sucrose, 45 to 55 percent maltose, 13 to 15 percent maltotriose, 15 to 28 percent higher sugars and dextrins.) If this is not the case, you may be no better off than with glucose. Remember, glucose itself is made from corn! It is not the origin but the sugar spectrum that makes the difference.

Another point to consider is that grain syrups (or dried extracts) may not impart the characteristic taste of the grain. The manufacturing process often involves a lot of refinement that removes much of the desirable aromatic fraction from the finished product. The only good way to evaluate the worth of these grain sugars is to try them and analyze your results.

*Malto-dextrin.* **Malto-dextrin** is the most complex fraction of the products of starch conversion. It is tasteless, gummy, and hard to dissolve. It increases mouthfeel (body) and wort viscosity, and adds smoothness to the palate of low-malt beers. Malto-dextrin is best thought of as an equivalent to dextrin malt for extract brews. However, it is again a refined product, lacking the aromatics, proteins, and other substances that contribute so much to the complexity of beer.

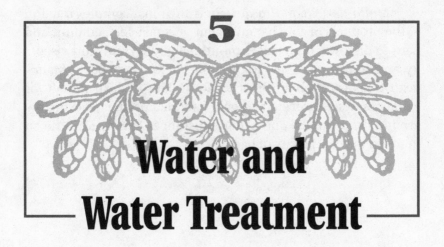

# 5

# Water and Water Treatment

**W**ater is the most difficult of the brewer's materials to understand. On the one hand, it makes up about 90 percent of the finished product, beer; on the other, at first glance it looks like a tasteless, nearly uniform liquid that serves merely as the medium in which the beer's flavor is contained. It is like a plain sheet of canvas waiting for the artist to paint something on it.

That perception is fundamentally true. Nonetheless, a brewer has to know what water is, and what is in it, in order to make good use of it. The wrong water, or the wrong water treatment, can lead to dire results in any brewery.

## Why Water Matters

Almost everyone knows that the chemical formula for water is $H_2O$. Most people can recall that this has to do with the water molecule: two atoms of hydrogen are bound to a single atom of oxygen, to form a molecule of a compound with properties that are totally different from those of the two elements that make it up. For instance, water is a liquid at room temperature; both hydrogen and oxygen are gases that can be liquefied only at very low temperatures, under high pressure.

Now, let us extend that concept. Just as two flammable gases combine to form a liquid that puts out fires, so various elements (and combinations of elements) may take on different properties, according to whether or not they are electrically charged. For example, chlorine is a poisonous, greenish-yellow gas that is widely used for disinfecting swimming pools and beer fermenters. But add an electron to that chlorine atom, giving it a negative electrical charge (electrons are negative), and it becomes a *chloride ion*, which is added to soup to enhance its flavor. You see, when salt is dissolved, it **dissociates** or *ionizes* into its components, a sodium ion ($Na^{+1}$) and a chloride ion ($Cl^{-1}$). So what you taste is not sodium chloride as such, but sodium and chloride ions working together on the taste buds of your tongue.

Two facts slightly complicate this picture. First, not all ions carry a charge of 1. For example, the calcium ion is missing two electrons, giving it a positive charge of 2, and so it is written $Ca^{+2}$. Second, not all ions are formed from single atoms. Some are composed of a bundle — a bound group — of atoms which, collectively, have a positive or negative charge. Examples are the sulfate ion ($SO_4^{-2}$), the nitrate ion ($NO_3^{-2}$), and the nitrite ion ($NO_2^{-1}$). Note that the last two are composed of the same elements, but nitrite has one less oxygen atom and a lower charge. Also, as you would expect, nitrate and nitrite have rather different properties.

All natural water supplies contain ions. They profoundly affect brewing in two critical ways: first, some ions affect the flavor of beer, for better or worse. Second, certain ions influence the chemical changes that take place during beer production. They do this by their effect either on the health of the yeast cells, or on the reactions that take place in the mash kettle and the boiler.

# The Concept of pH

If we could take a submicroscopic look at a sample of pure water — distilled water, consisting solely of $H_2O$ — we would see that it consists mostly of tightly bound molecules. However, we would notice that a few of the water molecules had ionized: broken up into hydrogen ($H^+$) and hydroxyl ($OH^-$) ions carrying an electrical charge. There are, of course, an equal number of each.

Suppose, however, we add a strong acid to the water: say, hydrochloric acid, HCl. It ionizes into hydrogen and chloride ions, $H^+$ and $Cl^-$. In this solution, the total of the electrical charges carried by the ions is still in balance, but we now have an excess of hydrogen as opposed to hydroxyl ions. Thus the solution is no longer balanced in that respect. Those $H^+$ and $OH^-$ ions are very aggressive chemically. They are always looking around for something with which to react. In fact, they are so active that the balance of those ions in the water determines its fundamental character — whether it is acid (excess $H^+$) or alkaline (excess $OH^-$).

The measure of acidic or alkaline character is *pH,* which stands for "power of hydrogen," referring to the hydrogen ion. Yet strangely enough, the pH scale is so designed that the greater the excess of hydrogen ions, the lower the number. A solution containing a strong acid might have a pH of 2. Conversely, a solution of a strong alkali, such as sodium hydroxide (NaOH), might have a pH of 13. The scale goes from 1 to 14, with 7 being the point of neutrality (perfect balance). Wine, which is somewhat acidic, will have a pH of 3 to 4. Beer pH is usually 4 to 4.5. Prior to fermentation, the wort should have a pH of 5.0 to 5.5, as should the mash. Ions in the brewing water have a great influence on the pH level.

## Strong and Weak Acids

One point that generates great confusion about water chemistry is that there are two different ways to measure the acidity or alkalinity of water, or a water-based solution. One is pH, as described above. The other is called *total acidity* or *total alkalinity,* which is a measure of the actual amount of acid or alkali in a given volume of water. You might think that this is just another way to measure pH, but it is not. This is because not all acids behave in the same way in water, and the same is true of alkalis.

Remember how I described salt dissolving into water by breaking apart into its component ions — the process of ionization. Salt ionizes just about totally in water. Strong acids act the same way. If you mix some sulfuric acid with water, it will instantly and almost completely break into hydrogen and sulfate ions. However, many acids, especially organic ones (organic means they contain carbon), do not ionize completely. Only a few percent of the molecules of tartaric acid or lactic acid will ionize in pure water. Most of the molecules remain intact.

This means that the acid content of a tartaric acid solution has relatively little to do with its pH. You can of course measure the pH with test strips or a meter, but that will not tell you how much acid is in the solution. In sensory terms, it does not correlate with how sour the solution will taste. You need to perform another measurement, called *titration,* to learn the total acid content. Titration is done by slowly adding a standard solution of a strong alkali (usually sodium hydroxide) to the acid solution. This procedure gradually forces all the acid in the solution to ionize, because the hydroxyl ions literally tear the hydrogen ions away from the acid molecules. At the end point of the titration, which is shown by an indicator which changes color at a certain pH, every bit of acid in the solution has been neutralized. Then, since you know how much hydroxide it took to do this job, you know how much acid there was in the solution you titrated.

This business of titration and total acidity is important because it lies behind a fundamental difference between wine and beer making. In wine, weak organic acids are a major flavor component, and so the critical measurement is total acidity. That tells the winemaker how sour his wine will be. For brewers, pH is the critical thing, because the malt enzymes require a certain pH range in order to make sugar from starch. However, water contains some weak alkaline compounds, and so the measurement of total alkalinity is important in assessing brewing water.

## Salts and Buffers

When we say *salt* we usually mean table salt, sodium chloride. But in chemistry, any compound formed by a reaction between an acid and an alkali is a salt. For example, potassium chloride can be thought of as the product of a reaction between a strong alkali, potassium hydroxide (KOH), and a strong acid, hydrochloric acid (HCl). The chemical equation is written KOH + HCl →HOH (same as $H_2O$, water) + KCl (potassium chloride).

Certain salts are weakly acid or alkaline in character, and they have the ability to buffer a solution; this means that, after reaching a certain concentration, they achieve a pH that is "natural" to them. Adding more of the salt will not change it. (Remember, we are talking here about salts that are mildly acidic or alkaline, not about strong alkalis or acids.) Now, if you add a strong acid to a solution containing a mildly alkaline buffering salt, the salt will react with it, consuming, so to speak, the hydrogen ions. But after the hydrogen ions are disposed of, the remaining buffer salt will maintain the pH of the solution about where it was before. Of course, if you add enough acid, all the buffer salt will be used up and the pH of the solution will drop.

Buffers are extremely useful in maintaining the proper pH of a solution where other chemical processes are at work. For example, they are used in photographic developers to hold the pH at a stable value while the silver salts of the emulsion are being reduced to metallic silver. Without the buffer, the pH of the developing solution would fall and reduction would come to a halt.

In other chemical processes, buffers are equally important. Many enzymes require a certain pH range to do their work. Malt contains a number of enzymes, and in order for the mash to succeed, these enzymes require a certain pH level. Fortunately, pale brewers' malt also contains natural phosphorus salts (phosphates), which act as acid buffers to maintain the mash pH at about 5.8. This is a little higher than optimum, but very close to what the malt enzymes prefer.

## Water Alkalinity

Most water supplies are, to some extent, naturally alkaline. There are two ways to measure this: pH and total alkalinity. Unfortunately, these two measurements do not correlate very well. Total alkalinity is basically a measure of the bicarbonate (written $HCO_3$) ion content. This ion is a weak alkali. Chemists measure the total alkalinity of water by titration using a strong acid, just as winemakers measure acidity of wine by titrating with a strong alkali. Total alkalinity is important because waters with a high bicarbonate content (total alkalinity) will overcome the weak acid buffering of the malt phosphates and raise the mash pH out of the proper range.

Water pH gives very little clue to the total alkalinity of water. For example, St. Louis city water has a very high pH, (over 9 most of the time), but moderate alkalinity (40 to 60 parts per million). Other water supplies often have a much lower pH (around 7.8 or so) but much higher total alkalinity (100 ppm or more). Thus a brewer needs to know exactly what is being referred to when the alkalinity of water is being discussed.

## Hard and Soft Water

Most discussions of brewing water start with some old adages about the "hardness" of water. Supposedly, "hard" waters are good for making dark beers, and "soft" waters are good for pale beers. Or is it the other way around?

The fact is, hardness is a concept that is not terribly useful. Technically, hardness refers to the content of calcium and magnesium ions in water. This is important because these ions interfere with the action of soap. Hard water means you need to use a lot of detergent to get your clothes clean.

Calcium and magnesium also influence mash reactions by dropping the mash pH slightly. They do this by causing the malt phosphates to *precipitate* (bind together and fall out of solution). This reaction includes the release of hydrogen ions, and thus the pH of the mash drops.

However, most hard waters also contain a fair amount of bicarbonate — a weak alkali, as explained above. This ion is more powerful than calcium in influencing the mash pH, so many hard waters, which contain both calcium and bicarbonate, will have the net effect of giving a pH that is too high.

If you start with distilled water (which is as soft as can be since content of all ions is zero) and "harden" it by adding calcium sulfate or calcium chloride, the net effect will be to make water that is good for brewing pale beers, because the mash pH will be lowered. However, adding calcium bicarbonate will have the opposite effect. You would have no luck at all making beer with this water, unless you compensate by making a dark beer. Dark malts are naturally acidic and will counteract the effect of the bicarbonate in the water.

Real breweries do not start with distilled water. They use the local supply, either surface water from a river or lake, or well water. All natural water supplies contain ions, mostly derived from the geologic formations through which the water has flowed. Thus, the mineral content of water is extremely complex, with trace amounts of many ions even in soft water. It is now time to look at these ions in some depth, so that you will understand what to look for in assessing your own water.

## Important Ions in Brewing

*Calcium* lowers mash and wort pH. It also assists enzyme action in other ways and is generally beneficial. Too much in blending water (used to "top up" after the boil) may cause haze. Also, excess calcium may cause too much phosphate to precipitate, thus robbing the wort of a vital yeast nutrient. Optimum range for all brewing water is considered to be 50 to 100 parts per million. However, this can vary depending on the malt, which always has some calcium of its own, and the concentration of other ions in the water. For example, some famous brewing waters (e.g., Burton) are also much higher than 100 ppm, though this is partly offset by the bicarbonates they also contain. Apart from lowering pH, calcium has no effect on the flavor of beer.

*Magnesium* will lower mash pH in the same way as calcium, but it is not as effective. It is an important yeast nutrient at levels of 10 to 20 ppm, but at 30 ppm or more, it gives a sharp, sour-bitter flavor. Malt contains a fair amount of magnesium and it is rarely necessary to add more to the brewing water.

*Sodium* has no chemical effect; it does influence flavor. Levels from 75 to 150 ppm give a round smoothness, which is most pleasant when paired with chloride ion. In the presence of sulfate, however, sodium creates an unpleasant harshness. The more sulfate you have in your water, the less sodium you want (and vice versa). In any case, 150 ppm is considered the upper limit for brewing water.

*Potassium*'s only chemical effect is to inhibit certain enzymes in the mash. Like sodium, it can create a "salty" flavor effect and should not be paired with sulfate. There is no reason to add potassium salts to brewing water.

*Manganese* ion (a trace) is important for proper enzyme action in the mash, but any appreciable amount is undesirable. Malt usually contains sufficient manganese, and more is not wanted in brewing water. Manganese and iron are responsible for the metallic taste of many well waters, and their flavor is very unpleasant in beer.

*Iron* may cause haze in beer and hamper yeast activity. Large amounts give a metallic taste to many well waters. It is not wanted in brewing.

*Copper,* like many metallic ions, is a vital yeast nutrient at low levels but can poison yeast if too much is present in the wort. Usually, copper from the water lines plus that contained in the malt provide all that is required.

*Nickel* causes foaming, as well as a metallic taste. The less the better.

*Tin* also causes haze and a metallic taste. It is not wanted.

*Lead* causes haze and is toxic. Depending on the chemistry of the local water, lead from old pipes may or may not pose a health risk. Obviously, the less the better.

*Zinc* is a yeast nutrient like copper, but too much gives a metallic taste. Malt usually supplies all the zinc required.

*Carbonate* ($CO_3^{-2}$) and *bicarbonate* ($HCO_3^{-1}$) are both alkaline. In water, when carbonate is in the presence of calcium, carbonate is only slightly soluble; it precipitates with the calcium as chalk. The predominant ion of alkaline waters is bicarbonate; however, on chemical analysis the two are usually lumped together and a single figure is quoted as "$CO_3$." This means the total amount of both ions has the same effect as the stated quantity of carbonate ion. This is the *total alkalinity* of the water supply.

Besides halting enzyme action, alkalinity harms beer flavor by promoting the extraction and formation of sharp, harsh flavor components from the hops. Carbonate-bicarbonate is tolerable only at low levels (under 50 ppm ideally) unless it is balanced by the calcium content of the water or by the acidity of dark malt in the grist.

*Nitrate* and *nitrite* should not be confused. Nitrate used to be considered harmful, but recent research has shown that the bad effects on yeast metabolism that were attributed to nitrate are, in fact, caused by nitrite in the wort. Several types of bacteria can reduce nitrate to nitrite, so that a so-called nitrate problem with fermentation is actually the result of infection by one of these bugs. If your water supply contains over 25 ppm of nitrate, your sanitation must be impeccable if you wish to avoid weak or incomplete fermentations. It is also possible for water supplies to become contaminated with nitrate-reducing bacteria, which will cause nitrite to appear in the water. This is a point on which you may want to question your water chemist. However, nitrate in and of itself is not a problem; it has no effect on beer flavor or brewing reactions.

*Silicate,* like nitrate, does not affect flavor. But it does cause haze and scale, and so is undesirable.

*Sulfate* has no chemical effect, but it imparts a sharp, "dry" edge to well-hopped beers. In the presence of sodium the dryness becomes positively harsh, and hop rates will have to be reduced if this combination cannot be avoided.

*Fluoride* is an ion added to public water supplies at the rate of 1 ppm to help prevent tooth decay. At that level, it has no effect, and even 10 ppm is harmless for brewing purposes.

*Chloride* may hamper yeast flocculation (clumping and settling). At levels of 250 ppm and above, it enhances the sweetness of beer.

# Chlorination

*Chlorine* is a gas added to water supplies to kill any stray bacteria that may get through the filters, or enter the water after it leaves the treatment plant. The combination of chlorine with certain organic compounds can result in formation of *chlorophenols,* which cause off-flavors at less than 1 ppm (some much lower) and are known carcinogens. Adding chlorine to any water will also produce a certain amount of *chloroform,* another potential health hazard. In the trade, chloroform is referred to as a trihalomethane, or THM. You can impress your water chemist by asking for the THM level, rather than using the prosaic term chloroform. In any case, the less chlorine they have to add, the lower the THM level will be.

## What Is in Your Water?

If your water comes from a municipal supply, you can get a free, complete analysis from the water company. When you call, explain that you need to talk to a water chemist in the lab, and that you need a water analysis. I have found that most chemists are sympathetic and will take a friendly interest in homebrewers. Before you run down your list, ask the chemist to give the range over which the numbers will fluctuate in a typical year; content of some ions varies quite a bit over time. Also ask for the figures on all the ions discussed in this chapter, as well as the chloroform level and the presence of chlorophenols. Finally, ask about pH and total alkalinity, and what kind of treatment the water receives. As a rule, municipal water supplies will have little or no problem with microbiological contamination, but you may wish to ask, just to be sure.

If your water comes from a well, you will have to take it to a laboratory for analysis. This will cost you some money, but it only needs to be done once. It is important to know whether the water contains iron or other metallic ions, though usually you can taste them if they are present. You will definitely want information about microbiological contamination. Without an analysis you are flying blind, and may waste far more in money and effort than you would have spent to have your water tested.

After reading this far and obtaining your analysis, you should be ready to evaluate your water supply and decide what should be changed.

In general, the most important specifications for brewing water involve:

1. Microbiological purity. You must be certain that your water does not introduce bacteria into your beer.
2. Chlorine content. Water actually used to make beer should be dechlorinated. However, water used for rinsing sanitized equipment should *not* be dechlorinated.
3. Total alkalinity. Under 50 ppm for pale beers ideally, with 75 being the absolute maximum. For darker beers, up to 150 ppm may be tolerated.
4. Calcium content. 50 to 100 ppm for pale beers; higher is tolerable.
5. Other ions. Metallic ions are generally undesirable; high levels of sulfate, sodium, or potassium may pose flavor problems. Nitrite interferes with yeast metabolism.

## Methods of Water Treatment

Depending on your water supply, there usually are a number of strategies that you can adopt to modify your water as required. In general, they fall under four headings: decontamination, dechlorination, demineralization, and ion supplements.

Most water supplies are decontaminated by the water company, and this is not a concern. If yours is not, there are UV lights that can be installed in the water line to kill bacteria. Boiling all brewing water also works. With either method, you have to watch your sanitation carefully to be sure that the water stays clean and germ-free after treatment.

Dechlorination can be accomplished by boiling or by carbon filtration. Both methods also remove chloroform. Carbon filters are more cost effective, but they can form a breeding ground for bacteria, and require periodic cleaning and maintenance. On the other hand, boiling carries high energy costs, and is time-consuming.

An appropriate demineralization method depends on what needs to be removed. If you only need to reduce total alkalinity, boiling will accomplish this, as will neutralization with acid; if there are other problems, you may need to employ more drastic measures, such as distillation or a resin demineralizing filter. Again, distillation involves boiling and is energy intensive.

Supplementation is simply a matter of adding the appropriate ions in the form of a salt — often a calcium salt, such as calcium chloride.

Now let us take a closer look at the various methods that have been mentioned.

**1** *Distillation Method.* Distillation or demineralizing filters offer total control of your brewing water. When water is distilled, all ions are removed. If you have a really intractable water problem — for example, nitrite or large amounts of sodium and sulfate — then these methods are the only way to solve it. However, I would not distill all the water, except as a last resort. Trace elements of many ions are helpful in various ways, so that (for example) simply adding gypsum to distilled water to make pale ale will not be as satisfactory as using a natural supply. You can usually dilute your tap water with a proportion of distilled water and thereby bring the content of harmful ions down to acceptable levels. In doing this, remember that all ions will be lowered and some beneficial ones may need to be restored.

**2** *Locating an Outside Source.* Finding another source may be the least expensive method of dealing with a difficult water problem. If you have a friend or relative in another town (especially one with a brewery) by all means investigate its water supply. However, do not assume anything. Get a water analysis. The only thing of which you can be sure is that the water supply is treatable. But you will need an analysis to figure out what needs to be done with it.

**3** *Filtration Method.* Carbon filtration removes all traces of chlorine, chloroform, and chlorophenols. If the ion content of your water is all right but you have chlorine-related problems, a carbon filter will solve them.

**4** *Boiling Method.* Boiling all the brewing water, and allowing it to cool overnight before racking it into a large container (e.g., a 10-gallon plastic pail) accomplishes several useful purposes. It kills all bacteria. It also eliminates chlorine and chloroform, which boils at 140°F. Finally, boiling uncouples the hydrogen atom from the bicarbonate ion, leaving a carbonate ion which, in the presence of calcium, will precipitate. Boiled bicarbonate water will, upon cooling, show a white deposit around the side of the kettle, somewhat like a bathtub ring, and on the bottom.

You can estimate the effect of boiling for decarbonation (removing bicarbonate) by the following formula: boiling will remove all but about 30 to 40 ppm of carbonate-bicarbonate; at the same time, it will remove 3 ppm of calcium for every 5 ppm of carbonate. For example, if your water has a total alkalinity of 150 ppm, boiling will remove 110 to 120 ppm of that amount. At the same time, the calcium content of your water will be lowered by 66 to 72 ppm.

One important point about the decarbonation reaction is that it requires time and oxygen. The water should be boiled for at least 15 minutes, preferably 30. The boiler must be uncovered so that chloroform can be driven off. Finally, the water must be aerated thoroughly before boiling. The best way to do this is by filling the kettles from your sink sprayer.

**5** *Ion Supplements.* Adding salts is the best way to adjust mash pH. If your water content is low in calcium, you can adjust the pH of a pale beer mash with USP-grade gypsum or calcium chloride. While it is possible to calculate these additions to a specific ppm value, it is simpler just to approach the problem empirically: add calcium to the mash, ½ teaspoon at a time, stir 5 minutes, and check the pH. Repeat if necessary. One teaspoon of either salt per 5 gallons of mash water is the most you should need.

Calcium carbonate can be used in the same way to raise the pH of a dark beer mash. This salt is not soluble in tap water, but when added to an acidic solution — such as a mash or wort — it will ionize, raising the pH. Still, it requires caution. It is sometimes better to accept a lower-than-optimum mash pH (as long as it is 5.0 or above) rather than add large amounts (over 2 teaspoons per 5 gallons) of this salt to the mash.

Other supplements are sometimes added to water in an attempt to duplicate the water supplies of famous brewing centers, such as Burton-upon-Trent. These include magnesium sulfate (epsom salts) and sodium chloride. These salts are not necessary for pH adjustment, and may have undesirable flavor effects. There are a number of articles in the brewing literature explaining how to calculate salt additions in order to approximate various types of brewing water, and those who want to attempt such work should consult them. However, it is not necessary to duplicate the original source water in order to make a particular style of beer.

**6** *Acidification Method.* Acidification is the simplest way to reduce the alkalinity of water supplies. However, the best approach is to proceed carefully, checking the pH at frequent intervals as you add acid. As a rule of thumb, I suggest bringing the pH of mash water down to 7.0 — no lower — and adding calcium if necessary to get the correct mash pH. However, sparging and blending water is another story. It is very desirable to keep the pH of the runoff during sparging at or below 5.7. The easiest way to assure this is to acidify the sparge water to a pH of 5.7. The amount of acid needed is very small.

There are two classes of acids used by brewers: mineral and organic acids. In general, the mineral acids are strong and stable. Sulfuric, hydrochloric, and phosphoric acids are the most common. Of these, phosphoric is both the least corrosive and least dangerous to work with. It also contributes phosphate, which is an important yeast nutrient. Organic acids are weak, and many, such as the wine acids, have inappropriate flavors. Lactic acid does not have this drawback, but it is unstable at high temperatures. For this reason my own preference, and practice, has swung toward phosphoric acid for brewing. Just be sure to get food grade — the kind sold for tropical fish tanks is not suitable.

# Examples of Water Treatment

Here are three examples to give you an idea of how to treat different types of water supplies. All of these are municipal supplies derived from surface or well water, and in each case the water has been purified and chlorinated, so that microbial contamination is not an issue.

These numbers show a surface water supply that was originally fairly "hard," with a fairly large calcium content. The water has been "softened" by lime addition, which drops the calcium content and total alkalinity, but leaves a high pH. This method of treatment is fairly common in the Midwest where many cities draw their water from rivers. The lime treatment not only removes calcium, but also many other metallic ions. Note, however, that

## *Water Supply from St. Louis*

| *Ion* | *ppm (parts per million)* |
| --- | --- |
| Bicarbonate | 20 – 40 |
| Calcium | 20 – 24 |
| Carbonate | 20 – 24 |
| Chloride | 23 – 25 |
| Fluoride | 1.0 |
| Magnesium | 16 |
| Nitrate | 2 – 16 |
| Nitrite | trace |
| Potassium | 5 – 7 |
| Silicate | 4 – 10 |
| Sodium | 20 – 50 |
| Sulfate | 70 – 150 |
| Total alkalinity | 40 – 60 |

| *Ion* | *ppb (parts per billion)* |
| --- | --- |
| Chloroform | 20 |
| Chlorophenols | nil |
| Copper | 5 |
| Iron | 10 |
| Lead | 20 |
| Manganese | less than 5 |
| Nickel | 5 |
| Tin | 5 |

pH = 9.5 (average)

the magnesium level is almost as high as calcium, and this can create flavor problems when paired with sulfate. Note also that the sulfate and sodium levels are fairly high.

Alkalinity is not a problem with this water. To dechlorinate the brewing water, a carbon filter is the best choice. However, remember that such a filter must be maintained properly. Also remember that water used for cleaning and rinsing equipment should not be filtered. An alternative to carbon filtration is to boil the brewing water.

Calcium supplementation is needed for pale beers, in order to raise the level to 50 to 100 ppm. One teaspoon of gypsum or calcium chloride per 5 gallons of mash water is sufficient. Calcium chloride would be preferred to gypsum, in order to avoid increasing the sulfate level of the water. For dark beers, usually no treatment is necessary. Very dark beers may require calcium carbonate in the mash. Sparge water should be adjusted to a pH of 5.7 with phosphoric acid.

Now let us look at another, naturally hard water supply. This time we will not give a full set of figures, but only those that are significant for brewing purposes.

## *Naturally "Hard" Water*

| Ion | ppm |
|---|---|
| Calcium | 160 |
| Carbonate-bicarbonate (total) | 100 |
| Chloride | 25 |
| Magnesium | 45 |
| Nitrate | 20 |
| Nitrite | trace |
| Potassium | 6 |
| Sodium | 75 |
| Sulfate | 250 |

pH = 7.7

This is a problem brewing water. The high levels of sulfate, magnesium, and sodium will give a very sharp edge to beer flavors. The alkalinity (carbonate-bicarbonate) will make it impossible to brew pale beers. All in all, the best treatment for such water probably is to dechlorinate it with a carbon filter, then demineralize it with a resin-type filter. As an alternative, it could be distilled.

Rather than demineralize this water completely, it would be best to demineralize about two-thirds of the total volume required for each batch of beer. The remaining third simply would be dechlorinated. The effect would be to reduce the content of all ions by two-thirds, which would bring them into an acceptable range for brewing. After blending, the water could be used for brewing all types of beers, and the only further treatment needed would be pH adjustment of the mash (by addition of calcium carbonate) for dark beers, and in all cases, lowering the pH of the sparge water (by acid).

Finally, to see what is possible with water treatment, let us look at the water of one of the world's great cities, London. (Note: This is *one* type of "London water."  Different districts in the city get their water from different sources and ion contents will vary accordingly.)

## *London Water Supply*

| Ion | ppm |
| --- | --- |
| Calcium | 52 |
| Carbonate-bicarbonate (total) | 156 |
| Magnesium | 16 |
| Sodium | 99 |
| Sulfate | 77 |

pH = 7.8

For the sake of simplicity we will assume that other ions pose no problem. The water is chlorinated and should be filtered through carbon as a preliminary step.

After dechlorination, this water would be excellent for brewing dark beers such as porter (which originated in London). However, pale beers pose a severe problem: the alkalinity is too high for a pale malt mash, and you cannot decarbonate this water by boiling.

Why can't we simply boil this water to precipitate the carbonate as chalk? Well, let's do the arithmetic. Boiling should eliminate about 120 ppm of carbonate (156 minus 35 residual). But, for that much carbonate to precipitate, we would need ⅗ of 120, or 72 ppm of calcium — a bit more than is actually there! Furthermore, this reaction is not 100 percent efficient. To get maximum precipitation of carbonate, you need an excess of calcium, ideally 40 to 50 ppm more than the reaction requires. In other words, you need to add 60 ppm of calcium ion to this water before boiling. With the sulfate content on the high side already, it would be better to add calcium chloride rather than gypsum for this purpose. About 1½ teaspoons of calcium chloride per 5 gallons should do the job.

An easier way around the problem would be to reduce the water alkalinity with acid. In this case, the best choices would be either phosphoric or hydrochloric acid. Remember that sulfuric acid would increase the sulfate content of the water. After neutralizing the water with acid, it could be used as is for brewing pale beers. Calcium content is not affected by neutralization, and since it is over 50 ppm, it will not need to be increased with calcium chloride. As in all these cases, reducing the pH of the sparge water is recommended.

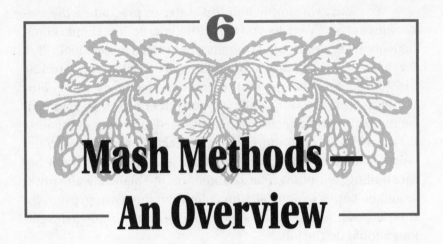

# Mash Methods — An Overview

**T**he first step in brewing beer is the chemical conversion of grain starch to sugar. This is accomplished in the mash tun. The basic chemical process is similar in all cases, but many mashing systems have been devised in different times and places in order to make the best use of the materials available. Homebrewers need to be aware of the different methods because they may influence the choice of equipment and even recipes. Also, there are a number of conflicting claims about these different methods. The following account is intended to give an objective picture of the choices, with information on both the advantages and disadvantages of each.

## Infusion Mashing

The simplest mash method is called "infusion mashing," or sometimes, "single infusion mashing." Infusion refers to the mixing, or infusing, of the crushed malt and other grains — the grist —

with hot water. The mixture is allowed to stand for 1 to 2 hours at a temperature (usually) of 145° to 158°F, for conversion, before the wort is drawn off and the grain is sparged with hot water.

The biggest advantage of infusion mashing is its simplicity. The mash temperature is not raised during the stand, so the vessel does not need to be heated. The correct mash temperature is achieved by preheating the mash water to exactly the right temperature so that, when it is mixed with the malt, the mash will settle in at the desired temperature. The mash tun can be made of many different materials. Furthermore, infusion mash tuns can be fitted with a false bottom screen so that they function as a combined mash/lauter tun. Using this method, the entire brewery can consist of only three vessels: the kettle, the mash/lauter tun, and the hot water tank (also called hot liquor tank, since "liquor" is a brewer's term for the treated brewing water). The hot water tank serves as a reservoir for hot water used during the sparge operation.

Infusion mashing originated in Great Britain, where it was well suited to British malts. Currently it is very popular with American microbreweries and brewpubs. Using modern American malt, an infusion mash can yield almost as much wort sugar as more elaborate methods while demanding far less capital outlay and floor space, both of which are at a premium in small breweries.

## Step Mashing

Step mashing is also called *step infusion,* or "upward infusion." This method is very similar to infusion, but the mash is mixed at a lower temperature and is put through a series of rests at progressively higher temperatures. This method allows the brewer great flexibility in setting the rests so as to take advantage of the many enzymes contained in the malt. Each enzyme has its own optimum operating temperature, so that infusion mashing always requires a compromise that attempts to get a good effort from several enzymes. Step mashing gives the brewer a great deal more latitude in manipulating conditions in order to get optimum results.

The disadvantage of step mashing, obviously, is that greater flexibility also means greater complexity in equipment. The mash tun must be heatable. This means it must be made of metal — normally copper or stainless steel — and fitted with a heat source. Also, the mash must be circulated or stirred while heat is applied in order to achieve an even temperature distribution. A false bottom screen will interfere with circulation, so the lauter tun must be a separate vessel.

For homebrewers, these constraints are not hard to deal with. Any large kettle can serve as a mash tun, and there are even ways to get around the circulation problem without having to add a fourth vessel as a lauter tun. For microbreweries, the usual solution is to add mash rakes to the kettle and use the kettle for mashing as well as boiling. The mash/lauter tun becomes a lauter tun only. However, this strategy still incurs additional complications and costs. Besides being fitted with rakes for stirring the mash, the kettle must also be equipped with a sump and oversized pumps and piping, so that the mash can be moved to the lauter tun. For most homebrewers, however, mash transfers can be accomplished with a bit of lifting and pouring, so these drawbacks are minor. The main disadvantage of step mashing is that it requires more time than a simple infusion.

## Double Mashing

Double mashing is a special method that was invented in North America to meet the requirements of the style of beer that developed here. American light lager beers typically use a large proportion of unmalted cereal grains — corn or rice — which must be cooked before their starches can be attacked by the malt enzymes. In addition to a mash tun, lauter tun, hot water tank, and kettle, a double mash requires a cereal cooker. This is a large kettle used to boil the cereal grain (adjunct).

Double mashing is far more complex than step mashing. Usually, both mashes are started at the same time. The main mash is mixed at a low temperature, while the milled cereal is mixed with a small amount of crushed malt and put through a rest at conversion temperature. Then the cereal mash is brought to a boil, and cooked for at least 20 minutes. The cereal mash is then combined with the main mash, with a resulting temperature in the conversion range.

The advantage of this method is that it allows the brewer to utilize raw cereal starches in beer. Rice and corn are far less expensive than malted barley, so if one's main products are mainstream American style beers, the economies in material costs quickly offset the added cost and complexity of the brewing equipment. For occasional, small-scale use, the main attraction is the ability to experiment with exotic materials like potatoes or millet. On a homebrewing scale, the costs are time, complication, and perhaps an additional kettle.

## Decoction Mashing

This method was developed in central Europe and is still used in that part of the world in brewing traditional, all-malt lager beers. The basic process involves mixing the mash at a low temperature, then putting the mash through a series of rests at progressively higher temperatures, just as with step mashing. However, the temperature rises are accomplished by removing and boiling (decocting) a portion of the mash, and then returning it to the mash tun.

There are a number of variations of this method. The classic system is *triple decoction,* where each decoction is taken and boiled for about 20 minutes, then returned to the mash tun for a 15 to 30 minute stand before the next decoction is done. Simpler variations involve only one or two decoctions, with additional temperature rests, if any, being accomplished by direct heating.

For all-malt beers, decoction gives the best rate of sugar extraction of any mash method. With poorly modified or unevenly modified malt, the gain can be very significant. Also, decoction will give a deeper color and a richer caramel flavor to dark beers. On the other hand, it is also the most complex and time-consuming system around. Even in Germany, most commercial breweries have gone to step mashing, or even simple infusion mashing, for brewing pale beers. Modern malting methods have reduced the extract advantage of decoction, while rising energy and labor costs have made it difficult to justify. Decoction is still favored for brewing dark beers, however, because of the effects mentioned above.

For the homebrewer, decoction mashing is the final frontier. Its benefits were greater in the old days, when malt was often unevenly modified. Still, there are reasons to try it, particularly with the amber and dark German lager beer styles. The equipment required is basically the same as for double mashing, but the time needed is greater.

Most homebrewers start with infusion, then move on to more elaborate mash methods as time and interest allow. Each of these methods has specific advantages for some styles of beer, and is worth exploring, but it is better for beginners to start with the simplest method first. By the time you understand its limits, you will know in which direction you want to move.

# 7

# Equipment for Wort Production

**M**ost of the major items of equipment for wort production can be bought off the shelf from either discount and hardware stores, or homebrew supply shops. It is also possible to save money by building some of these items yourself. If you start out with a basic set for extract brewing, such as the one listed in Chapter 3, you can move into grain brewing just by adding a few pieces of equipment.

Eventually, you may wish to increase your batch size to 10 or 12 gallons. This involves a good deal of expense, but it cuts your work in half, and gives you the opportunity to move your brewery out of the kitchen. There are several ready-made systems available, of varying quality and sophistication. However, many homebrewers still choose to cobble up their own hardware, farming out tasks beyond their competence (e.g., stainless steel welding) to friends or acquaintances.

There are limits to what you can learn from books. While the general principles of design and operation are established, the value of a piece of equipment will often boil down to execution and details. In other words, if you want to buy a certain piece of equipment ready-made, there is no substitute for actually seeing it in operation. If this is not possible, the next best thing would be reports from current users. For homemade designs, get as much specific information as possible about how the item is made and how well it works. In this general handbook, I can offer some helpful yet basic guidelines. I have not tried or even seen every piece of equipment available, and more are being invented every day, so it behooves the homebrewer to do some research in the field.

## Malt Mills

Large commercial breweries use sophisticated mills containing three sets of cast-iron rolls. Each set of rolls is set to a smaller gap than the one above it. The malt is coarsely crushed in the first set of rolls, and the milled malt falls onto a screen. The screen holds back the broken husks, which are blown or otherwise diverted off to the side, while the large, coarse pieces of the malt interiors (grits) fall through into the second set of rolls, where they are crushed into even finer pieces. The crushed grits then pass through the third set of rollers. At the end of the process, the interiors of the grain have been milled into flour, while the husks remain in large pieces that provide a buoyant, open filter bed in the lauter tun.

Very few microbreweries, and no homebreweries that I know of, have a mill that even comes close to the capabilities of the large, six-roll malt mills. The two-roll mills used in most micros are designed for milling feed grain. Like the mills available for homebrewers, they do a decent job of crushing the grain without pulverizing the husks, but they leave most of the grain interiors as coarse grits.

The crush of the malt is of the utmost importance, as it greatly influences the brewing methodology and even the specifications of the equipment in the brewhouse. Coarsely crushed grits mean a long conversion stand, and therefore a long sparge will be required in order to get a reasonable rate of sugar extraction from the grain. They also require different dimensions for some key components, such as the screens on the false bottom of the lauter tun.

For homebrewers, the old standby is the Corona grain mill, a crude but effective instrument with two significant drawbacks. First, it takes a lot of muscle power to crush a brew's worth of grain in it. This can be remedied by adapting the drive mechanism to accept an electric drill. The second drawback is that many examples give an uneven crush. The rotating plate wobbles as it turns, rather

*Crushing the malt using a hand-cranked grain mill. Note the adjusting screw and the lock nut, which must be loosened before the adjusting screw can be turned.*

than maintaining a consistent gap from the fixed plate. This can be remedied to some extent by carefully grinding the back of the moving plate so that it is aligned parallel to the fixed plate.

In recent years, several roller mills have been designed and marketed for homebrewers. Some of them work better than the Corona, but others do not. In any case, they are all two-roll designs and share the inherent limitations of the breed. I urge reserved caution in buying one of these mills. Either try it before buying, or if that is not possible, be very certain there is a no questions asked, money back guarantee.

## Kettles

If you brew with grain malt, you need a kettle with a capacity at least 2½ gallons larger than your batch size. For example, a 7½ gallon size is recommended for 5-gallon brews. Depending on the rate of evaporation and other factors, an even larger capacity may be needed.

*Roller mill*

For the common 5-gallon batch size, the cheapest kettle is still the 8.25-gallon enamelware canner, which is widely available. This unit is perfectly adequate. However, the best materials available, and the only ones used in commercial breweries, are copper and stainless steel. Copper has excellent heat transfer characteristics, but is very costly. Stainless steel is cheaper and less subject to corrosion, but has poor heat transfer characteristics and is difficult to cut and weld.

Many large homebrew systems are based on kettles and other brewing vessels built from 15.5-gallon stainless steel beer kegs. Damaged kegs are often available at scrap prices and can be modified to make a good brew kettle. The two required modifications are to cut off the top of the keg and to weld a tap on the bottom. The tap is necessary for safety reasons. A keg containing 10 gallons of liquid weighs over 100 pounds and cannot be emptied by inverting it, as a smaller kettle can.

## Hot Water Tank

Batch size determines the requirements for a hot water tank. For 5-gallon brews, almost any kettle equal to the batch size can be used. For 10-gallon brews, where the volume of water is too heavy to move easily, it is best to have a second kettle complete with tap. Volume should be equal to the batch size.

## Mash/Lauter Tun

Once again, there is a big gap between 5- and 10-gallon systems. For 5-gallon batches, the simplest lauter tun is a pair of plastic buckets, one fitted inside the other. The outer bucket has a tap fitted at the bottom. The inside bucket has its bottom drilled out with hundreds of holes. If you are doing it yourself, I recommend a 3/16-inch bit, and drilling the holes on 3/8-inch centers. Alternatively, a mesh bag, and some sort of support to hold the bag above the tap, will also work.

A system using this sort of lauter tun requires a separate mash tun, which can be any 5- or 6-gallon kettle. It is possible also to build combined mash/lauter tuns, and this is the best choice for a larger homebrewery.

There are two basic types of mash/lauter tuns. One is made from an insulated plastic picnic cooler. This type is suitable only for infusion or decoction mashing, though it can be used only as a lauter tun for step mashing. The key to this type of mash lauter tun is a copper manifold made from sections of ½-inch copper pipe and fittings (see illustration). The pipe has slots cut in the bottom with a hacksaw, at ½- or ¾-inch intervals. The manifold should not be soldered together, as it must be disassembled for cleaning.

One important point here is that this type of mash/lauter tun should not be too large for the batch size. The depth of the grain bed must be at least 4 to 5 inches, drained. This means that, for 5-gallon batches, the maximum area of the bottom is only about 1 square foot. A larger size means a thin grain bed, which will make it hard to get adequate filtration of the wort during runoff.

The other basic type of mash/lauter tun is made from a kettle or keg, fitted with a tap at the bottom. The tap is attached to a loop of flexible ¾-inch copper tubing, slotted like the manifold described above. This option is more versatile because the loop does not interfere with stirring, so the mash tun can be heated. The other option is a false bottom made of stainless or copper plate. The bottom can be drilled or slotted. Slots are harder to cut, but work better than holes. Holes should be ³⁄₁₆-inch on ⅜-inch centers. The ultimate false bottom is a v-wire screen as found in commercial brewery vessels. The advantage of a false bottom plate is that it can be removed easily for cleaning. However, a vessel with a false bottom cannot be heated. It requires a separate mash tun for step mashes.

# Grant

Any type of lauter tun must be fitted with a tap so that the wort can be drawn off into the kettle. However, you need a buffer vessel in between the lauter tun and the kettle, because the cloudy

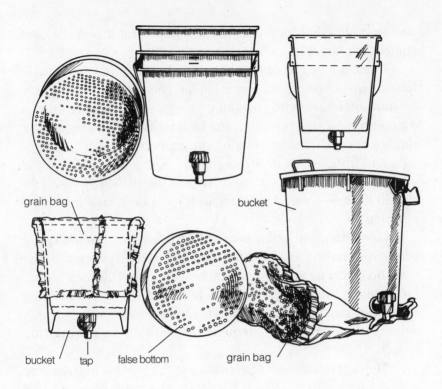

grain bag

bucket

bucket   tap   false bottom   grain bag

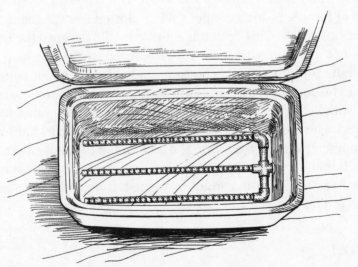

*Lauter tuns. A lauter tun for large-batch brewing can be made from several food-grade plastic buckets or a 48-quart picnic cooler fitted with a manifold of slotted copper pipe.*

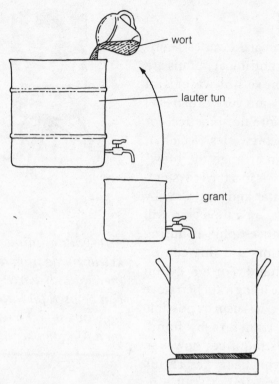

*With this homebrew lautering setup, you can draw wort from the grant and return it to the lauter tun until the wort is clarified, using a quart pyrex pitcher. Then you can just leave the grant tap open and run the wort into the kettle. If you can set this all up with the kettle on a burner, you can get the wort to boiling point by the time you have collected your desired volume.*

---

first runnings should not be run straight into the kettle. They must be recirculated through the grain bed until a filter that clarifies the wort is formed. The key to recirculation is the *grant*, a small vessel that sits directly under the lauter tun tap.

The grant can be made of stainless steel, copper, or food grade plastic. It should have a capacity of ½ to 1 gallon, and it should be fitted with a tap near the bottom. In use, it may hang from the lauter tun tap or be supported from the bottom.

# Pumps

In commercial breweries, stainless steel centrifugal pumps are used to move hot water and wort. They are very expensive, and therefore not practical for most homebreweries. Usually, it is better to arrange the brewhouse vessels in a tower system, so that water and wort flow by gravity. The only time wort will need to move uphill is during recirculation and this can be done by hand. For a 5-gallon brewhouse using a kitchen stove for heating, it is usually possible to make transfers by hand. Caution is required, however, when moving heavy vessels full of dangerously hot (140°F or above) liquid.

*A 14-gallon stainless steel kettle, made from a commercial half-barrel beer keg, can be used for large-batch brewing. It is shown sitting on a King Kooker burner.*

*A tower brewhouse setup for large-scale brewing*

# Heat Sources

Most 5-gallon homebreweries are based in a kitchen and use the stove. This setup works well in most cases, although gas stoves are easier to modulate than electric ones. Larger homebreweries generally use burner/kettle stand units specifically designed for the purpose. It is possible to build such items using surplus water heater burners. They can also be bought ready-made. Be sure the burner matches your fuel source (natural gas or bottled propane). Ideally, a 10-gallon tower brewhouse should have three burner units, one for the hot water tank, one for the mash/lauter tun, and one for the kettle. This removes the need to move hot kettles or burners around, and makes it possible to start heating the wort as the kettle is filled.

While moving the brewery out of the kitchen is desirable, you must consider ventilation when setting up a brewhouse in the basement or garage. You need a hood (or at least a large window fan) over the burners, and some provision for the entry of makeup air to burn with the gas. Improper or inadequate flue venting may be deadly.

# Measuring and Testing Equipment

It is important to have a small scale that is marked in quarter-ounce increments or better. Postage scales are one possibility. A large 10- to 20-pound scale is nice, but you can measure out large quantities by volume if need be.

Every homebrewer needs a thermometer that can measure from 32° to 212°F. The two basic types are spirit and bimetal. With either, the scale must be large and must be calibrated in 1- or 2-degree increments. Spirit thermometers are the glass tube type. Bimetals have a dial readout (or, in expensive models, digital) and are superior in that they react much faster and are usually easier to read. Many are adjustable so that, if dropped, they can be recalibrated.

It is best to check the accuracy of any thermometer by comparing it with a mercury fever thermometer. These narrow-range devices are usually accurate within .2°F. Fill a quart pitcher with

water at 100°F, or as close as you can mix it; after stirring to equal-
ize the temperature and giving your thermometer plenty of time
to settle in, take your reading with the bulb or stem in the middle
of the container. Immediately immerse your fever thermometer
alongside it and watch the mercury until it stops rising. At this
point, remove and read it, and note any discrepancy. If, for example, your brewing thermometer reads 100°F exactly and your
fever thermometer reads 102.8°F, you know that at mash temperatures your readings will be at least three degrees low. If you encounter such a large discrepancy, you should check it further
against wide-range instruments of high accuracy.

Another essential item is the *hydrometer*, which measures
the weight of a liquid compared to an equal volume of water. This
relative weight can be measured on several scales, but the one
most homebrewers use is the specific gravity, or S.G., scale, which
directly compares the liquid with water at a standard temperature, usually 60°F. A beer wort with a specific gravity of 1.050 (usually read as "fifty") will weigh, pint for pint, 1.05 times as much as
pure water. The other common scale is the Balling, or Plato, scale.
It converts this comparison into a percentage of sucrose (cane
sugar) that would raise the specific gravity by the measured difference. The assumption is that the excess weight of a beer wort is due
to the sugar dissolved in it. This is only partially true, as beer wort
contains many other dissolved materials in addition to sugar.

Hydrometers need a fairly tall container in which to float,
and the glass or plastic sample jar is best for this. Also, like thermometers, hydrometers should be calibrated. Simply float the
instrument in tap water at exactly 60°F. It should read zero (1.000
on the S.G. scale). In taking the reading, follow the directions that
come with the hydrometer. In some cases, you have to read the
point at the top of the *meniscus* (the curve where the water rides
up the stem). In other cases, you ignore the meniscus and sight
straight across the surface of the water. Either way, if the reading
is off, you must note the error and correct all your readings to account for it.

Since hydrometers are only accurate at one temperature,
they are furnished with a table for temperature correction. In

reading specific gravity, it is best to cool the wort to near room temperature before reading it so that any temperature correction you need to apply will be small. Furthermore, if your hydrometer is off at 60°F, you will have to apply two corrections to readings at other temperatures.

There is one more complication to using a hydrometer. When you float the instrument in a liquid saturated with gas — such as fermenting beer — bubbles will cling to it and lift it. The beer must be de-gassed by repeatedly stirring the sample and spooning out the foam, until no more gas evolves. This is the only way to get an accurate reading.

You need a way to measure the pH of the mash, runoff, and sparge water. The choices are digital readout pH meters and paper or plastic test strips. The former are much better and much more costly. The strips work on the principle of a color change when they are immersed in a solution. They are adequate for homebrewing but have two drawbacks. First, they tend to read low — for example, 5.3 when the actual pH is 5.5. Second, they can be hard to read, especially in artificial light. It is best to read them by a window, against a neutral white background. The plastic strips made by Merck are best because they are easier to read and have a wider range than ordinary pH papers.

The last measuring tool you need is a logbook. Instrument readings quickly lose their value unless they are recorded systematically. A number of brewer's log form books are available. Whichever one you pick, be prepared to make modifications and additions. The more information you record about your specific procedures, the more useful your log will be.

# 8

# What Happens in the Mash Tun?

**H**aving looked at the materials and equipment that are used in wort production, it is now time to look at the process itself. In this chapter we will discuss the scientific basis for the ancient art of brewing. Remember that the science came later, and while it has brought about improvements, it has not fundamentally altered malting or brewing practices. You don't need a background in biochemistry to make good beer, but if you understand a bit about what is going on in your mash tun, you can choose to alter your procedures in order to get the results you want.

## The Mash-In

Mashing-in is just a brewer's term for mixing the *grist* (crushed malt and adjunct flakes) with water in the mash tun. Once this is done, enzymes are released into solution and the amazing transformation of grain and water into sweet wort begins. Mashing-in may be done at a variety of temperatures. Infusion mashes are mashed-in at about 150°F; decoction and step mashes are mixed at lower temperatures and raised through a series of steps. There are practical reasons why these different procedures were developed.

# Enzymes

The first thing we need is a clearer picture of what defines an enzyme. In the discussion of malt, we mentioned that the raw barley is germinated in order to trigger the production of enzymes, which break down complex organic molecules into simpler ones. In brewing, this is true, although a biologist would say we are selling these compounds short. Actually, enzymes are large protein molecules that bring about all the many chemical changes that sustain life. Every living cell contains numerous enzymes that catalyze the reactions by which each produces energy, grows, and multiplies.

Like all proteins, enzymes are fragile. They can be destroyed by heat. Very few enzymes can survive at 212°F and many are deactivated at much lower temperatures. They also require certain conditions in order to work. The most important of these to brewers are temperature and pH. In fact, the acid rest of a pale malt mash is the story of using one enzyme to set the right pH so that other enzymes can do their jobs.

# The Acid Rest

Pale lager malt is rich in *phytin,* a complex organic phosphate containing both calcium and magnesium. Malt also contains the enzyme *phytase,* which is active at temperatures of 86° to 128°F. A traditional decoction mash begins with a stand at around 95°F, which allows this enzyme to break down phytin into calcium and magnesium phosphates (which precipitate) and phytic acid. Phytic acid is very weak, but it has a strong affinity for calcium ions that react with it, both to form calcium phosphate and to release hydrogen ions in the process. Inorganic malt phosphates also react with calcium to release hydrogen ions, but the phytic acid reaction is more efficient. The malt itself contains enough calcium to sustain the reaction. This means that a mash in which phytase is active does not need much calcium in the brewing water in order to lower the pH. Active phytase makes it possible to brew pale lager in very soft (low-calcium, low-total alkalinity) water without adding a calcium salt.

This description exactly fits the water of Plzeň, in the Czech Republic, where the first pale lager was brewed in 1842. The water is very low in both carbonate and calcium, and a triple-decoction system is employed. The first rest is devoted solely to reducing the pH of the mash.

Pale ale and dark beer (lager or ale) mashes never have used an acid rest. Historically, dark beers could be made only from alkaline water, and relied on the acidity of the dark roasted grains to lower the mash pH. It is impossible to brew pale beers from such water, as the bicarbonate alkalinity completely overpowers the weak action of phytase. In modern practice, if dark beers are brewed from low-carbonate water, the mash pH can be raised, if necessary, by adding calcium carbonate.

Pale ale is usually mashed by a single-temperature infusion but an acid rest would not help in this instance. The long kilning given to this malt deactivates phytase so the only phytic acid present in an ale mash is that formed during malting. Ale brewers, therefore, have always had to rely on the calcium content of their brewing water to bring about the desired reduction of pH.

In recent times, the general trend has been to simplify and shorten the mash, and only a few traditionalist lager breweries still use an acid rest. The reaction can take hours to lower the pH, and the cost in time and energy is high. It is quicker and simpler to add some calcium to the mash water in the form of gypsum or calcium chloride.

## Proteins and What They Do

It is almost impossible to draw a simple diagram of a protein, because in shape and size this type of organic matter is enormously variable and complex. However, the basic building blocks of any protein are amino acids, which are themselves rather impressive substances. Twenty-two different amino acids are found in malt proteins, and they vary widely in their makeup. However, all amino acids contain carbon, hydrogen, oxygen, and nitrogen, and they all have one part of their structure that is identical to that of every other amino acid. This section, which is represented by the formula below, is what enables amino acids to link together to form proteins:

$$NH_2\text{-CH-COOH.}$$
$$|$$
$$R$$

*Molecular structure of an amino acid*

(The *R* in the formula stands for the remaining part of the molecule and varies from one acid to another.) Because this segment is identical, any two amino acids can join by forming a *peptide bond.* What happens is that one of the hydrogen atoms at the $NH_2$ end of the substructure combines with the OH part at the other end of a second molecule, thus creating a molecule of water and leaving the two amino acids joined like this:

$$NH_2\text{-CH-CO-NH-CH-COOH.}$$
$$|\qquad\qquad|$$
$$R\qquad\qquad R$$

This is the generic formula (so to speak) for a *dipeptide,* the simplest sort of protein. Other proteins are formed in the same manner, but hundreds of amino acids can be linked together to form huge molecules of virtually infinite variety. Still, the heart of them all is the peptide bond.

One way to classify proteins is according to the number of amino acid molecules they contain. The simplest are the di- and tripeptides, which, as you would expect, contain two and three amino acids respectively. Somewhat larger proteins are given the general name *polypeptides,* and even bigger proteins are called *peptones.* Finally we get to the largest proteins and have to draw a distinction. Some of these gigantic molecules are soluble in water and are called *albumins;* those that are insoluble are called *globulins.* Malt contains proteins of all sizes, including both globulins and albumins. The reason protein breakdown *(proteolysis)* is important is that, in general, the larger proteins are not wanted in beer, whereas the small and medium-sized ones are desirable. There are several reasons for this.

First, there is the matter of yeast nutrition. Yeast is a simple organism and cannot break down complex proteins. It requires a ready-made supply of amino acids in order to efficiently synthesize the complex proteins that make up much of its cellular structure. Fortunately, brewers are only too happy to cater to this need by inducing the breakdown of proteins during malting and mashing. One of the most common tests of wort quality is its content of amino acids.

The medium-sized proteins (polypeptides and peptones) are not useful to the yeast, but we want them in our beer for other reasons. They contribute to the body or palate fullness of the beer, and they are also responsible for head retention. By reducing surface tension, they increase the stability of the bubbles that are formed as the carbon dioxide gas comes out of solution in the glass. The result is the head of foam and resulting Belgian lace so prized by beer drinkers.

On the other hand, proteins are also responsible for haze. Large peptones and albumins can clump together, or flocculate, to form large, insoluble particles that scatter light and thereby cloud the beer. Haze is not the sole responsibility of proteins, because tannins derived from the malt husks also play a big part. As a rule, reducing the number of large protein molecules in beer will make it less prone to haze.

The only way the brewer can assist the breakdown of proteins in the mash is to set conditions favorable for the activity of the proteolytic enzymes and let them work. In other words a brewer should run a protein rest.

## Enzymes and Mash Conditions

There are at least eight enzymes in malt that can break down proteins, and they all do precisely the same thing. Enzymes break the peptide bonds that hold the molecules together. They do this by reversing the process described previously, that is, they attack the CO-NH link where two amino acids are joined together, and, after making the separation, they take the two ions of a water molecule (H and OH) and stick them onto the NH and CO groups respectively. Because a water molecule is used in this process, it is called *hydrolysis.*

The fact that there are eight enzymes capable of this little feat does not mean that they are identical in any other way. Each has its own preferences as to pH and temperature. Also, the complex shape of an enzyme makes it resemble a lock. Only proteins (keys) of a certain shape and size will fit into it. Enzymes that can only break down small proteins are called *peptidases;* those that prefer to work on larger proteins are called *proteases.* Since these enzymes all work together in the mash kettle, there is no practical reason for discussing ideal operating conditions for each one. It is enough to know that the optimum pH for both proteases and peptidases is 4.6–5.2. Optimum temperature range is 122° to 140°F for proteases and 113° to 122°F for peptidases. It follows that the traditional protein rest temperature of 122°F is a good compromise for maximum breakdown of both large and small proteins, while the pH of a typical mash (5.3) is only a bit high.

Actually, that pH is not as much higher as it seems. The pH readings are usually taken — and always specified in this book — with the wort or mash sample at room temperature. At high temperatures, however, the pH values of the mash are displaced downward a little, so that 5.5 at room temperature translates into an actual working pH of 5.2 in the mash kettle at 150°F. A room temperature reading of 5.5 translates into an actual working pH of about 5.3 at 122°F, so you can appreciate that, even at the high end of the range, we are very close to optimum conditions for proteolysis.

There are good reasons to avoid lower pH values in the mash. First of all, the recommended room temperature value of 5.3 is favorable to the action of the starch-converting enzymes that are also at work in the mash tun. Furthermore, low mash pH values render large proteins more soluble, and this is not desirable. It reduces the *hot break* — the coagulation of proteins and tannins in the kettle. Sometimes it is necessary to accept mash pH values as low as 5.0 with dark beers, but they should never deliberately be set that low.

As with the acid rest, recent trends in lager brewing have favored elimination of the protein rest. Modern pale malts are well and uniformly modified. In an all-malt wort, there are almost always plenty of amino acids available for yeast growth. The haze problem is probably the best reason to utilize a protein rest, and, for homebrewers who are trying to make a clear beer without filtration, it is still worthwhile. It is unavoidable when using the double mash or decoction methods; however, an over-long protein rest can cause problems with foam retention and a thin body, so if you choose to include a protein rest, keep it to half an hour or less.

## Starch Conversion

The acid rest and protein rest are optional steps in brewing. You can, if you choose, simply omit them. Most microbreweries and many larger commercial breweries do so, and yet, with modern materials, they manage to make good beer. But there is no getting away from starch conversion. The transformation of starch to sugar is one of the turning points of making beer. The following discussion will explain how temperature and pH variations affect the outcome. But right at the start, you need to understand that brewing is not like tinkering with a watch, where if you make one false move the whole thing comes apart in your hands. It doesn't work that way in starch conversion and homebrewing. Temperature control is important during starch conversion, but remember that mistakes are correctable. There is a good deal of leeway built into the process.

## Starches, Dextrins, and Sugars

Almost all the carbohydrates in malt and wort are based on one simple sugar, glucose. This compound is called a "single sugar" because it is the simplest sort of molecule that has the basic characteristics of a sugar, including the sweet taste. In the older chemistry texts, glucose was usually represented as a chain of six carbon molecules linked together by single bonds, with oxygen, hydrogen, and hydroxyl groups bound to each carbon. However, almost all glucose molecules actually exist as rings, with the first and fifth carbon atoms sharing an atom of oxygen (see illustration). The sixth carbon and its associated atoms are not part of the ring. For reasons to be explained shortly, the structure of glucose is extremely important. Glucose is what both humans and yeast cells metabolize to produce energy. Yeast can also ferment fructose, which has the same chemical formula as glucose ($C_6H_{12}O_6$) but a different ring arrangement (in fructose the second and fifth carbons share an oxygen atom, and both the first and sixth carbons are outside the ring). However, the preferred food is glucose.

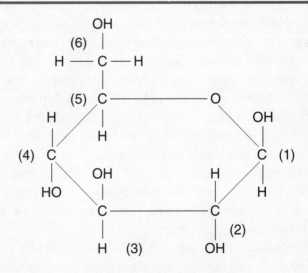

*Molecular formula of glucose*

*Molecular formula of maltose*

The complex sugars, starches, and dextrins that have been mentioned from time to time in this book are built up from glucose molecules. The illustration shows the simplest of these compounds, maltose. As you can see, it is formed from two glucose molecules by removing a hydrogen ion from the first carbon of one glucose and the hydroxyl ion from the fourth carbon of the other. The result is a pair of glucose molecules linked by an oxygen atom between them, and a molecule of water. Note how similar this is to the linkage of amino acid molecules to form proteins.

The link between the two glucose molecules is called a 1-4 link, after the carbon atoms involved. Large carbohydrates can be built up by 1-4 links to make molecules that resemble a string of beads, each bead being a glucose molecule. Long strings are starches; shorter strings are dextrins. When the lengths get short enough, we can name the compounds according to how many glucose molecules they contain. They can be considered true sugars because they taste sweet and dissolve freely in water. *Maltotetraose*, for example, is a string of four glucoses hooked together by 1-4 links.

There are other ways that glucose molecules can be joined together. *Beta glucans* are long strings containing a mixture of 1-4 and 1-3 links. They tend to be gummy and increase the viscosity of beer wort. In a well-modified malt, most of the beta

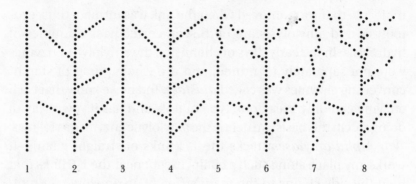

*Malt Starches and Enzyme Action. 1) Straight-chain starch (amylose). 2) Branched starch (amylopectin). 3) Beta glucans (looks like amylose, but contains both 1-3 and 1-4 links). 4) Amylopectin under attack by dextrinase. 5) Amylose being attacked by beta amylase. 6) Amylopectin attacked by beta amylase. 7) Amylose attacked by alpha amylase. 8) Amylopectin attacked by alpha amylase.*

glucans are broken down during germination, but the use of raw barley in the grist will often yield a wort of high viscosity due to the presence of beta glucans.

Long strings of glucose connected only by 1-4 links are called **amyloses.** There is another type of starch molecule that has side chains branching off the main string, rather like limbs branching off the trunk of a tree. These starches are called **amylopectins** and are worth noting because the branches are joined to the main string by a 1-6 link. Both these starches can be classed together because they are insoluble. Short-branched strings are somewhat soluble and increase wort viscosity, in a manner similar to beta glucans. For this reason these dextrins are now also called "alpha glucans."

# The Amylases

**Amylases** are enzymes that break the various bonds that hold starches, dextrins, and complex sugars together. They all work in the same way as the proteolytic enzymes, replacing the water molecule that was removed when the link was formed; thus, pro-teolysis and amylolysis are both seen correctly as examples of hydrolysis. In the early days of chemistry, the amylolytic enzymes were not separately identified, and the whole group of starch-converting enzymes was called *diastase.* Today, we know that each enzyme can only break one type of link, and has its own way of doing so. On this basis, we define the amylolytic enzymes as follows:

*Alpha amylase* attacks the 1-4 links of straight chains. It works any place along such a chain, except near the 1-6 links that hold the side chains to the main string of an amylopectin mol-ecule. Because it attacks the bonds at random, alpha amylase may break off molecules of glucose, maltose, maltotriose, malto-tetraose, or even long dextrins and alpha glucans.

*Beta amylase* also attacks the 1-4 link, but it has different work habits. It seems to view the amylose molecule as a sort of banana, and systematically takes bites off the end! It works *only* on the end of a chain, and always breaks off two glucose molecules at a time. This means that the products of beta amylase are mal-tose and what are called "limit dextrins." The latter are dextrins that are formed because, like alpha, beta amylase cannot break the 1-6 branching links and has to stop eating when it has bitten off a straight chain down to the point where it branches.

*Dextrinase* attacks the 1-6 links only. Thus its effect is to make amylose molecules out of amylopectins. Since these bonds pose a limit to the other enzymes, you can understand why its role, though less appreciated than that of alpha and beta amy-lase, is very important. Unfortunately, dextrinase rarely survives in the malt kiln, because it is extremely sensitive to heat. Few, if any, 1-6 links can be broken in the mash kettle. The brewer must rely on the maltster to supply a fully modified malt that has un-dergone a long period of dextrinase activity during germination.

*Beta glucanase* attacks the 1-3 links in beta glucan strings. Like dextrinase, it is somewhat underappreciated because its work is normally done during malting. However, it does survive low-temperature kilning. Beta glucanase is active at relatively low tem-peratures and is rapidly destroyed in the starch conversion range. Thus, to reap its benefits, a low-temperature rest must be included in the mash schedule. In fact, the activity of glucanase and beta amylase is just as significant in the so-called protein rest as is protein breakdown.

I think you can see how all these enzymes work together. It is only by their combined efforts, during malting as well as mashing, that a satisfactory wort can be produced.

## Practical Considerations

Each of the amylases has its own preferences as to temperature, pH, and other environmental factors. This means that we can set mash conditions to favor the action of one enzyme over another in order to regulate their relative contribution to the finished wort. This is especially true when using a simple-infusion mashing system. Conditions that favor beta amylase activity will produce a highly fermentable wort, rich in maltose. Conditions that favor alpha amylase will yield more maltotriose and complex unfermentable sugars and dextrins.

In practice, the optimum conditions determined in the laboratory for each enzyme are of little use to the brewer. For example, beta amylase works best at a low pH (around 5.0). But in the mash kettle, beta depends on alpha amylase. In practical trials, running the mash at a pH of 5.0 gives a less fermentable wort than using a somewhat higher value. This is because alpha amylase works better at higher pH levels. Similarly, mash temperature must be compromised to allow alpha and beta amylase to work as a team, if one wishes to produce a highly fermentable wort. Beta amylase works best and survives longest at around 140°F, but malt starch does not fully gelatinize until it reaches 149°F, and, until this happens, much of the malt starch is not accessible. (*Gelatinization* is the process by which starch granules break up and disperse evenly throughout a liquid. If you have ever used cornstarch or flour to thicken a sauce, you were observing gelatinization.) For complete starch conversion, therefore, the mash *must* be brought to at least 149°F, which also benefits alpha amylase. Alpha amylase works best at higher temperatures, with its maximum activity at 158°F. In the mash tun, then, the conditions that produce

the most fermentable wort are a pH of 5.3 to 5.4, and a temperature of 149°F. At higher temperatures, beta amylase is destroyed
more rapidly and alpha activity is greater, so that mash temperatures as high as 159°F can be used to make a less fermentable
wort and, consequently, a thicker, maltier beer. A high pH (around
5.7) also favors alpha over beta amylase.

Another variable is time, but this is related to temperature.
The hotter the mash, the more quickly beta amylase is deactivated, and the more active alpha amylase is. With highly diastatic
lager malt, all the starch will be converted to sugar within 20 minutes at 158°F. A longer rest will allow further breakdown by the
enzymes and give a more fermentable wort. At a lower mash temperature, starch conversion will take longer because alpha amylase activity is subdued. Forty-five minutes may be required at 149°F.

Especially when dealing with coarsely crushed malt, which
is typical of both microbrewery and homebrewing operations,
temperature has an influence on the yield of sugar from the grain.
The coarse grits require a long time to absorb water, and a relatively high mash temperature will allow the grits to swell and their
starches to gelatinize more quickly. What this means, in practice,
is that for maximum yield with typical American brewers' malt,
an infusion mash must be run at a high temperature, around
158°F, in order to get the maximum amount of extract from the
malt. Such high mash temperatures will also yield a wort of high
viscosity and low fermentability, which, for many styles of beer,
is not what is desired.

These considerations become even more complicated when
one is dealing with a malt of low enzyme content, such as Munich,
Vienna, or British ale malt. These malts have had a large proportion of their amylases destroyed on the kiln, and the loss of beta
amylase is always greatest because it is more sensitive to heat than
alpha. Nonetheless, alpha is also seriously reduced, and mash
temperatures must be low enough to allow the remaining fraction of this enzyme to survive long enough for starch conversion
to go to completion. If this occurs, the results will be low extract
and possible starch haze in the finished beer. With these malts,
mash times must be prolonged to compensate for the lower level

of enzyme activity. Yet, no matter how one manipulates conditions, it is just not possible to get the same degree of fermentability with a high-kilned malt as with a low-kilned one.

High mash temperatures favor alpha amylase and give a less fermentable wort. A slightly high mash pH (5.7) also helps alpha amylase and gives a less fermentable wort. Short mash times give the amylases less time to break down dextrins and likewise give a less fermentable wort. To get maximum fermentability, these conditions must be reversed. Use a long, low-temperature mash schedule and set the pH around 5.3. When working with high-kilned malts, long mashes and low temperatures (150° to 153°F) are necessary to assure starch conversion.

Another factor influencing enzyme activity is the stiffness (thickness) of the mash. A thin mash — say, 2.5 quarts of water per pound of grain — ultimately favors a more complete breakdown of carbohydrates in the kettle. However, because the enzymes are more diluted, breakdown takes longer to achieve. On the other hand, a stiffer mash — around 1.33 quarts per pound — initially favors starch breakdown; however, as amylolysis proceeds, the increasing concentration of sugars in the mash inhibits further enzyme activity. A stiff mash also favors breakdown of proteins in the mash kettle. It provides one other benefit in that it protects the enzymes better. At any given temperature, the thinner the mash, the faster the enzymes will be deactivated.

# The Uses of Complexity

Some of the compromises that are forced on a brewer by the chemistry of amylolysis can be avoided by adopting a step mash or decoction mash procedure. Even if protein breakdown is not needed or desired, a low temperature rest (131° to 145°F) will enable the brewer to get a better yield of extract and a more fermentable wort. This is because a rest in this range will allow the glucanase and beta amylase enzymes to work for a longer period of time (in the case of glucanase, to work at all) before they are destroyed by the high temperatures of the main starch conversion rest.

A decoction mash (single or double) has the same effects as a step mash, with the added benefit that boiling a fraction of the mash (typically ⅓) bursts and gelatinizes all the starches contained in that fraction, making them available to the malt enzymes. In practical trials, even with well-crushed, well-modified malt, decoction gives a higher yield than other mash methods, and the difference is much more significant when working with coarsely crushed malt, or malt that has been unevenly modified.

There are, however, criticisms that have been leveled at complex mash systems. First, the time and energy costs are great. Today, even in Germany, pale beers are usually made by the infusion method. Second, complex mash systems require more, or at least more sophisticated, equipment. From a brewing viewpoint, decoction is especially criticized because the repeated boils of the mash extract more color from the grain and somewhat darken the finished beer. However, this can actually be an advantage when making amber and dark lagers, where the sharp flavors of roasted malts (e.g., black or chocolate malt) are not desired. When attempting to make these beers by infusion mashing, it is hard to get the appropriate color from high-kilned and caramel malts alone. Another effect of boiling the mash is the extraction of tannins from the grain husks, which can lead to an astringent, grainy character in the beer. The pH of the mash inhibits this action to some extent, but a high quality, low-tannin barley is certainly an important requirement for decoction mashing. However, most of the cases of grainy flavors in beer can be traced to improper sparge techniques.

In the end, the choice of a more elaborate mash method must be left up to the individual brewer. As in many aspects of this art, there are no perfect answers, for every attempt to improve in one area also incurs risk in another. Advanced homebrewers sometimes become ardent partisans of one particular mash system, but it is important to understand that the complexities of brewing chemistry do not allow for absolute certainty about what is "best" in all cases. It depends on your materials, your equipment, and your aims, especially the type of beer you have chosen to brew.

# Sparging

Once starch conversion is complete, the solid part of the mash — husks, small particles, and flourlike fines — is redundant. It needs to be separated from the liquid part of the mash (the sweet wort) before the boil. This is because the *draff*, as this solid fraction is called, contains large amounts of protein, lipids (fatty substances), silicates, tannins, and usually unconverted starch. If the mash were boiled without being sparged, a large proportion of these substances would be extracted into the wort, causing fermentation disorders, haze, poor head retention, and astringency.

Please do not think that every last particle of draff needs to be removed during sparging. If a few teaspoons of solid material are carried into the kettle, little harm will be done. In defining an ideal sparge, however, we have to say that one of the aims is to leave all the solid mash material in the lauter tun.

In an ideal sparge, all soluble matter should be carried into the boiler. In other words, every last bit of sugar should be rinsed out of the draff, so that you get the full brewing value from your malt and adjuncts. This goal is, unfortunately, unattainable. Sparging, like any sort of rinse, is a process of dilution, and one reaches a point where it would require several gallons of additional water to wash out a few ounces of sugar.

In practice, sparging must be limited. You can collect only a volume of wort equal to the final volume you want in your fermenter (in other words, your batch size), plus as much additional liquid as you can boil off in 75 to 90 minutes.

One old brewers' rule of thumb is to sparge with no more water than was used in mixing the mash. This is a good guideline when thin mashes are used, as in decoction or double mashing. As the mash is sparged, the wort thins out and its pH rises. This in turn causes large amounts of tannin to be leached out of the husks. The result is an unpleasant, "grainy" astringency in the finished beer. One way around this difficulty is to restrict sparging. However, graininess can also be minimized by lowering the pH of the sparge water. Many breweries routinely adjust their sparge water to a pH of 5.7 using phosphoric, sulfuric, or hydrochloric acid.

The other factor in tannin extraction is heat. High temperatures during the sparge will dissolve tannins and also unconverted starches and other undesirable substances. For this reason, most breweries hold their sparge water to no more than 168°F, and some use a lower temperature.

## Wort Clarity

There is some controversy about how clear the runoff from the lauter tun should be. The lipids contained in the cloudy first runnings have positive value as yeast nutrients. On the other hand, they also are precursors of many so-called staling compounds that degrade the flavor of packaged beer. Some large commercial breweries have experienced fermentation troubles that were traced to over-clarifying the runoff from the lauter tun. However, few microbreweries or homebrewers are able to clarify their wort as well as the bigger brewers can. In addition, they usually brew all-malt beers, which means their worts have a high level of yeast nutrients.

There is a simple, practical test of whether your wort is over-clarified. If you are getting normal lag periods and fermentation times, there is no need to deliberately reduce the clarity of your runoff. On the other hand, if your beer is liable to oxidation, paying more attention to wort clarity may be helpful.

# 9

# Mashing and Lautering

**T**his chapter explains the process of making wort from barley malt and adjuncts. It is of necessity a somewhat general overview. No two breweries are alike, and there are many aspects of procedure that are more or less dictated by available equipment. You also will find that your own methods will change as you become more proficient.

## Crushing the Malt

Crushing is the best word to describe the milling of barley malt. For efficient sparging, it is important not to grind the malt to flour. The husks should be split open so that water can permeate the pieces of starchy endosperm. Malt enzymes can act only in solution, and, if grains are left intact, their extract potential will be lost. On the other hand, if the husks are pulverized, the wort will be very hard to run off.

If you have ever seen or used a hand-cranked grain mill, you know that it represents a serious compromise from the ideal malt mill. It can work satisfactorily, but it requires careful adjustment, and you must not expect perfect results. Some grains will just be cut in half by the plates, and the husks will be powdered to some extent. A great deal depends on your malt. The more uniform the grains are in size, the easier it is to get a good crush. With some malts, you may have to accept an adjustment that leaves a few of the smallest grains intact.

I hope you have the idea that an over-coarse grind is preferable to an over-fine one. With this in mind, I suggest the following setup procedure. The first time you use your grain mill, wash it carefully in lots of detergent to remove all traces of the packing grease. Rinse and dry each part, then coat the sleeve-bearing surface and the ball-bearing well with grease (I prefer long-fiber wheel-bearing grease because it will not run) and reassemble, being careful not to get the grease onto any areas that will come into contact with the grain. Now clamp the mill to a table and tighten the adjusting screw until you can just feel it touching the ball bearing and beginning to push the outer (moving) plate toward the inner (fixed) one. Back the screw off one full turn and fix the adjustment by tightening the wing nut. Check to see if the gap between the plates is fairly uniform, regardless of the position of the handle. If not, you can improve things by disassembling the mill and grinding or filing the mating surfaces on the outside of the rotating plate and the adjusting screw. To get an even grind, the rotating plate must remain parallel to the fixed plate throughout its rotation.

Once you have the mill set up, crush a cup of malt and examine it. If there are a lot of whole grains, tighten the screw a half turn and run another cup of malt through. If, on the other hand, there are not many whole or half husks in your trial cup of grain, back off the screw half a turn for your second run. Repeat this procedure again, if necessary. By the time you have crushed three cups of grain, you should be close to the optimum setting. Fine-tune by adjusting the screw by quarter, or even eighth, turns until you get what seems to be a good setting.

When you have proven your adjustment by crushing a load of grain malt and brewing with it, mark it on the adjusting screw. The setting for pale malt will also work for special malts, but wheat and rye malt require a finer crush, and if you ever use these materials, you will have to tighten the screw considerably — probably about half a turn.

The adjustment procedure for standard roller mills is essentially the same as for hand-cranked. Besides setting the gap between the rolls, you must make sure that the rolls are aligned so that the gap is uniform from one side to the other.

In crushing malt, it is best to mix dark specialty grains into the grist during the middle of the grind. Hold back a pound of pale malt and run it through the mill at the end. This will "flush out" dark grain flour from the machinery. Dark grain residue from the mill can noticeably affect the color of a pale beer, brewed immediately after a darker one.

# Preparing the Water

With so many choices of water treatment, it is impossible to outline a specific procedure for preparing water before mashing. If your procedure involves using acid to reduce the pH, remember that pH papers are accurate only at room temperature. Hot water samples must be cooled before checking.

All breweries require a large supply of hot water — ideally, about twice the volume of the batch size. In most homebreweries it is possible to heat a large amount of water in a hurry, so elaborate preheating rituals are not required. However, it is important to have your sparge water ready to go at the end of the mash cycle.

Mash water should be brought to the ideal temperature for mashing-in, called "strike temperature," in the mash tun. For infusion mashing in a heatable kettle or mash/lauter tun, prepare 1 gallon of water for every 3 pounds of grain. Strike temperature should be about 11°F, higher than the desired mash temperature.

Picnic-cooler type, insulated mash/lauter tuns must be preheated before use. The water temperature should be about 180°F, and the volume must be at least ⅔ the total capacity of the tun:

for example, 14 quarts for a 21-quart cooler. After running in the preheat water, cover the vessel and let it stand for 20 minutes before returning the water to your kettle or hot liquor tank. Then make up the volume of mash water to the correct temperature, tempering the hot water with cool treated water if necessary.

## Mashing-In

The basic mash-in procedure is quite simple. Put the correct amount of prepared water into the mash tun, check the temperature, and correct if necessary. Then stir in the grist. When all the grist is in, stir thoroughly, then check the temperature and adjust if needed. If the mash is too hot, the simplest way to reduce it is with cold water. If the mash is not hot enough, either turn on the heat under the mash tun or, if the mash tun cannot be heated, add some boiling hot water.

In adjusting the mash temperature, be cautious. Be sure you have stirred thoroughly and given your thermometer plenty of time to settle in. Also, when using hot or cold water, add it a little at a time and keep stirring. There is no need to panic. When heating the mash tun on a stove or burner, apply heat in short bursts and check frequently. The temperature will continue to rise for several minutes after the burner is turned off.

With the mash temperature set, you can turn your attention to pH. After the mash stands for a few minutes undisturbed, the grain solids will begin to settle. With a stainless steel spoon, skim a bit of the clear liquid from the surface and allow it to cool for a few minutes before checking. Remember that pH papers are accurate only at room temperature. After checking with a pH paper strip, discard the sample. Also try to read the color comparison in good, natural light, against a white background. If you are lucky enough to have a pH meter, be sure to follow the instructions for calibration and temperature compensation.

If the mash pH is outside the proper range of 5.2 to 5.6, you should add calcium carbonate (to raise it) or calcium chloride or calcium sulfate (to lower it). In either case, ½ teaspoon at a time is recommended. Recheck pH after each addition. In some cases, with very dark beers, you may have to accept a mash value as low as 5.0. Under no circumstances should you add more than 2 teaspoons of calcium carbonate to a 5-gallon mash.

## Maintaining and Boosting Temperature

A single infusion mash should be held at conversion temperature of 150° to 158°F for at least one hour. If using high-kilned malt, such as British pale ale malt, as the base of the grist, 1½ hours is needed. During this stand, the mash tun must be kept covered except when stirring.

An uninsulated heatable mash tun or mash/lauter tun should be stirred and checked for temperature every 15 to 20 minutes. An insulated picnic-cooler type tun should be stirred and checked after half an hour. This type should not need a boost to maintain conversion temperature. Uninsulated tuns may need heating, using short bursts as described above.

## Step Mashing

A step mash is essentially the same as a single infusion except that the grist is mashed in at a lower temperature, typically 122° to 131°F. The proportion of water to grist is the same. Normally a strike temperature 9° to 10° hotter than the desired mash temperature will do the trick. The mash is held in this temperature range for 30 minutes for protein rest. Then the mash is boosted to starch conversion temperature of 150° to 155°F.

The best way to boost the mash temperature is by applying short bursts of heat (2 to 4 minutes) with careful checking and lots of stirring between bursts. As you approach the target conversion temperature, use shorter bursts of heat to avoid overshooting. After you gain some experience, you will be able to regulate the heat applications in order to achieve what is called a particular "ramp" or rate of increase. For step mashing, a ramp of 1 to 2 degrees per minute is normal.

One variation is a short rest of 15 minutes or so at around 140°F on the way from the protein rest to conversion rest. This intermediate rest gives the beta amylase extra time to work and will increase the fermentability of the wort.

## Testing for Conversion

Many brewers use an iodine test to check for conversion. The procedure requires a clean white dish and some iodine solution. Tincture of iodine from the drugstore can be used, but special solutions made for the purpose are better, and may be available from some homebrew or lab supply houses.

The technique requires you to withdraw a few drops of liquid from the top of the mash and put them on a dish. Put a drop of iodine next to the mash liquid and observe where they run together. A color change to blue indicates that starch is still present and mashing must be continued.

This test is often used with double mashing or decoction mashing, where it is desirable to end the starch conversion rest as soon as the test reads negative (i.e., no starch). However, with imperfectly crushed malt (such as almost all homebrewers have), a lot of starch is bound up in coarse grits. It takes a long time for the grits to yield up their starch as sugar. If the conversion rest is ended when the iodine test is negative, a large proportion of starch will remain unconverted, and the yield of sugar will be low. For single infusion or step mashing, it is better to work by time, rather than trusting the iodine reaction.

## The Mash-Out

With step mashing, the last step is a temperature boost to 165° to 168°F for a short stand, normally only 5 minutes. This high temperature rest destroys all remaining enzymes and fixes the balance of sugars and fermentability in the wort. It also allows the wort to be run off more easily, because sugar solutions are thinner and less viscous at higher temperatures. If you are using a mash/lauter tun that can be heated, a mash-out will be beneficial even for single infusion mashes. However, it is not necessary.

# Decoction Mashing

Decoction mashing differs in several important respects from infusion and step mashing. One fundamental difference is that a considerably thinner mash should be made: only 2 pounds of grain for every 1 gallon of water. The entire process is considerably longer than other methods.

The classic triple-decoction mash starts with what is called "mixing" or "doughing-in" the grist with a small amount of cold water. The mash is raised to its first acid rest stage by adding boiling water slowly until a temperature of around 95°F is reached. Subsequent boosts, to 122°F, 150°F, and 168°F, are achieved by decocting a portion of the mash, boiling it for 20 minutes, then returning it to the mash tun. The stand between adding one decoction and taking the next is normally 15 minutes. However, conversion is checked with the iodine test before taking the last decoction.

A double-decoction mash omits the dough-in, boiling-water infusion, and acid rest. The grain is mashed-in with the water at a temperature in protein rest range. Because of the larger proportion of water to grain, the strike heat of the water should only need to be 6°F to 8°F above mash-in temperature. The boosts to conversion and mash-out are achieved by decoctions. Alternatively, there may be two decoctions taken between protein rest and the end of conversion, perhaps with rests at 122° (mash-in), 140° to 145° (for beta amylase), and 155° to 158° (for alpha amylase). The lower temperature rests last for 15 to 30 minutes, while the high temperature conversion rest is ended as soon as starch conversion is complete (checked by the iodine test). The final boost is done by directly heating the entire mash. This method offers a great deal of control of fermentability and high extract potential.

A single-decoction mash likewise may be done in two different ways. The grist may be mashed-in at starch conversion temperature, and then raised to mash-out temperature by decoction; or it may be mashed-in at protein rest temperature, raised to conversion by decoction, and then raised to mash-out by direct heat. The latter method is preferable, as direct heat is more reliable.

In removing the decoction, you should take as much as possible of the solid fraction of the mash. Take only enough liquid to make the decoction stirrable. Stir the decoction frequently during boils, in order to prevent scorching and sticking. You will want to apply fairly high heat in order to bring the decoction to a boil as quickly as possible, but, once it boils, lower the flame somewhat. Some experimentation is required to determine how much of the mash to take for each decoction. For this reason, a beginner should use a main mash tun that can be heated if necessary, in case the decoction does not raise the mash to the desired temperature.

Decoction mashing is elaborate and there are few fixed rules. Homebrewers who pursue it should first learn the basics by doing some infusion and step mashing, and by studying the information in the materials listed in the bibliography. Homebrewers who attempt decoction mashing should also be prepared for some surprises.

# Double Mashing

Double mashing is an offshoot of decoction mashing. In this case, however, the decoction is prepared separately. It consists of a very thin mash of the milled adjunct (rice or corn meal) along with 10 to 15 percent of the crushed pale malt. This grist is mashed-in using only 1 to 1½ pounds of grist per gallon of water, at starch conversion temperature (155° to 158°F). After a stand of 15 to 20 minutes, the mash is brought to a boil and boiled until the starch is gelatinized — that is, completely dispersed to a sticky, uniform mass with no hard starchy grits remaining. This typically takes about 20 minutes.

As soon as the adjunct mash is mixed and settled in at the conversion temperature, the main mash is mixed, using the remaining crushed malt and a minimum of water — 1 gallon for every 4 pounds of grist. The main mash is mixed at about 113°F normally, but the temperature must be set so that when the boiled adjunct mash is added to it, the entire mash will settle in at about 155°F. The main mash simply sits for an extended protein rest until the adjunct mash is ready to be added to it.

Normally, the main conversion rest lasts only until starch conversion, verified by the iodine test, is achieved. Then the mash is raised to mash-out temperature by directly heating the tun.

As you can see, double mashing is similar to decoction mashing in its complexity as well as its methodology. Once again, homebrewers need to prepare themselves well before attempting it.

# Preparation for Sparging

Preparation for sparging is simple. The lauter tun must be set in place with the grant under the spigot, and the kettle is set below the grant. Also, your volume of sparge water must be prepared and raised to the proper temperature. If you do a mash-out, 163°F is recommended. If you omit the mash-out, 168°F is preferred. The higher temperature will help because it will raise the temperature of the mash as the sparge goes on, and will assist the runoff.

The pH of the sparge water is adjusted in the same way as the pH of the mash, except that acid, rather than calcium salts, is used. If it is convenient, adjust the pH before heating the water. Proceed slowly, because if you go too far, the only way to reverse yourself is to add more water to the hot water tank.

At first, it is best to make up a volume of sparge water equal to your batch size. Usually, this will give you enough to make your required volume of wort. Later, with experience, you can make up just the quantity you need for a particular recipe. In general, the more water you use for mashing, the less you will need for sparging.

If your lauter tun has a false bottom, you should add prepared, heated sparge water to a level just covering the screen or plate. This is called "foundation water" and it helps with the initial runoff. Foundation water is not necessary if the lauter tun has a runoff system of slotted pipe or tubing, or, of course, if you are using a combined mash/lauter tun.

The last step in preparing for sparging, if you are using a separate lauter tun, is to transfer the mash to the lauter tun. Be careful when pouring from one vessel to another because the mash is hot enough to cause serious injury. After transfer, stir the mash briefly, then let it stand for 15 minutes so that the solid fraction can settle to the bottom.

## Clarifying the Wort (the Vorlauf)

The first step in sparging is to recirculate the wort by drawing it off and returning it to the top of the lauter tun. Begin by running the wort out at a moderate rate, around 1 quart every 2 minutes. The method is to open the tap from the lauter tun, then put a 1-quart pitcher under the tap of the grant and open it wide. This should allow you to drain the grant. When you have 1 quart or so of wort in the pitcher, close the tap of the grant and gently pour the cloudy wort on the surface of the mash, but do not pour too slowly. Collect another quart in the same manner. Keep repeating the cycle of collecting and returning the wort. As recirculation continues, the wort should clarify. If your runoff rate is right, the wort should be sufficiently clear — not absolutely bright, like a filtered beer, but fairly clear with only slight haze, and almost no chunks or grits — after about 15 minutes. If it takes much longer than this, or if the wort will not clear, you will need to increase the runoff rate. On the other hand, if the wort clears very rapidly, you may be draining off the wort too fast. This can cause problems because the filter bed that has been formed by the draff in the lauter tun will be packed too tightly.

One problem often encountered during the vorlauf (and later) is that pieces of draff will partially, or even totally, block the lauter tun valve. The cure is to swing the valve wide open for an instant and then close it again. Depending upon the type of valve on your lauter tun, blockage can be a major nuisance. If it presents serious difficulties you may have to replace the valve with another type. Butterfly valves and ball valves are the easiest types to work with.

## Running Off the Wort

Once the wort is clear, you can run it straight into the kettle. The flow rate should be somewhat slower than the rate during recirculation. During runoff, as the depth of wort above the filter bed drops, the bed itself will tend to pack down and you want to minimize this. One rule of thumb is to set the runoff rate so that it takes 10 to 20 minutes to complete the operation. The rate must be set with reference to the sparge rate (see below), because you cannot run off the "first wort" faster than you will run off the sparged wort. Runoff is complete when there is about 1 to 2 inches of wort standing on top of the filter bed.

## Sparging

Sparging is simply a matter of continuing the runoff, while pouring or gently running water on the surface of the grain bed to keep it covered. The flow of water must not agitate or cut a channel in the filter bed.

Runoff rate during sparging should be increased slowly. The filter bed is like an accordion, and will tend to open up as the wort thins out. To keep the grain bed compressed, suction must be maintained. If the bed opens up, it will release some of the fine material trapped in it, which will cloud the wort.

The reason for a slow initial runoff is to avoid compressing the filter bed too much. The more compressed it is at the start of sparging, the more difficult it will be to maintain suction and keep it from opening up during the sparge.

It is good practice to have a clear, open tube extending upward from the runoff outlet, between the lauter tun and the valve. This tube gives a visual indication of suction on the grain bed. To use it, mark the level at the end of the runoff step, and maintain that level or lower throughout the sparge.

Add water to the top of the grain bed at a rate that just matches the rate of wort outflow. This will maintain the level of water an inch or two above the surface of the grain bed.

One very important rule is that sparging should take at least 45 minutes. If it takes less, your efficiency will suffer. It takes time to leach the sugars out of the grits and husks that make up the filter bed. This means, for example, that if you need to collect 5 gallons of wort during the sparge, your average runoff rate should be 20 quarts in 45 minutes (20/45), or .44 quarts per minute, average. In practice, your runoff rate at the start of the sparge should be considerably slower than this, since you will have to increase it gradually as the wort thins.

During the sparge, it is a good idea to cut a cross-hatch pattern in the surface of the filter bed from time to time. This will help prevent the formation of cracks and channels and ensure that the water percolates straight down through the spent grains. Be sure not to cut too deep — leave the bottom 3 to 4 inches of the bed undisturbed.

If possible, you should arrange your equipment so that the kettle is sitting on its burner during the sparge. Then you can turn on the heat and bring the wort to a boil just as you finish collecting it. It will take some practice to get the timing down, but this is an easy way to speed up your brewing operation. One trick you should remember is to stir the wort thoroughly but gently when you turn on the heat. The heavy first worts on the bottom of the kettle scorch easily and should be diluted to avoid this problem.

Overall, the recirculation/runoff/sparge operation recommended here will take about 1½ to 2 hours. It is possible to do it faster, but the trade-off is poor wort clarity and/or poor extraction of sugars.

# 10

# Hops

**T**he hop is a bitter herb that is used almost exclusively for brewing. In earlier times, a number of herbs and spices were used to balance the natural sweetness of beer, but hops were found to have superior preservative abilities, and, during the Middle Ages they gradually spread throughout northern Europe. These days, their bitterness and aroma are an expected part of any beer's flavor.

The hop plant is *dioecious,* that is, the male and female flowers grow on separate plants. Because the species can be propagated by cutting, the male plant is expendable. Except for a few males used in cross-breeding programs, male hops have been outlawed in all hop-growing nations outside of Great Britain. The reason for this banishment is brewing value. Only the female flowers (or cones) contain the bitter resins and aromatic oil for which the plant is prized. If the female plant is pollinated, much of its energy will be expended to produce a crop of useless seeds. The seeds also contain tannin, which can give beer an astringent flavor.

Hops are grown in many varieties, usually named after their place of origin. Hallertau is the district north of Munich where the hops for the classic Munich beers are grown. Saaz hops come from the Zatec area in western Bohemia, near Pilsen. These varieties are examples of the aromatic or *noble hops,* which are prized for their fine flavoring qualities. They are still going strong today, but, in the past century, another type of hop, the *high alpha* or bittering hop, has been bred and cultivated as well. High alpha hops are so named because they have been bred to be high in alpha acid or humulone, the soft resin that is the main contributor in bittering beer. Ounce for ounce, they will often give double or triple the bitterness of the noble hops.

Early work in hop breeding focused on increasing bitterness, but, more recently, disease resistance, storage stability, and agricultural properties have also gained importance. Fungus diseases have ravaged the hop gardens of Europe for decades, and the raising of resistant strains is often a matter of economic survival for the brewing industry. In its native fields, the Hallertau hop has been virtually wiped out by downy mildew.

*Hops*

The more recent work in hop breeding stems from a growing recognition by brewers that hops are far more than a simple bittering commodity. The number of aromatic substances in hops is very large, and many of these components, though present in tiny quantities in the finished beer, exert a great influence on its flavor. Noble hops were never abandoned entirely even by the large commercial breweries, and today they seem to be staging a comeback. As a result, hop-breeding programs seem to have been refocused. In the

United States, we have new varieties such as Liberty, which combine the excellent aromatic and flavoring properties of the noble German hops with superior disease resistance and yield per acre.

## Hop Specifications

The most important specification of hops is the alpha acid content, stated as a percentage of the weight. Since alpha acids, also called *humulone,* are responsible for around 90 percent of the bitterness in beer, in practice we can duplicate any level of bitterness we want in a recipe by maintaining a consistent amount of alpha acid from batch to batch.

A related specification, less frequently available, is the percentage of *beta acid,* or *lupulone.* This resin has an unpleasant, clinging bitterness but is almost entirely insoluble at normal wort pH values (5.5 or lower), and it can generally be ignored.

A more important specification is the amount of *cohumulone,* stated as a percentage of the total alpha acids. Both humulone and lupulone are actually found in three different forms in the hop cone; they differ slightly in the arrangement of a few atoms in their chemical structure. The three are called humulone, cohumulone, and adhumulone. (The three types of lupulone carry the same prefixes.) Cohumulone is important because it is slightly different from its two partners; it is more soluble, or, to be technically accurate, it isomerizes to a greater extent. This means that hops high in cumulone will yield a little more bitterness than will those with low cumulone levels.

Cohumulone is believed also to impart a more clinging, harsh bitterness to finished beers. Hops that are high in cohumulone are mostly the newer, high-alpha varieties, and beers made with these hops certainly show this characteristic. Low-cohumulone hops are for the most part low-alpha, noble varieties with fine aromatic and flavoring properties.

Another important hop specification is keeping quality, which is usually rated on a verbal scale (poor, fair, good), according to how fast the alpha acids oxidize when the hops are stored at room temperature. Even though hops are dried in an oven

# Hop Specifications

| Variety | Alpha Acid | Beta Acid | Cohumulone of Alpha Acid | Storageability (of Alpha rem. after 6 mos. @ 20°C) | Total Oil (ml/100g) |
|---|---|---|---|---|---|
| **Aroma Hops** | | | | | |
| Cascade | 4.5–7.0 | 4.5–7.0% | 33–40% | 48–52% | 0.8–1.5 |
| Crystal | 2.0–4.5 | 4.5–6.5 | 20–26 | 50 | 1.0–1.5 |
| Fuggle | 4.0–5.5 | 1.5–2.0 | 25–32 | 60–65 | 0.7–1.2 |
| Hallertauer | 3.5–5.5 | 3.5–5.5 | 18–24 | 52–58 | 0.6–1.0 |
| Hersbrucker | 3.5–5.5 | 5.5–7.0 | 20–30 | 55–65 | 0.6–1.2 |
| Liberty | 3.0–5.0 | 3.0–4.0 | 24–30 | 35–55 | 0.6–1.2 |
| Mt. Hood | 5.0–8.0 | 5.0–7.5 | 22–23 | 50–60 | 1.0–1.3 |
| Perle | 7.0–9.5 | 4.0–5.0 | 27–32 | 80–85 | 0.7–0.9 |
| Spalt | 3.0–6.0 | 3.0–5.0 | 20–25 | 45–55 | 0.5–1.0 |
| Tettnanger | 4.0–5.0 | 3.0–4.0 | 20–25 | 55–60 | 0.4–0.8 |
| **Bittering Hops** | | | | | |
| Willamette | 4.0–6.0 | 3.0–4.0 | 30–35 | 60–65 | 1.0–1.5 |
| Centennial | 9.5–11.5 | 3.5–4.5 | 29–30 | 60–65 | 1.5–2.3 |
| Chinook | 12.0–14.0 | 3.0–4.0 | 29–34 | 65–70 | 1.5–2.5 |
| Cluster | 5.5–8.5 | 4.5–5.5 | 36–42 | 80–85 | 0.4–0.8 |
| Eroica | 11.0–13.0 | 4.0–5.5 | 36–42 | 55–65 | 0.8–1.3 |
| Galena | 12.0–14.0 | 7.0–9.0 | 38–42 | 75–80 | 0.9–1.2 |
| Northern Brewer | 8.0–10.0 | 3.0–5.0 | 20–30 | 70–85 | 1.5–2.0 |
| Nugget | 12.0–14.0 | 4.0–6.0 | 24–30 | 70–80 | 1.7–2.3 |
| **Selected Imported Hops** | | | | | |
| Czech Saaz | 3.0–4.5 | 3.0–4.0 | 24–28 | 45–55 | 0.4–0.7 |
| UK East Kent Goldings | 4.0–5.5 | 2.0–3.5 | 20–25 | 65–80 | 0.6–1.0 |

Hop Specifications provided by Hopunion USA Inc., Yakima, WA.

(called an *oast*), rather like malt, they will not last. Some varieties (including Hallertau and other highly desirable types) will deteriorate noticeably in only a few weeks. Such hops must be stored in a freezer to maintain their quality and bittering power.

## Forms of Hops

There are at least three ways to buy hops: as loose or whole-leaf hops, pelletized or powdered hops, and hop extract. They differ in important respects.

Loose hops are compressed into bales after drying. The degree of compression is important, because extreme pressure will burst the **lupulin glands** (tiny yellow specks found on the petals) which contain the bitter resins and aromatic oil. This exposes them to oxidation. Hop merchants who specialize in selling to microbreweries and homebrew supply shops will sell whole compressed hops in quarter bales of 50 pounds each, and sometimes in smaller quantities. They are broken down into smaller packages by the retailer. The chief disadvantage of whole hops is their bulk, which makes them difficult to store and, perhaps, depending on your brewing system, difficult to remove from the wort after boiling.

Pelletized or powdered hops are made by removing extraneous stems and grinding the cones to a fine powder, which is then compressed into pellets. Pellets have several advantages. First, they will yield a somewhat larger percentage of their alpha acids in the kettle, and require a shorter boil time to do so. Second, they may be easier to remove from the wort after boiling. Finally, they are much more compact for a given weight, which makes them easier to store.

There is some controversy about the quality of hop pellets. On the one hand, the processing bursts the lupulin glands and exposes the delicate aromatic substances to heat and air, and, therefore, some oxidation. On the other hand, the pellets, once formed, present far less surface area exposed to air than do the natural cones; therefore, they tend to be more stable in storage. In practice, they can tolerate unfavorable conditions better than whole hops. Nonetheless, some large breweries and many smaller ones continue to shun them, feeling that whole hops impart superior aroma. Still, many excellent beers have been brewed from hop pellets, and, given properly handled examples of both types, the differences are small.

The third form of hops is hop extract. Most of these products are made by chemical processes (such as dissolving in hexane or boiling in highly alkaline water) which extract only bitterness. They are mainly of interest to commercial breweries that want to simplify their process. The best hop extracts are made by dissolving the hop resins and oils in liquid carbon dioxide. This treatment not only isomerizes the resins, but also dissolves the aromatic oils. You can add such an extract to your beer at bottling time to increase both its hop flavor and bitterness.

## Hop Varieties

There are a large number of hop varieties in production. New varieties are being tried constantly, and over time production of many types has risen or declined according to brewers' preferences. Here is a listing of some popular and not so popular hops, with brief descriptions.

*Brewer's Gold.* An early, high-alpha strain with a coarse flavor and aroma.

*Bullion.* Similar to Brewer's Gold.

*Cascade.* Low to moderate alpha, floral aroma, coarser in flavor than the true noble hops.

*Centennial.* Formerly called CFJ 90. Similar to Cascade with a higher alpha acid.

*Chinook.* High alpha, coarse flavor, distinct piney aroma.

*Cluster.* An old American variety, combining low alpha and undistinguished aroma. Cascade was bred as a replacement.

*Comet.* High alpha, coarse flavor and aroma.

*Eroica.* High alpha, better aroma than others of its type.

*Fuggle.* A noble British hop. Low to moderate alpha, distinct spicy aroma.

*Golding.* There are several subtypes of this noble British strain. The classic aroma hop for pale ale, with a distinct earthy note.

*Hallertau.* A noble German hop, one of the favored varieties for Bavarian lagers. Low alpha, fresh mild aroma.

*Hersbruck.* Another noble German hop, on a par with Hallertau.

*Jura.* See *Hersbruck.*

*Liberty.* An American-bred Hallertau derivative, superior in agricultural characteristics but with the genuine German noble hop character. Low alpha.

*Mt. Hood.* Another American-bred Hallertau replacement, similar in character to Liberty.

*Northern Brewer.* Medium to high alpha, more pleasant flavor and aroma than most of the other old high alpha types.

*Nugget.* A high alpha type that is low in cohumulone.

*Perle.* Medium alpha, bred as a replacement for Hallertau. Flavor and aroma are not as fine as some of the later derivatives.

*Saaz.* The noble Bohemian hop. Low alpha, poor storage stability, but the unique, pungent aroma makes this the first choice for Pilsners among German, as well as Czech, brewers.

*Spalt.* A noble German hop. Low alpha, more assertive aroma than Hallertau.

*Styrian.* A noble hop of former Yugoslavia. Low to medium alpha, sharper flavor and aroma than German hops.

*Tettnanger.* Noble German hop. Excellent aroma, mild flavor.

*Willamette.* American-bred Fuggle derivative, virtually identical in all respects.

## Buying and Storing Hops

Bad hops are no bargain at any price. Remember that hops are far more delicate than malt. Talk with dealers about their storage practices before buying. Ideally, they should at least refrigerate their hops and date the packages. Make sure all hops have been analyzed for alpha acid content. Some wholesalers and retailers have developed special packaging, i.e., sealed foil/plastic laminate bags filled with nitrogen. This packaging, properly implemented, eliminates the need for refrigeration. You may find the slight extra cost of this packaging worthwhile.

Hops with fair or good storage properties will keep for several months in a refrigerator. However, unless they are double-wrapped in airtight material, they can absorb odors and should not share space with fish, potato salad, or other pungent foods. The best place to store all hops is in a freezer. This is the only sure way to prevent the deterioration of delicate types such as Hallertau.

## Hop Rates and Hopping Schedules

Alpha acid analysis is the most important hop specification because it enables brewers to control the bitterness of their beer. Every type of hop will vary in alpha acid from one year to the next, and one type may go up in alpha while another goes down. Setting hop rates in terms of ounces per batch will give wildly inconsistent results.

The simplest way to utilize the alpha acid content information is through the system of *alpha acid units,* or AAUs. These units are also called *homebrew bitterness units,* or HBUs. Both terms mean the same thing. One AAU is the amount of alpha acid contained in 1 ounce of hops with an alpha content of 1 percent, or .5 ounce of hops with an alpha content of 2 percent, and so on. If a recipe calls for 8 AAU of hops, for example, then this would require 2 ounces of 4 percent hops, or 1 ounce of 8 percent, or 1½ ounces of 6 percent.

In recent years, many more elaborate systems of calculating hop rates have been devised. These systems attempt to predict the actual bitterness of the beer, which is stated in *International Bitterness Units* (IBUs). One IBU is 1 part per million of isomerized alpha acid. It is a measured quantity that can be determined in a laboratory.

Systems that calculate IBU are difficult to apply. In a real brewery, anywhere from 1 to 40 percent of the alpha acid in the hops will find its way into the finished beer, depending on the form of the hops, the length of time they are boiled, the configuration of the brew kettle, the pH of the wort, and many other factors. Some of these factors can be accounted for in a formula, but not all. To cover the unknowns, all such formulas must include a factor for utilization efficiency, at which either the brewer or the formula writer has to guess. The only way to establish it is to have a finished beer sample — or better, several samples — analyzed in a laboratory.

In practice, homebrewers find that they have to adjust the hop rate of their recipes according to their own taste. This being the case, the AAU system works as well as any and is, therefore, followed in this book.

Hopping schedules are another difficult and controversial topic. What works for some brewers would not even be considered by others. For example, ale brewers often add hops as soon as the boil begins, and this may mean a hop boil of 2 hours. Lager brewers object to this, pointing to experiments that show that such long boils damage the flavor of the beer, and may even decrease the bitterness of the finished product. In this case, it seems that the safest course is to restrict the hop boil to no more than one hour.

Many breweries add hops in several lots at different stages of the boil. The aim of this practice is to retain different fractions of the aromatic oils, and there is no doubt that altering the hopping schedule has a subtle influence on the hop flavors of the finished beer.

The most extreme example of this practice is the use of finishing hops, which are added for aroma at the very end of the boil. Since they are not boiled, their contribution to bitterness may be very low, depending on how the wort is handled subsequently. Another way to get aroma from hops is dry hopping, in which hops are added to the secondary fermenter or cask. Ounce for ounce, dry hopping gives a stronger hop aroma to the beer than finish hopping, but the character is different and you must choose on the basis of taste. The recipes in this book reflect the traditional hopping practices followed in breweries that produce the particular style of beer.

# Making Adjustments

The toughest part of adjusting hop rates revolves around the use of finish hops. The brewing method has an enormous influence on their utilization. At one extreme, a brewery uses hop pellets exclusively. Pellets do not require a lot of time to yield their bitterness. In fact, if the wort is whirlpooled and settled for a total of 30 minutes before cooling, the finish hops will yield almost as much bitterness as hops that have boiled for 1 hour. At the other extreme, if you use whole hops for the finish and begin cooling the wort after 5 minutes, you will get very little bitterness out of them.

For the sake of consistency, all of the recipes in this book are based on the assumption that the brewer will be using whole hops for the finish. If your methods are different, you will have to make an adjustment in the earlier additions of boiling hops.

For example, a 5-gallon recipe for Czech pilsner calls for 12 AAU of hops total, and 1½ ounces of finish hops. If your Saaz hops are 4 percent alpha, this means 1½ ounces contains 6 AAU. That is the finish amount. The remaining 6 AAU are divided between the other additions 45 and 15 minutes before the end of the boil (3 AAU or ¾ oz. each). However, if you are using whole hops for the finish, you should figure that you will only get half the hop extraction from the finish addition. Again assuming that your whole hops have the same alpha as your pellets, that means you would count the 1½ ounce finish addition as 3 AAU. The other two additions should then total 9 AAU, or 4½ AAU each.

If whole finish hops are added shortly before cooling is begun, you may have to make a more extreme adjustment, figuring they will yield almost no bitterness. In any case, your first attempt at the recipe must be regarded as a trial run. You can expect to make adjustments based on the taste of the finished beer.

# Kettles, Wort Coolers, and Other Equipment

**T**his chapter deals with the equipment needed for boiling and cooling wort. This stage of brewing ends the process of wort production and sets the stage for fermentation. It is the step at which malt extract brewing begins and is, therefore, of interest to all homebrewers. While it is simpler than the prior step of wort production, it is important nonetheless, and good equipment will make it faster and will give you better results.

## Kettles

If you are using malt extract, it is possible to make up a concentrated wort and boil it in a small kettle, then dilute it before fermentation. However, for all grain brewing the kettle must be considerably larger than the batch size. This is also a better option for extract brewing, because boiling all the wort has a number of benefits, not the least of which is eliminating the risk of contamination from dilution water. Kettles should be 50 percent oversized. A 10-gallon batch size (or brew length as the jargon has it) would ideally require a 15-gallon kettle.

The best materials for a kettle are copper and stainless steel. Copper has excellent heat transfer characteristics and for centuries was the material of choice. In England, brew kettles are still called coppers, even though most of them are now made of stainless steel.

Stainless steel has now displaced copper in commercial breweries, for two reasons. First, a stainless steel kettle costs about half as much as a copper one. Second, it stands up better to the strong corrosive chemicals that are used in automated cleaning cycles.

Homebrewers have to clean their kettles by hand, so the toughness factor is not much of an issue. However, cost is a factor. The best kettle for 10-gallon batch homebrewing is a 15.5-gallon beer keg with its valve end removed. Such kettles can be made quite cheaply if you can find some surplus kegs at scrap prices.

For 5-gallon batches, the cheapest alternative is still an 8¼-gallon enamelware canning kettle. The enamel will chip eventually, but a few bare steel spots will make no difference.

Aluminum generally is frowned upon for brew kettles. It is never used commercially because it is soft and easily corroded by caustic cleaning chemicals. It also is believed to impart a metallic taste to beer. This belief has been challenged, but as of this writing no trials have actually been performed to settle the issue. In any case, stainless and copper are superior on other grounds.

In many systems, the kettle is fitted with a tap at the bottom to draw off the wort. This is recommended to avoid lifting the vessel and makes it easy to control the flow rate, which is especially important if you use a counterflow wort cooler.

# Hop Strainers

If you use whole hops in your beer, you need some way to separate them from the wort after boiling. In commercial breweries, a large vessel with a screen false bottom, called a "hop back" or "hop jack," is often used. This is not practical for homebrewing because the taps and tubing used to move wort are too small and would be plugged by hop cones.

For 5-gallon batches where the wort is cooled in the kettle using an immersion wort cooler, hops can be removed by suspending an ordinary stainless steel strainer over an open bucket and pouring the wort through. This is risky because of the exposure to air and requires cleaning an additional vessel, but it works. For larger batches or for use with a counterflow cooler, the best arrangement is to fit the bottom of the kettle with a perforated screen or a loop of slotted copper tubing. This allows the wort to be drawn off through the kettle tap.

## Wort Coolers

Arrangements for wort cooling range from very rudimentary to very sophisticated. Once you move past the stage of putting the hot kettle in a tub full of cold water, there are two basic choices. They differ mainly in where you put the coolant in relation to the hot wort.

An immersion cooler is a coil of copper or stainless steel tubing, usually with a ⅜-inch outside diameter. This coil is made to fit inside the kettle. It is put into the kettle about 10 minutes before the end of the boil. Then, when the boil is over, water is circulated through it until the wort reaches the desired temperature.

The advantages of an immersion cooler are simplicity and cost. Furthermore, it is relatively easy to control the final temperature by placing a dial thermometer in the wort and observing it during cooling. In addition, there is no danger of picking up contamination from the cooler coils, because the outside surface is sterilized by the boiling wort immediately before use. The disadvantages are that cooling is slow, and the wort is out in the open — or, at best, partially covered — during a period of time when it is especially vulnerable to spoilage organisms.

Counterflow coolers are used almost universally in both large and small commercial breweries. Homebrewing versions are constructed with the same type of metal tubing used for the immersion chiller; however, the metal tube is placed either inside a length of hose or a large chamber, and cooling water is run through this outer casing in one direction while the wort flows through the metal tubing in the opposite direction. As the wort flows, it gives up its heat to the water. The process is quite efficient, bringing the wort from near boiling to fermentation temperature in the few seconds it takes to flow through the cooler.

The counterflow cooler has obvious advantages in being a quick, closed system that does not expose the wort to air while it is being cooled. There are two disadvantages. The first is that it is more costly and difficult to build. More important than cost, however, is that the wort is on the inside of a small metal tube that cannot be inspected or cleaned by hand. During cooling, considerable solid matter is formed, and some of this will be deposited on the walls of the tubing. In practice, counterflow coolers must be cleaned with strong protein solvents to remove every trace of soil. If this is not done, eventually they will become a source of contamination and off flavors. In commercial breweries, counterflow wort coolers (generally known as heat exchangers) and filters are the two most common reservoirs of infection.

Those who are looking for precision and repeatable results should fit the wort outlet of a counterflow cooler with a tee that will serve as a well for a dial thermometer. Then, by controlling the flow rate of coolant and/or wort, a precise temperature can be set and maintained.

## Coolant Sources

The best source of cooling water is the nearest tap. Unfortunately, in many parts of the country the water is too warm to be used for wort cooling during part, or even all, of the year. One alternative is to make up an ice water bath in a picnic chest or a plastic bucket. Run lengths of plastic tubing from the ice water bath to your wort chiller water inlet and outlet, and put a small pump in the line at some point. As long as you keep adding ice periodically to maintain a 50/50 mix, the coolant temperature will remain relatively constant.

A practical alternative with an efficient counterflow wort cooler is to chill a quantity of cold water in advance and run it on a one-way basis; in other words, send the hot outflow water down the drain. Depending on your setup, this may eliminate the need to use a pump and certainly will eliminate the need for a large supply of ice. To cool 10 gallons of wort, you will need at least 10 gallons of cold water at 34°F, and if your cooler is inefficient, you may need a lot more than 10 gallons of cold water.

If you need to rely on a limited supply of coolant, and this includes the ice water bath, you will have to do some trial runs using boiling hot water as your "wort." *Ad hoc* engineering is part of the game, and you have to be sure your system will work before you trust a brew to it.

# 12

# What Happens in the Kettle and Wort Cooler?

**I**n this chapter, we will look at the chemical and physical changes that take place when wort is boiled and cooled. This seemingly simple process brings about profound changes and fixes the basic character of the beer.

## Boiling

The main purposes of boiling are: (1) to destroy any enzymes in the wort, (2) to sterilize the wort, (3) to remove by evaporation certain undesirable aromatic components of the wort, (4) to extract the bittering and aromatic elements from the hops, and (5) to clarify the wort by coagulating proteins and tannins. In some cases, especially with strong beers, concentrating the wort is also an important goal. Finally, boiling darkens the wort, though this is incidental rather than a deliberate aim of the brewer. Hop extraction and protein coagulation are complex chemical reactions and need to be examined in some depth.

# Extraction of Hop Compounds

Both aromatic hop oil and bitter hop resins (alpha and beta acids) are extracted into the wort during the boil. Hop oil contains many volatile compounds, including hydrocarbons and esters. These are largely evaporated with the steam during long boils. The practice of adding a portion of the hops near or at the end of the boil is aimed at retaining some of these substances and thus increasing the hop nose and flavor of the brew.

One factor that greatly influences the retention of volatile hop constituents is ventilation during the boil. If the wort could be boiled in a fully closed vessel, the resulting beer would have a very strong hop aroma, even if no finishing hops were used. In real brew kettles, which are partially closed, some of the volatile hop elements will condense on the lid and fall back into the kettle. So, obviously, to minimize hop aroma, the boiler should be as open as possible. This means that the amount of finishing hops you will need depends not only on how much hop aroma you want, but also your equipment. The more vigorous your boil and the more open your kettle, the more hop oil will be evaporated. Once you have made a few batches, you can rely on your own taste and experience in deciding how much finishing hops to use.

It is not a good idea to try to retain hop aroma by keeping the kettle as closed as possible, and just simmering the wort. You need a vigorous boil in order to extract hop resins, coagulate protein and tannin, and boil off undesirable aromatics like dimethyl sulfide that are derived from the malt.

Unlike the aromatic oil, hop resins do not simply mix into the wort. Alpha and beta acids are only slightly soluble in room temperature water, and if they did not undergo changes in the kettle, they would precipitate when the wort was cooled and leave almost no bitterness in the finished beer. Fortunately, boiling causes hop resins to *isomerize,* which means that they are changed into what can be thought of as different forms of the same chemicals. Isomers contain the same numbers of the same atoms — so that their chemical formula is the same — but the atoms are arranged a bit differently. As a result, the chemical properties of different isomers are not uniform. For example, the single sugars glucose and fructose have the same chemical formula, $C_6H_{12}O_6$, but different structures and chemical properties. In the case of alpha acids, which are responsible for about 90 percent of the bitterness of beer, the isomers formed during the boil are bitter, like their precursors, but fortunately are more soluble.

Isomerization is not easy to accomplish. Not only is a long, vigorous boil needed, but the mechanical action of the hops rolling through the wort seems to help by breaking up the droplets of hop resin. Many commercial brewery kettles are fitted with percolators or mechanical agitators in order to increase the motion of the wort, partly for this reason. Still, even with a rolling boil, isomerization is far from total. Usually only around half of the alpha acids are isomerized during a 1-hour boil; of this fraction, some will precipitate with the hot and cold breaks while more will be adsorbed onto the yeast cells during fermentation. In fact, what brewers call "hop utilization" (the percentage of alpha acids that is isomerized and remains in the finished beer) can be as low as 10 percent and seldom exceeds 40 percent.

Hop utilization is affected not only by the vigor of the boil, but also by its length. The longer the wort is boiled with the hops, the more of the bitter resins will be isomerized. However, this is not a linear progression. According to one experiment, boiling the wort with the hops for 30 minutes gave over 80 percent of the isomerization achieved in 2 hours. Furthermore, the chemical changes that take place during boiling are not limited to simple isomerization. Various alpha and beta acid derivatives may undergo further changes as the boil continues, with the result being that bitterness actually may decrease, or, even worse, harshly bitter compounds may be formed. For this reason, it has long been the practice in most Continental breweries to restrict the hop boil to 1 hour at most. (Note: This is the boiling time *after* the hops are added. Hops are added at intervals over the last hour of this period.)

Another factor affecting utilization is the wort pH. The higher the pH, the greater the isomerization of hop resins. In fact, many hop extracts are made by heating the hops in a strongly alkaline solution (pH around 11) where almost 100 percent of the alpha acids can be isomerized. In the brew kettle, such conditions are not possible, and there are other reasons for avoiding high pH worts. For one thing, the undesirable changes mentioned in the previous paragraph take place much faster if the wort pH is over 5.7; so, to avoid harsh bitterness, you must adjust the wort to a value lower than this. The best flavor is achieved when the wort pH is 5.0 to 5.4. On the other hand, a very low wort pH reduces utilization and has other deleterious effects, such as making a good hot break nearly impossible.

The final variable that can affect utilization is wort gravity. In a high gravity wort, the concentration of sugars acts to block isomerization. High gravity beers always suffer from this phenomenon, and must be brewed using hop rates higher than would be needed for a normal strength beer of similar bitterness.

The best way to sum up this discussion might be to quote the diet pill advertisements: your results may vary! Since so many factors can influence hop utilization, your best hope for consistent results is to standardize your methods. If you want to experiment, do not change more than one factor at a time. If, for instance, you buy a larger boiler, make your first brew in it according to an old, tested recipe. Then you can compare results to see how much utilization has been affected.

## Protein Coagulation

One of the drollest facts of brewing chemistry is the way that almost anything can cloud your beer. Beers that are kept too cold in a refrigerator may throw a haze; but when you heat a clear, sweet wort, the same thing happens. As the wort approaches the boiling point, it will become murky.

Actually, different properties of protein are responsible for these reactions. Chill haze is formed as protein and tannin molecules come out of solution and *flocculate* (clump together) to form light-scattering particles. In the boiler, heat causes water molecules to be uncoupled from the larger proteins. This is called "denaturing," and it is exactly what happens when you cook an egg white. The result is that these huge protein molecules become insoluble and cloud the wort.

After being denatured, protein molecules do not automatically flocculate. In fact, wort can stand at the boiling point for any length of time and, unless it is agitated, will remain turbid. The rolling action of the boil bumps the protein molecules into one another, causing them to clump together. This fact has been demonstrated by repeated experiments and is another reason why agitators are used in commercial breweries. Homebrewers rely on the natural kicking of the wort to do the job.

The flocculation of proteins during the boil is called the "hot break" and its results are remarkable. As the boil continues, more and more material will break out of suspension, and the wort will lose its turbidity. If you hold a spoonful of the boiled wort under a light, it will appear crystal clear, with obvious particles of break floating in it. This simple visual test is one of the best ways of assessing your brew. If you do not get a good hot break, something — very likely the wort pH — is wrong and will have to be corrected. A low wort pH (below 5.0) will make a good break impossible and, for this reason, even more than the effect on hop utilization, should be avoided.

So far we have been talking as if proteins alone were responsible for the hot break, but this is not true. Tannins (also called *polyphenols*) from both the grain husks and the hops also play a role. These compounds, which are all based on the 6-carbon phenolic ring, tend to link together, or *polymerize,* somewhat as glucose molecules join to form starches — though the bonding mechanism is different. In any case, polymerized polyphenols will, under certain conditions, associate with large protein molecules, forming very large structures that are seen as break particles. In the boiler, the main force inducing tannins to link up with proteins is electricity. Tannins have negative electrical charges and are attracted to positively charged proteins. Different proteins are positive at different values of pH, which may help explain why low pH worts do not break well. It also explains why, helpful as it is, the hot break alone cannot fully "hazeproof" beer. Nonetheless, a good hot break will produce a beer that is less prone to haze than a similar brew that did not break well.

While hot break consists mainly of protein/tannin complexes, it also contains measurable amounts of lipids (fatty compounds) and other substances. Many of these break components are harmful to either the fermentation or the flavor of the finished beer. It is important to separate the hot break from the wort before it is pitched with yeast. This is the reason almost all commercial breweries put wort through a whirlpool before cooling it. The spinning action causes the break to be deposited in a mound at the center of the vessel bottom. Then the wort can be drawn gently off from an outlet at the side.

# Caramelization

When subjected to heat, sugars and amino acids can combine to form complex substances called "melanoidins." These chemicals have a dark color and strong flavor. Melanoidins are formed in malt during the kilning operation and the higher proportion of them is what gives high-kilned malts (and beers brewed from them) their deep color and rich flavors. Melanoidins are also formed in solutions, and beer wort is, of course, loaded with sugars and amino acids. It is not surprising that it darkens during the boil.

The two factors that most affect wort darkening (since temperature is practically a constant) are time and concentration, or specific gravity. Of these, the second is by far the more significant. A high gravity wort will darken much more during a 1-hour boil than a normal gravity wort during a 2-hour boil. Thus, if you are striving to produce a light colored beer, you must use a large boiler so that your wort gravity will be as low as your recipe permits. Even if you are not concerned with color, remember that *caramelization*, as this reaction is called, will also affect flavor. The caramel taste produced in the boiler is different from, and less pleasant than, the flavor produced during the curing of malt.

A shorter boil time and a full wort boil both help reduce caramelization and are desirable when making pale beers. With any beer, it is a good idea to stir the wort gently as it is first run into the kettle. You want to be sure the heavy first runnings are not allowed to lie at the bottom of the kettle.

# The Cold Break

After the wort boils it must be cooled to fermentation temperature before it can be pitched with yeast. During the cooling operation, the clear, hot wort will become cloudy. This is the result
of the same protein/tannin interaction described earlier. Some
of the compounds formed will remain in solution at high temperatures, and only precipitate during cooling. One of the most
dramatic results of using a counterflow chiller is the way hot wort
will flow crystal clear into the device, only to emerge as muddy
(or nearly) as the Missouri River!

The faster you can drop the temperature of the wort, the better. A long, slow cooling does not give a good cold break, and this
in turn may lead to hazy beer. You should try to get the wort down
to fermentation temperature within 1½ hours after the end of the
boil for this and other reasons, such as inhibiting bacterial growth.

# Other Cooling Factors

Most of the bacteria that are classified as wort spoilers grow best
at temperatures from 80° to 120°F. Slow cooling methods give
these bugs an excellent opportunity to multiply in the wort. Obviously, the best practice is to drop the wort from a very high temperature (which the bugs cannot survive) to a very low one (which
puts them to sleep) as quickly as possible. A good counterflow
chiller is ideal in this respect.

With many worts, there is another factor to consider. Pale
brewers' malt contains substantial amounts of *S-methyl methionine* (SMM) and *dimethyl sulfoxide* (DMSO), two compounds that
are changed to dimethyl sulfide (DMS) upon heating. Large
amounts of DMS are produced during the boil but are driven off
with the steam. When boiling ends, so does expulsion of DMS,
but it continues to be formed as long as the wort is hot. Dimethyl
sulfide has an aroma of cooked vegetables that is not desirable in
many styles of beer. For this reason, hot wort should be cooled as
rapidly as possible after boiling.

# 13

# Boiling, Trub Separation, and Cooling

**W**hile boiling is a simple process, it requires attention and some experience with your own equipment. There are several factors that you need to think about in planning the operation.

## Evaporation Rate

One factor that you have to think about in planning your boil is your evaporation rate. When you buy or make a new kettle, it is a good idea to do a trial boil with plain tap water to gauge your rate of evaporation. Simply measure in a quantity of water — say, 6 gallons for a 5-gallon batch size — and boil it for the normal time of 75 to 90 minutes. Then cool the water using your normal procedures and measure it again. Ideally, you should get at least 10 percent evaporation in a 75-minute boil, which, for our example, would be .6 gallons. The final volume after boiling thus would be 5.4 gallons or less. Knowing your evaporation rate will enable you to collect the proper amount of wort in the kettle at the start of the boil so that you get the right amount of wort at the end. This will enable you to avoid having to dilute your wort with treated sterile water — a big hassle — or, even worse, ending up with a larger volume of wort than you can handle.

## Conducting the Boil

The kettle may be partially covered to minimize heat loss during the preboil phase, but you should never cover a kettle of wort completely. In fact, as the boil approaches and a layer of foam begins to appear, the best practice is to remove the lid — at least until the boil settles down. With a really vigorous boil, you may have to spray down the foam with a hose to prevent it from boiling over. On the other hand, if your heat source doesn't have enough power, partially covering the kettle may be necessary in order to maintain a vigorous rolling boil.

A grain beer wort should be boiled for 75 to 90 minutes. For making dark, high gravity beers, the boil may be extended to 2 hours if needed for more evaporation. Sometimes longer boils are used, but they may adversely affect the wort quality.

In general, the lighter the wort, the bigger the break particles. Also, worts produced by infusion or step mashing will yield more break in the kettle than those made by decoction. Regardless of mash method, a 75-minute boil will yield a wort that is very bright, with visible particles of hot break suspended in it. Worts that do not break bright are a sign of problems — low wort pH or starch carried into the kettle. Some grains, such as wheat malt or rye malt, always make a wort that appears rather cloudy when it is run into the kettle; but the wort should break bright during the boil.

Hops normally are added during the last hour of the boil, and the recipes in this book call for the first addition 45 or 30 minutes before the end. Some breweries add a fraction of the hops before the wort boils, to keep down the kicking and foam buildup. This works with whole hops, but pellets have the opposite effect: the tiny particles serve as nucleation sites for the formation of bubbles, and the result is increased foaming. Because of the flavor problems that may be caused by overboiling the hops, it is better to control foaming by other means, even if you elect to use whole hops.

Finish hops are added immediately after shutting down the boil. As soon as possible after they are added, the kettle should be covered, so as to retain the volatile aromatic hop constituents. Just be sure that the boil has stopped; otherwise covering the kettle will cause it to boil over.

## Trub Separation and Running Off the Wort

Regardless of whether you cool your wort in the kettle or put it through a counterflow chiller, the most practical way to separate pellet hop residue and trub is by stirring the hot wort with a long spoon to set up a whirlpool action. The solid matter will settle into a mound in the center of the kettle bottom. You can then gently draw the wort from the kettle using either a siphon tube (metal if the wort is hot) or the tap fitted to the kettle bottom.

With whole hops, it is possible to pour the wort through a strainer into a bucket, but this is not recommended. It is dangerous if the wort is hot, and the hot wort will be aerated, which will hasten oxidation of the finished beer. Even if the wort is cool, there is still the problem of getting trub material into the fermenter, and this also adversely affects the beer. Using a hop screen or slotted tube, you can let the hops settle to the bottom to form a loose bed. They will then retain and filter out the hot break as you draw the wort off.

A somewhat controversial practice is sparging whole hops with hot or cold water as appropriate. On one hand, whole hops retain a good deal of wort, and the sugar will be lost with them if they are not rinsed. On the other hand, hot break is always washed through in the spargings. If you want the best possible wort quality, it is better to omit the hops sparge.

Similarly, when working with hop pellets, you must watch the kettle and stop the runoff as soon as you see solid matter being pulled into the wort outlet (tap or siphon tube). With a good whirlpool and gentle runoff, wort loss will be minimal.

# Methods of Cooling

As mentioned above, the best methods to avoid oxidation of the hot wort are either to use the immersion chiller right in the boiler or, with a counterflow device, to rack the hot wort straight from the boiler into it. These procedures are quite straightforward. The immersion cooling method is simpler, because you can monitor the wort temperature with a thermometer suspended in the kettle.

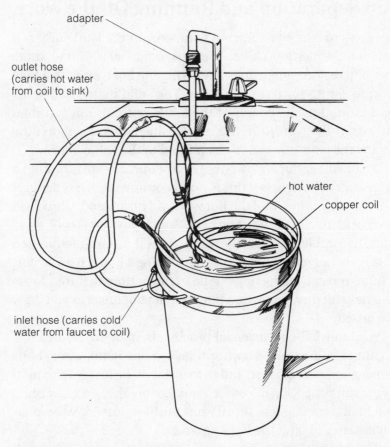

adapter

outlet hose
(carries hot water
from coil to sink)

hot water

copper coil

inlet hose (carries cold
water from faucet to coil)

*Cooling the hot wort with an immersion chiller. The inlet hose is connected to the faucet and carries cold water to the cooler. As it flows through the coil, the water picks up heat from the wort and then flows back to the sink through the outlet hose.*

With a counterflow cooler, you must try to monitor the temperature of the wort flowing out of the cooler and adjust it as necessary by controlling the flow rate of the wort and/or coolant. The runoff rate should be slow: ideally, it should take about half an hour to run off the wort. This is important because a rapid runoff will pull solid material into the wort stream, and, if you are using whole hops, it will pack the hop bed down and may stop the flow.

In order to get a trouble-free runoff with whole hops, it is important to allow the hops to settle gently to the kettle bottom before beginning runoff. If this is not done, the results will be the same as a rapid runoff: trub carryover at first, followed by blockage.

## A Note on Sanitation

Cleaning and sanitation procedures are discussed elsewhere, but it must be mentioned that wort cooling is the beginning of the "cold side" of the brewing process. Once the wort is cooled below about 140°F it is vulnerable to attack by various bacteria and wild yeast that can ruin its flavor. It is vital, therefore, starting with the cooling step, to keep the wort away from air as much as possible, because air contains dust particles on which bacteria and yeast spores ride. If you cool wort in the kettle, keep it covered during the process. Also be sure that every implement and instrument that touches the wort is clean and sanitized. Finally, pitch the yeast and aerate the wort immediately after cooling. The best procedure is to run the cooled wort directly into a clean, sanitized fermenter to which you have already added your pitching yeast.

# 14

# Yeast

**C**enturies before the study of chemistry began, the basic transformation of malt starch to sugar and then to alcohol was empirically understood. Yet the role of yeast was missed completely. The grayish-tan scum that rose to the surface of the fermenter was regarded as a useless by-product, to be skimmed off and disposed of as quickly as possible. Even after microscopes were invented and scientific inquiry began, it took many decades before Louis Pasteur was able to demonstrate, in the face of considerable opposition from his fellow scientists, that the production of alcohol during fermentation is a vital function of the living yeast cell. He called the process *la vie sans air,* a description that is still considered accurate today.

A little later, the Danish brewer Jacob Christian Jacobsen wished to improve the quality of his beers. He had become a friend of the great Munich brewmaster Gabriel Sedelmayr, and was familiar with the excellence of Bavarian lagers. Realizing that yeast was the key, he persuaded Sedelmayr to give him two pots of the treasured fungus, which he managed, with great effort, to keep alive and healthy during the two-day coach trip from Munich to Copenhagen. Jacobsen began to brew outstanding beers, and the Carlsberg Brewery (named for his son) gave Denmark its reputation of being an important brewing nation.

It is worth recounting this bit of brewing history because we need to appreciate that all the hard work of brewing takes place inside the yeast cell. Brewers make the wort, but yeast makes the beer. Your job as a brewer is to provide the nutrients and physical conditions that will allow your yeast to flourish. If you take care of your yeast, it will take care of you.

## Yeast Characteristics

The first thing to understand is that brewers' yeasts belong to two different species, *Saccharomyces Carlsbergensis* (commonly known as "lager yeast") and *Saccharomyces Cerevisiae* (commonly known as "ale yeast"). Though they cannot be distinguished visually, it is possible to tell them apart by other means. Lager yeast will ferment *raffinose* (a triple sugar found in raw barley), whereas ale yeast will not. This difference is the basis of the tests that large brewing laboratories use to distinguish the two species.

It is often said that ale yeast is top-fermenting, while lager yeast is bottom-fermenting. However, this distinction no longer holds, even among deliberately cultured strains. Some ale yeasts will drop to the bottom, rather than forming a "pancake" on the surface of the wort. In this respect they behave exactly like lager yeasts.

In brewing jargon, this characteristic is called "flocculence," which means clumping together to form large masses. Some yeasts flocculate early in the fermentation; they are then carried to the surface by the evolving carbon dioxide gas. Yeasts that flocculate later in the fermentation, when $CO_2$ production is slow, will fall to the bottom of the tank. There are also yeasts that never flocculate at all. That causes problems with beer clarity, and such strains are seldom selected deliberately for brewing.

Another practical distinction between ale and lager yeast is cold tolerance. Most ale yeasts go dormant at 55° or 60°F, while lager yeasts will work happily, if slowly, at lower temperatures, some down to near freezing. Once again there is a lot of variation from one strain to another, but this generalization holds for the most part.

A final distinction between the species is their creation of fermentation by-products. Again, this is a characteristic of individual strains, but there is one aspect that concerns the expected flavor of ales versus lagers. This is the production of *esters.* Esters are a class of organic compounds with strong aromas: certain esters are responsible for the characteristic aromas of bananas, pineapples, and other fruits. British ale yeasts often produce noticeable amounts of these fruit esters and are highly prized for this quality. Lager yeasts, on the other hand, produce smaller quantities of esters, and an obvious fruity aroma is not expected or desired in lager beers.

There are other by-products that are more characteristic of ales than lagers. The most famous is *diacetyl,* which has a strong butter or butterscotch aroma. Diacetyl is produced early in the fermentation, and then reabsorbed by the yeast and reduced to flavorless compounds later on. Yeast strains differ markedly in their diacetyl reduction ability. Some ales and a few lagers (such as the famous Pilsner Urquell) contain perceptible amounts of diacetyl, but as a rule modern brewers consider it a fault. This is because certain bacterial infections and other errors in brewing technique will increase diacetyl levels, and so this parameter serves as a quality check. However, it is important to remember that diacetyl is a flavor that is a natural by-product of yeast fermentation, and in some beer styles it is an optional or even required flavor component.

The other significant by-products are *fusel alcohols* and *fatty acids.* Some fusel alcohols give a harsh aftertaste at the back of the tongue; fatty acids have flavors described as soapy or goaty. In general, these tastes are not considered desirable, but again there are exceptions. The characteristic clove flavor of Bavarian wheat beers is produced by the fusel alcohol *4-vinyl-guaiacol* and is considered a hallmark of the style.

The last characteristic of yeasts is their ***attenuation,*** or their ability to metabolize wort sugars. Attenuation is the drop in specific gravity that takes place as the yeast converts sugar into carbon dioxide and alcohol. Malt sugar is not a single substance. There are actually many different sugars in beer wort. Some of them — the single and double sugars glucose, fructose, maltose, and sucrose — can be fermented by all strains. Most can also ferment the triple sugar maltotriose to some extent. Other minor sugars, such as raffinose, depend on the species. In general, lager yeasts will ferment a wort more completely than ale yeasts will, often yielding a terminal gravity two to four points lower (for example, 1.008 versus 1.011) for an identical wort.

## Forms of Yeast

Yeasts come in two forms for homebrewing use. They can best be described as *dry* and *wet*. Dry yeasts are granules packed in foil pouches, similar to baker's yeast. One or two packets contains sufficient live yeast to ferment an average batch of homebrew. All that is required is to rehydrate the yeast cells in warm water to make a slurry that is ready for pitching. The practical advantages are obvious.

Unfortunately, dry yeasts also have some disadvantages, which have to do with purity and stability. The yeast is propagated in large amounts using basically the same equipment and techniques as those used to produce baker's yeast. It is fed a strong solution of molasses and various nutrients, and the medium is aerated continuously so that the cells multiply furiously. When the yeast has multiplied sufficiently, the

*Forms of yeast. Brewer's choice liquid culture in foil packet (left); dried yeast in foil packet (right).*

*A liquid yeast "smack pack" before the inner bag of wort is broken (left) and afterward (right), as the yeast starts to work and the bag begins to swell.*

medium is drained off and the wet mass is dried in a low temperature oven. It is then granulated and packaged. This technique is efficient but primitive; the kill rate can be quite high. Naturally, the manufacturer will try to select a strain that is strong enough to survive the treatment, but it may not have the best brewing qualities. Another concern is that propagation conditions are not sterile. All dry yeasts are contaminated with wild and mutant yeasts to some extent, and usually with bacteria as well.

This means that dry yeast is something of a gamble. The viability of the cells and the degree of contamination vary widely. Even among the better brands, there are great differences from one lot to the next. However, there are some dry ale yeasts that usually make a good beer. Unfortunately, lager yeast does not take as well to the drying process, and a true dry lager yeast with satisfactory brewing characteristics has yet to appear.

Wet yeasts are pure strains cultured in a laboratory and packaged in a medium designed to ensure their survival. These days, they usually are sold in a "smack pack" that contains a small envelope of wort sealed inside the foil pack that contains the wet yeast. When the wort envelope is broken, the yeast revives and begins to grow. Usually, wet yeasts are free of contamination and represent a pure strain of yeast as used by major commercial breweries. A great variety of strains is available.

The disadvantages of wet yeasts include perishability and difficulty in use. The packs must be kept refrigerated and used before their expiration date. Even so, bad conditions during shipment, especially heat, may destroy them. Since the packs contain only a few cells, they must go through an intermediate stage where the culture is "stepped up" in sterile wort, in order to get enough cells to pitch a batch of homebrew. At this stage, you must be very careful to avoid introducing contamination. Finally, wet yeasts are costly enough to make one-shot use an expensive proposition. Fortunately, with some planning and care the yeast can be repitched from one batch to another, which brings down the cost per batch.

## Choosing Yeast

Ale brewers can choose between the simplicity of dry yeast and the variety and potential superiority of wet yeast. Many more varieties of wet yeast are available, and usually it is possible to find one or more that is used commercially for the same type of beer you intend to brew. Since new varieties are being introduced constantly, any listing would be difficult to keep timely. Fortunately, the laboratories that propagate and package wet yeast also provide information about them. The names given often provide hints about the sort of beer for which they are best suited, and further descriptions are often provided as well.

On the other hand, the manufacturer's information seldom tells the whole story. For example, the description of Wyeast Labs ale yeast #1007 is that it is a strong flocculator. What this does not tell you is that this yeast will, indeed, flocculate early and rise to the top, giving a huge pancake of yeast on the surface. However, if this pancake is not skimmed, the yeast will fall back into the beer and will not subsequently fall to the bottom. In short, the yeast is suitable for open, but not for closed, fermentation. It is difficult to collect enough yeast from the bottom of the fermenter for repitching, and it is difficult to clarify the finished beer if the yeast pancake is not skimmed. On the other hand, it produces beer with a gentle fruity note and, from a sensory standpoint, makes an excellent all-around ale yeast.

Another example is the Wyeast strain #2124, labeled as "Pilsner yeast." This yeast does, indeed, make excellent pilsners, but the name does not tell you that this is the famous Weihenstephan strain #3470, used by many German and American breweries. It also does not indicate that it is just as suitable for making a malty, Bavarian-style lager as it is for a hoppy pilsner. In fact, in one controlled split-batch comparison (same wort, different yeast) it proved superior to two other strains that are labeled specifically as German lager yeasts. These tests were done brewing Maibock and Oktoberfest style lagers, two high gravity, malty brews.

One of the most intriguing aspects of homebrewing is experimenting with different yeasts, observing how differently they behave and how much they influence the flavor of the finished beer. One good reason for joining a homebrewing club, and patronizing a good supply store, is the information you can gain about different yeast strains. I, personally, have tried only a handful of the many strains available, so I prefer not to comment on the relative suitability of those strains I have not used.

# 15

# Yeast Propagation and Maintenance

There are many excellent strains of yeast available for homebrewing. One of the great freedoms you have is the ability to experiment with them and select just the strain you want for a particular style of beer. Commercial breweries, even small ones, usually have to settle on one or two strains and use them for all their beers. There are too many headaches and risks involved in dealing with multiple yeast strains. The situation is completely different for a homebrewer. Because you brew less frequently, there is little additional trouble involved in working with many strains of yeast. The number of propagation steps is smaller when you only need enough yeast for a 5- or 10-gallon batch.

## Propagating Yeast

Theoretically, you could add a single yeast cell to a batch of wort, and it would just keep dividing until there were enough cells to do the fermenting. However, this does not work in practice. It is impractical to sterilize large volumes of wort or large brewing vessels. There will always be a few stray microbes that manage to get into your brew. Once the yeast is pitched, it will grow and basically crowd out its competition; but if your pitching yeast is too small in volume or too weak to quickly take over the wort, other microbes may gain a foothold and play havoc with the flavor of your beer.

Propagation serves two purposes. It increases the number of yeast cells, and it assures that they have high *viability* (a microbiologist's term meaning strong and full of fight). With dry yeast, you can buy enough yeast cells to pitch directly into your wort, but you still have to do some preliminary work to get them into shape for the task ahead.

# Rehydrating Dry Yeast

This is a simple procedure, but it must be done correctly for best results. Dry yeast is — well — dry, and if not clinically dead is at least in a sort of fungal coma. The many complex chemical transformations that make a cell alive can take place only in a liquid environment. Water must get into the dry, shriveled cells to start them up again.

It used to be thought that the best way to rehydrate a yeast cell was with wort, the idea being that, besides water, the yeast would benefit by an abundance of all the nutrients it needs — the sugars, amino acids, and trace minerals found in wort. However, research has shown that the sugar in wort actually interferes with the dry yeast cell's ability to absorb water. That is why rehydration in plain water is now recommended.

The best way to rehydrate dry yeast is to boil a pint of tap water for 10 to 15 minutes, then let it stand to cool until it reaches about 95° to 105°F. This method will get rid of all chlorine and/or microbes in the water. Once the rehydration has begun, the yeast slurry should be agitated every few minutes to assure that the cell walls have ample contact with the water. The slurry is ready to pitch after 15 minutes.

# Propagating Wet Yeast

Wet yeasts come in various forms, but in all cases the packages contain relatively few cells, and the cells are in a stressed, weakened condition due to starvation. The nutrient (wort) envelope contained within the smack-pack-type container is intended to allow you to give the cells an initial feeding and restore their vitality without breaking the sterile seal. This type of package is easy to work with, but the yeast still needs another stage of propagation after you have activated it (following the instructions of the manufacturer) and it has puffed up. The best way to achieve this propagation is in a ½-gallon or 1-gallon jug using sterile wort.

To make sterile wort, you need some malt extract and normal brewing equipment, plus canning jars and lids and a canning kettle or large pressure cooker. The pressure cooker is preferable because it allows you to reach a temperature of 250°F, high enough to kill not only live microbes (212°F will do that) but also spores. However, if all you have is a canning kettle, don't despair. Just allow your jars of canned wort to sit for a week or so before using them. If any jars pop their lids or show other signs of spontaneous fermentation, that means that spores were not killed, and you should discard them.

All canners and pressure cookers come with instructions on method. For pressure cooking, 15 minutes at 15 psi is recommended. For canning in a kettle, 30 minutes at a simmer with the kettle covered is adequate.

The wort can be made up without hopping or boiling. Just dissolve malt extract in some brewing-quality hot water and dilute to about S.G. 1.025. Normal strength wort is not necessary for propagation. Depending on the type of yeast (ale or lager) and your batch size, you will need different sized canning jars. Dry malt extract is more versatile because you can make up just what you need. Hot break will deposit on the bottom of the jars, but it is easy to decant the clean wort off of it.

Recommended propagation steps using a reactivated smack pack (50 ml) of yeast are as follows:

5-gallon batch size: ale yeast, 1 stage, 1 pint.
Lager yeast, 2 stages, 1 cup, 1 quart.

10-gallon batch size: ale yeast, 2 stages, 1 cup, 1 quart.
Lager yeast, 2 stages, 1½ cups, 2 quarts; or 3 stages, ½ cup,
2 cups, 2 quarts.

Propagation requires careful cleaning and sanitizing of the propagation vessel. A ½- or 1-gallon glass jug is best, depending upon the total volume required. Work carefully but quickly in a clean room, as dust-free as you can make it. After sanitizing and rinsing the jug, keep it upside down until you begin to work. Sanitize a funnel, scissors, and all other tools. Dip the smack pack and jar of sterile wort in the sanitizer, rinse them off, and set them, along with all implements, on a clean, smooth surface that has been wiped with the sanitizer. Set up the jug, put the funnel in its mouth, pop off the lid of the wort jar, and decant the wort. Immediately shake up the smack pack, cut the top off, and pour in the contents. Remove the funnel, cover the jug with a piece of foil or a plug of sterile cotton, and swirl vigorously for at least 5 minutes to aerate the wort. Aerate several times during the next day or two until the wort shows obvious signs of fermentation.

During propagation the jug should be kept at room temperature (68° to 75°F), regardless of whether it is ale or lager yeast. When the wort is obviously fermenting, it is ready to pitch or be stepped up to the next size volume of wort. Periodic aeration must be continued through all stages of propagation. Be sure to schedule your brewing so that the final volume of propagated yeast can be pitched while in active fermentation. Normally, each step takes 24 hours, though the first stage may take longer, especially with a large quantity of wort, as in the 1-stage propagation of ale yeast in a 1-pint starter volume.

Many other systems of wort propagation exist. Erlenmeyer flasks are often used instead of canning jars, and the yeast is inoculated directly into the first flask, which minimizes the chance of contamination during transfer. This is definitely recommended, especially for the first stage of propagation when starting from a slant rather than a smack pack (see below). A small jar such as a baby food jar could be used instead of a flask. The Erlenmeyer flasks must be covered with small squares of foil; screw-type lids are not available. Because the flask is not airtight, its sterility is questionable if it is stored very long. The flasks should be made up just before starting each propagation sequence. Homebrewers who do a lot of yeast propagation find it more convenient to make up a dozen or more jars of canned wort at a time.

Whenever you pour sterile wort or yeast slurry from one container into another, always wipe the mouths of both vessels with 70 percent alcohol using a swab or cotton ball, then flame with a propane torch. This will ensure that you do not pick up contamination from the container surfaces during the transfer. If any other implements are used, such as a funnel, make sure they are spotlessly clean and sanitized before use.

## Maintaining Yeast

Advanced homebrewers often want a way to maintain their favorite yeast strains at home. This is a lot of work, but it eliminates the need to buy a fresh smack pack every time they use a different yeast. The standard method of yeast maintenance, used by most major breweries and yeast laboratories, is based on growing yeast on a solid medium called "agar" (named after the solidifying agent, a seaweed derivative that forms a gel at room temperature). *Yeast agar* is made up with malt extract and sometimes other nutrients. It is possible to buy kits with petri dishes and test tubes already poured with yeast agar and all other special equipment required. These kits include good instructions and are usually cheaper for homebrewers than buying the separate components, which are only available from laboratory supply houses, in large quantities.

When working with these kits, you will be storing the yeast on a slanted agar surface in a test tube. The yeast is harvested with a device called an "inoculating loop." Propagation is started by swirling the loopful of yeast into a jar containing 50 ml of sterile wort. Once this tiny volume is fermenting, you step it up in a flask (included in the kit) in which you have made up 250 ml (about half a pint) of sterile wort. From there on, you can do a further step or two as required for your batch size and yeast type.

airlock

½-gallon jug

*This is a "second starter" culture, made by pitching the activated yeast into a quart of sterile wort. Note the layer of yeast on the bottom of the jug.*

Yeast slants must be stored in a refrigerator. They only keep about 6 months before they start to lose viability, so each strain of yeast needs to be recultured several times a year. This is a lot of work, and it helps to explain the high prices that commercial yeast laboratories, which maintain hundreds of strains, charge for their slants.

Very advanced homebrewers often trade slants. In some clubs, different members are responsible for maintaining particular strains that they can then supply to fellow club members. This is a good way of cutting down the burden of yeast maintenance.

Another way to maintain yeast is to use the Yeast Bank™ kit. A bit of your first stage propagation culture is mixed with a liquid called "freeze shield" and stored in a small container in your freezer. These kits also come with good instructions.

The yeast bank kit is simple because it does not involve working with agar. The chief disadvantage is that you are freezing a sample of your pitching yeast that may, at this stage, contain a few bacteria or wild yeast cells. Part of the maintenance procedure with agar slants involves diluting the yeast starter with sterile water and streaking the dilution on an agar petri dish. Each colony (about one billion cells) that grows on the dish comes from a single yeast cell. Thus the streak method lets you isolate the yeast from any stray contaminants, and reestablishes the purity of the culture.

## Repitching Yeast

The simplest of all methods for keeping a yeast going is simply to repitch some of the slurry recovered from one fermenter into another. This system has always been used by commercial breweries. The only problem it poses for homebrewers is that repitching must be done frequently. Yeast slurry must be kept refrigerated in a sanitized jar and repitched within 24 hours after collection. Since top-fermenting ale yeasts rise to the surface in the first few days of fermentation, you may have to brew twice a week to keep a yeast of this type going. The other way of collecting yeast — from the bottom of the fermenter — may not be possible with these strains because so little yeast is deposited there. If you collect yeast from the bottom of the fermenter, you should only repitch it within 2 weeks of the prior pitching. You may be able to stretch this to 3 weeks with lager yeasts. This rule assumes that the beer is cooled at the end of active fermentation (3 to 5 days for ales, 6 to 8 days for lagers). If you cannot cool your beer, you must rack it off, and recover and repitch the yeast as soon as primary fermentation is over.

Do not repitch slurries from dry yeast. Because all dry yeasts contain some degree of contamination, and because the contaminating organisms will grow from one pitching to the next, the only safe course is to use dry yeast on a one-shot basis. Also, you should use caution in repitching yeasts derived from pure cultures (whether you made them or they came from a smack pack or other commercial source). Lager yeasts tend to get old and tired, and, even if contamination is not suspected, they should not be repitched for more than five generations. Ale yeasts tend to hold up better, and some strains can be repitched successfully dozens of times; but you have to be very sure of your cleaning and sanitation before trying this.

## Rousing Yeast

If your yeast has been sitting around for too long, either in the refrigerator or on the bottom of the fermenter, there is an alternative to getting a new culture and propagating it up to pitching volume. The procedure is called "rousing," and it is basically the same as the last step of propagation. Simply make up a volume of sterile extract wort, identical to what you would use for propagating, and pitch about ⅓ of your normal yeast slurry volume into it. (Recommended pitching rates for yeast slurries will be found in Chapter 19.)  Aerate it well, keep it under an airlock at room temperature, and 24 hours later you should have a sufficient volume of strong, active yeast cells ready to pitch.

## Yeast Feeding

Feeding yeast means periodically adding a small amount of sterile wort to a yeast slurry stored in the refrigerator. This method is often advocated as a way of keeping a slurry alive between pitchings. Claims of extending the storage life to several months have been made.

Yeast feeding has been criticized because of the danger of contaminating the culture when you open the storage jar and pour in the wort. The same charge could also be made against rousing yeast. Everything depends on the care you take to make sure that everything is kept clean and sanitary. Whether you are rousing or feeding yeast, first tighten the lid and swirl the container in a sanitizer solution. When you open it, flame the mouth of the jar before pouring out the slurry.

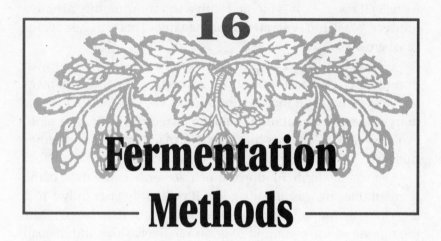

# 16

# Fermentation Methods

**T**his chapter presents an overview of the commonly used methods of fermentation for lagers and ales. The basic steps are outlined first, followed by various practical methods of implementing these steps. There are a number of options, some of which require more equipment and work than others.

## Steps of Fermentation

Fermentation can be broken down into four steps or stages:

1. Aeration and pitching of the cooled wort;
2. Lag period and primary fermentation;
3. Secondary fermentation; and
4. Clarification rest and lagering.

The first stage is straightforward. As soon as the wort has been cooled to fermentation temperature or pitching temperature (usually the same), it is pitched with a suitable quantity of active brewers' yeast and is aerated or oxygenated. This is necessary for yeast growth.

The second stage begins with a brief period of yeast growth during which the yeast consumes all oxygen in the wort. This takes only 6 to 24 hours. It then begins to ferment, and this first or primary stage of fermentation builds to a vigorous pace. The rapid evolution of $CO_2$ gas is a sure sign. Normally primary fermentation lasts 3 to 5 days for ales, 6 to 8 days for lagers.

Secondary fermentation is much slower, because most of the fermentable sugar is already gone. It ordinarily lasts only 1 to 3 days for ales, but may last a week or even a month in lagers. During this stage, the evolution of gas is relatively slow, and the cap of foam that covers the surface of the beer during primary fermentation disappears. The transition from primary to secondary fermentation is quite marked. In ales, especially, it often takes place over only a few hours.

Clarification and lagering is the final stage, when essentially all the sugar has been consumed. The beer usually clarifies because the yeast flocculates and falls to the bottom of the vessel. However, not all the yeast cells flocculate, and, in lager beers, those that remain suspended in the beer continue to work slowly, bringing about important changes in the flavor of the beer. This stage ends when the beer is filtered — or, in the case of unfiltered beers, when it is consumed.

# Aeration and Pitching

Yeast can be added to the wort before or after it is aerated. The choice depends on the brewing equipment. Some breweries aerate the wort using an aeration stone that sits in the wort line on the cold (wort out) side of the wort cooler. An aeration stone is similar to the aerating stones used in tropical fish tanks. It is made of stainless steel rather than stone, but it works the same way: air is pumped into the porous stone, which breaks up the flow into very fine bubbles. This encourages the dissolution of gas into the wort.

If an in-line aeration stone is used, yeast is pitched into the fermenter before the wort cooling operation begins, and the wort is cooled and immediately aerated on the way from the kettle to the fermenter. However, some breweries use a separate vessel for aeration. This is called a "flotation tank," and is fitted with one or more aerating stones at the bottom. The cooled wort is run into the flotation tank and aerated before being moved into the fermenter. Yeast may be pitched into the flotation tank or into the fermenter. The idea behind the flotation tank is that the aeration brings about half of the cold break material to the surface, where it floats (hence the name of the vessel). The wort is then drawn off the bottom of the tank, leaving this fraction of cold break behind. This procedure has been shown to give more stable beer; in other words, if the wort is treated in this way, the final filtered beer will have a longer shelf life because it is less prone to oxidation.

A final option is to aerate the wort in the fermenter itself. This is simpler for homebrewers than either of the other methods, and it works perfectly well. The only problem with it is that the simple methods of aeration normally used, such as agitating the fermenter, do not fully saturate the wort with air. Some alternatives, such as pouring the wort back and forth between two buckets, compound the problem by exposing the wort to airborne microorganisms. However, a clean, sanitized stone can be placed in the bottom of almost any homebrew fermenter and removed when aeration is over.

One controversial practice is the injection of oxygen rather than air into the wort. Many commercial breweries do this, but it is not practical for most homebreweries. Bottled oxygen is expensive and somewhat hazardous. Also, as further explained in Chapter 19, pure oxygen is a double-edged sword. It may give better yeast growth than air, but too much can kill the yeast.

## Open versus Closed Fermentation

Fermenters can be either open or closed at the top; if closed, they must be fitted with an outlet tube to allow $CO_2$ to escape. Closed fermenters are a recent development, and they have become very popular in microbreweries. They are favored because they allow the entire fermentation to take place in a single vessel, which means less equipment cleaning, and reduced risk of contamination because of fewer transfers.

Open fermenters have been used for centuries and generally work quite well. During the primary fermentation, the beer is covered with a layer of foam (and, with some ales, yeast) that protects it from stray airborne microorganisms. However, the beer must be transferred to a closed vessel for secondary fermentation when the head disappears. Open vessels are still favored in breweries that use top fermenting ale yeasts, because the yeast can be skimmed off the surface rather than allowed to drop back into the beer when the head collapses. With some strains, skimming is the only way to collect enough yeast for repitching: very little settles to the bottom.

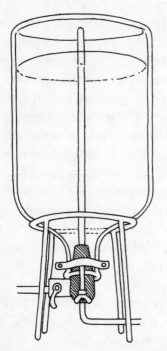

*This fermenter setup turns a carboy into a "poor man's unitank."*

An alternative to open fermentation for top fermenting yeast is the use of a closed system loosely patterned after the Burton Union system employed by some British breweries. The beer ferments in a closed vessel of a size that closely matches the amount of wort. (Normally, closed fermenters are at least 30 percent larger than the batch size, in order to allow head space for the foam.) The yeast pancake is expelled through the vent tube and then can be collected and repitched. The problem is that a lot of wort is expelled along with the yeast. The Burton Union system includes a trough where the yeast will separate from the beer, and the beer then runs back into the closed fermenter through a pipe. This means a good deal of air exposure that negates the sanitation advantage of a closed fermenter.

Homebrew systems based on the Burton Union method do not return the expelled beer to the fermenter. This is more sanitary, but it means substantial beer loss, especially with vigorous top-fermenting yeast strains. There is less loss with bottom-fermenting yeasts but also no advantage over using an oversized closed fermenter.

## Single- versus Two-Stage Fermentation

As the last section makes clear, the choice of single- or two-stage fermentation is tied up with the yeast you are using and the type of fermenter you have chosen. Top-fermenting yeasts require either a Burton Union (blowoff) system or two-stage fermentation with an open primary fermenter. Bottom-fermenting yeasts will work with either open or closed fermenters.

Most homebrewers who use two vessels for fermentation move the beer to a closed (secondary) fermenter as soon as primary fermentation is over. The alternative is to rack the beer after secondary fermentation, which allows more yeast to drop out and may diminish the risk of old-yeast flavors in the beer. However, this is possible only if both the primary and secondary fermenters are closed.

If you are recovering yeast for repitching, one advantage of two-stage fermentation with bottom yeast is that you can recover the yeast when it is most vigorous. If it lies at the bottom of the vessel for a week or two during secondary fermentation, it can lose vitality or even begin to *autolyze* (feed on itself), creating sulfury off flavors. This deterioration happens quite rapidly at higher temperatures. If you have refrigeration and can cool the beer as soon as fermentation is over, the threat is much reduced.

The key to the success of single-stage fermentation in microbreweries is the use of the cylindro-conical fermenter, also called the "unitank." These vessels solve all the problems associated with single-stage fermentation and serve for primary and secondary fermentation as well as lagering or cold aging of the beer. The unitank is a cylinder with a conical bottom. The walls are fitted with jackets, and a coolant (usually a glycol-water mix) is circulated through these jackets to control the temperature of the beer inside. The cooling may be controlled by a thermostat that opens and closes the coolant valves as required to maintain the preset temperature.

The advantage of the conical bottom is that the yeast that drops out of suspension can be drawn out by opening the valve

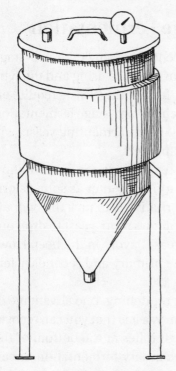

at the bottom of the cone. Thus, the yeast can be removed as needed for repitching. Because the vessel is cooled when fermentation ends, the yeast will keep for at least a week and the unitank serves as a yeast reservoir in addition to its other functions. However, real top-fermenting yeasts do not work well in most unitanks, because the top of the vessel is closed and the yeast pancake cannot be skimmed off.

## Clarification and Cold Storage

*The unitank fermenter is a cylinder with a conical bottom so that the yeast that drops out of suspension can be drawn out by opening the valve at the bottom of the cone.*

With unitanks, the beer is cooled and allowed to mature in the same vessel in which it was fermented. Most home-brewers, however, have to move the beer to a closed vessel, either at the end of the primary or secondary fermentation. This is the custom in both traditional ale and lager breweries. With lager brewing, there is no definite line between secondary fermentation and cold storage (lagering); the yeast continues to work slowly as the temperature drops. Therefore, lager beers are usually moved to lager tanks at the end of primary fermentation, and the secondary fermentation takes place as the temperature is lowered slowly, over a period of a week or so, to 32°F. Ales are "crash cooled" to near the freezing point over a much briefer period (24 to 36 hours). Because ale yeasts go dormant at low temperatures, the idea behind crash cooling is precisely to encourage the dazed yeast to flocculate and settle out. Lager yeasts also settle out slowly during the lagering period.

Obviously, in the days before refrigeration, lagering was a difficult proposition. At that time, lagers were only brewed in central Europe, and only during the winter, when ambient temperatures in the breweries could be kept cool enough for fermentation. Lagering was done in caves that were cool all year-round, and blocks of ice, cut from the surfaces of frozen lakes and rivers during the winter, were used for supplemental cooling. With ales, no attempt was made at crash cooling. The fresh beer was casked soon after fermentation ended, and then underwent a brief secondary fermentation and conditioning before being shipped out to the pubs. Most homebrewers still handle their unfiltered ales in this way, except that bottles are more usual than casks as the final vessel. The modern use of refrigeration for ale is largely tied to the practice of filtering, and the consumer's demand for crystal clear beer.

# 17

# Fermentation and Lagering Equipment

**T**he equipment for fermentation and lagering can be very elaborate or very simple, depending on the type of beer you want to make. As with the equipment for wort production and boiling, there is a great deal of latitude, and it is possible to put together a set of equipment that fits almost any budget. However, we have now entered the "cold side" of the process, where the introduction of stray microbes can lead to spoiled beer. For this reason, it is better not to skimp too much, because the cheapest equipment often comes at the price of increased risk of infection.

## Aeration Equipment

A prime example of the "cheap is dangerous" principle is the vital step of wort aeration. One common method of aerating the cooled wort is to pour it back and forth between two buckets, which is an invitation to infection. This method does not work very well, nor does fanning the wort down the side of the fermenter.

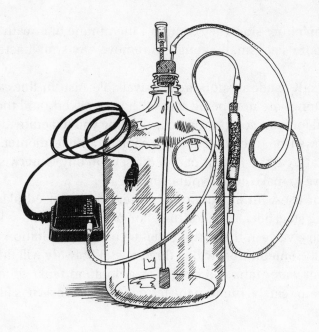

*Wort aeration assembly. The wort aerator consists of a cork fitted with an airlock and a length of ¼-inch copper tubing. The copper tube is attached to a length of polyethlene tubing, which in turn connects to an aquarium aeration stone. In use, the aerator is inserted into the starting tank.*

Shaking the fermenter is better, but there is a serious risk that the cork or lid will pop off; also, fermenters are heavy. All told, aeration stones are the best alternative.

The old standby is the aquarium aeration stone with tubing and a small air pump. With this device, you can quickly and easily saturate the wort with air. There are two problems that must be considered, however: sanitation and odor. The stream of air put out by an aquarium pump smells like rubber. The best way to remove the odor is with a carbon filter. You can make one from a length of plastic hose, a couple of corks, and short lengths of copper or stainless steel tubing. Put a wad of cotton in the end, away from the pump, to catch the dust. A sterile air filter also should be put in the line. These items look like a plastic disk with hose barbs on either side; they contain a membrane filter with a very small pore size, small enough to remove any stray bacteria or spores.

Ready-made aerators are also available. Also, in-line carbonating stones are now being sold for homebrewers, and they can be used for wort aeration as well, allowing you to aerate the wort as it flows from the kettle or wort cooler to the fermenter. Make sure that a carbon filter is part of the set you buy. Otherwise, you will have to make one of your own.

For use with an aerator, a somewhat oversized plastic or stainless steel bucket (or, for 10-gallon batches, a stainless keg fitted with a valve at the bottom) can be used as a flotation tank if desired. Homebrewers with a three-vessel brewery will find that their hot water tank can double as a flotation tank. Otherwise, the aerator can be put into the fermenter as soon as it is filled.

## Fermenters

The standard fermentation setup for homebrewing is a plastic 7- or 10-gallon open bucket, used as a primary fermenter, plus a 5-gallon glass carboy, as a secondary fermenter. This system has been used to brew many batches of excellent beer. The weak point is the plastic bucket, which should be replaced after a year or two. No matter how gentle and careful you are, plastic will get scratched as you clean it, and scratches are a perfect lodging place for sludge, which, in turn, will eventually become a home for unwanted microbes. If you choose to use plastic, the best buckets include a tight-fitting lid with a grommet that will seat an airlock. This makes them practically the same as a closed fermenter, except that they can be opened for cleaning or skimming.

For an oversized primary fermenter, a 7-gallon carboy is the best choice, and is easy to find at homebrew supply stores. Most homebrewers, when they move up to 10-gallon batches, simply split their wort into two equal volumes and keep right on using glass carboys for both primary and secondary fermentation.

There are several alternatives for large batch homebrewing. One is to use a half-barrel size stainless steel keg. This option can be relatively inexpensive, assuming you can find kegs at scrap prices. There are drawbacks, however. First, it is difficult to see inside the keg, and therefore hard to know whether you have gotten it clean. Second, working on scrap kegs involves some risk as they may be under pressure. To avoid injury, never try to remove the valve/spear assembly from a keg unless you have vented it first. If you don't know how to do this, find someone who does. It requires special tools.

An auxiliary item used with fermenters is an airlock. These devices are cheap and easy to find. A range of stoppers is available from most homebrew supply shops to fit the airlock to almost any size opening. If you have an open fermenter that cannot take an airlock, at least use a lid of some kind to cover it.

One interesting device that has been on the market for some time is the brewcap. This invention, along with a modified milk crate, allows you to ferment in an inverted 5-gallon carboy, drawing yeast off the bottom just as with a unitank. It is quite simple and ingenious, though there are a couple of drawbacks. The first of these is the beer loss that comes with any system where the fermenter volume is the same as the amount of wort you put in it. A second drawback to a brewcap is, while it resembles a unitank, an inverted carboy has a very shallow "cone" angle, which makes it hard to pull all the yeast out. This means there will be considerable yeast carryover into the next vessel.

Several part-time entrepreneurs are now making unitanks in ½- and 1-barrel sizes, suitable for advanced homebrewers. Some of them even have jackets for circulating coolant. If you are in the market for a truly professional quality fermenter, you should investigate this option. However, a jacket is not likely to be useful unless you also have a convenient supply of cold water and the willingness to invest further time and money wiring and plumbing the jacket and thermostat connections. It would be simpler to put the unitank in a suitable refrigerator, and to equip the refrigerator with a wide-range thermostat (see next section) to control temperature.

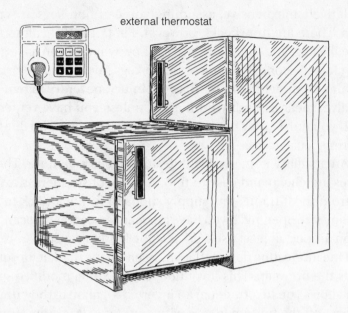

external thermostat

*You can enlarge a refrigerator for use in brewing by building a plywood addition in the lower compartment and insulating the box with 2-inch rigid styrofoam paneling. An external thermostat can be used to control the temperature of a fermenting refrigerator.*

## Refrigerators

Regardless of what types of fermenters you have, a dedicated brewing refrigerator is a very useful accessory, since it allows you to control temperature during fermentation. Because it is not opened and closed frequently, a normal refrigerator can be expanded (see illustration) to accommodate a large number of 5-gallon kegs or other vessels. Most refrigerator thermostats allow temperatures of only about 45°F maximum, so you probably will have to get a wider, higher range thermostat to use in place of, or in line with, the one in the refrigerator. One popular plan is to use a plug-in type thermostat and leave the refrigerator's internal thermostat set on maximum cooling. Suitable thermostats are available from Grainger and other sources.

It is really best to have two refrigerators, one of standard size equipped with a high-range thermostat, the other an expanded one with only the normal thermostat. The wide-range refrigerator holds your fermenter(s) during primary and secondary fermentation, when temperatures are high and need to be controlled; most homebrewers will only have one batch of beer at a time in active fermentation. The other refrigerator can be set permanently at 32° to 34°F, and is used for cold storage and lagering of beer in 5-gallon soda kegs.

## Soda Kegs

The 5-gallon soda keg is, for most homebrewers, the best lagering tank available, and it is also excellent for dispensing finished beers. If you own a few of these tanks plus some fittings, hoses, and a small $CO_2$ tank, you can carry out a range of operations including filtering and dispensing with minimal air pick-up and maximum efficiency. Soda kegs can be stacked lengthwise in a refrigerator like cordwood, making excellent use of the space available. The only drawback is that some of the internal fittings are hard to clean without disassembly.

## Siphoning Equipment

The most usual method of beer transfer is with a siphon. Racking tubes and hoses are available at all homebrew supply shops. There are now some devices on the market that will allow you to start the siphon without putting the hose in your mouth and sucking. Since the human mouth is full of *lactobacilli* —a genus of bacteria well known for spoiling beer — this is a close encounter of a kind you might want to avoid. The only time you want beer in your mouth is when you're drinking it.

# 18

# What Happens during Fermentation?

**F**ermentation is the most complex step in the brewing process. The simple chemical breakdowns that take place in the mash kettle look like child's play compared with the biochemical reactions in the fermenter. Working with sugars, amino acids, and a variety of trace elements and vitamins, the yeast cells create an amazing array of compounds. Brewers need to appreciate that all the really hard work of beermaking is done for us by a microorganism that has no awareness of our keen interest in its activities. Brewers make wort, but yeast makes beer.

## What Is Fermentation?

One way to understand fermentation is to look at what it is not. It is not the normal way that living things obtain energy. The ordinary method is *respiration,* which is a form of oxidation, as is burning coal or wood. It involves taking oxygen (from the air, as a rule) and combining it with fuel. In living cells the fuel is a single sugar — glucose, usually — and the results are an equal quantity of carbon dioxide and water. The chemical equation is

$$C_6H_{12}O \quad + \quad 6\,O_2 \quad \rightarrow \quad 6\,CO_2 \quad + \quad 6\,H_2O$$

$$\text{(glucose)} \qquad \text{(oxygen)} \qquad \text{(carbon dioxide)} \quad \text{(water)}$$

As you know from standing near a fire, oxidation releases a lot of energy. That is why respiration is such an efficient life process. However, it is limited by the availability of oxygen. What do you do if your air supply is cut off? The usual answer is, you die. But yeast and some other organisms have found a way of surviving in the absence of air. They go into *anaerobic metabolism* (without air) and ferment sugar rather than oxidize it. The equation is

$$C_6H_{12}O_6 \quad \rightarrow \quad 2\,C_2H_5OH \quad + \quad 2\,CO_2$$

$$\text{(glucose)} \qquad \text{(ethyl alcohol)} \qquad \text{(carbon dioxide)}$$

This process releases relatively little energy to the cell, as might be expected when you consider the complexity of alcohol, the end product. The chemical breakdown is far from complete. Still, it is the best that can be done without oxygen. Yeast cells are so adapted to "life without air" that, in the presence of large amounts of glucose, they will not even attempt to respire — even when there is oxygen available! This phenomenon, known as the "Crabtree effect," will be discussed later.

Now it is time to look more closely at the normal life of yeast cells in beer wort. This is divided into three stages: lag period, respiration and growth, and fermentation. Please remember that more than one stage may be going on at the same time. Yeast cells do not march in step like soldiers. However, for the sake of clarity, we must describe these stages in sequence.

# The Lag Period

This is when brewers' hands sweat. Yet, despite the appearance of inactivity, the yeast are not idle. They are busy preparing for the hard work ahead. The main activity of freshly pitched cells is to secrete enzymes that will allow amino acids and sugars to be transported through (permeate) the cell wall. This transport system is vital because, without it, all subsequent activity is impossible. Each of the common wort sugars needs a separate enzyme to allow it to permeate, and in the case of *sucrose* (ordinary table sugar), three are required: the first, *invertase*, is excreted through the cell wall and breaks the bond holding the double sugar together; then two permeases are formed that allow the resultant glucose and fructose molecules to enter the cell. Maltose and maltotriose, on the other hand, are transported into the cell first, and then are broken into glucose molecules within the cell.

These facts have an important implication. The separate transport enzymes explain one of the yeast mutations occasionally experienced in breweries. Attenuative strains can become unattenuative because they lose the gene that governs the synthesis of maltotriose permease — the enzyme that brings maltotriose into the cell.

Yeast must build up food reserves before growth and fermentation can take place. The cells store fuel in the form of *glycogen*, a starchy material built up from glucose. Yeast also must take in amino acids from which they can synthesize proteins. The reason glycogen storage is needed is that reproduction — which is the cell's first concern — requires tremendous amounts of energy, and, in order to make it possible, the yeast will refuse to do anything else until the glycogen reserves are built up. Similarly, proteins (built up from amino acids), oxygen, trace minerals, and lipids (fatty compounds) are needed in order to create the materials for the cell wall and many internal structures.

The Crabtree effect is important because it short circuits the normal process of energy storage and reproduction. Instead, the yeast go directly into fermentation. The normal cycle of growth is delayed and, to some extent, suppressed. As a result, the cell count in the wort does not increase as much as it should, and the fermentation will be feeble and protracted. Because of the Crabtree effect, beers formulated with large amounts of sugar are prone to difficult fermentations.

# Growth and Respiration

Actually, yeast cells do not grow like higher organisms. Instead, they multiply. Although capable of sexual reproduction under extraordinary circumstances, their usual method of multiplication is "budding," which is a form of cell division. As noted earlier, the process of synthesizing new material and duplicating all the discrete "organs" of the cell requires not only amino acids, lipids, minerals, and vitamins, but also oxygen. Most of the oxygen consumed by yeast — and they consume *all* the wort contains — is used to synthesize sterols and other complex fatty substances that are vital components of the cell wall and other structures.

This explains why oxygen is so desirable in a freshly pitched wort. A strong growth of yeast is needed before fermentation begins. After a vigorous growth phase, the majority of the cells in the wort will be young, and yeast cells are like people: only the young can be strong. For a rapid, complete fermentation, you need lots of healthy young yeast cells in your wort.

The factor limiting yeast growth is always either amino acids or oxygen; more frequently, the latter. It should be noted, though, that yeast *can* grow without oxygen to some extent, if the wort is rich in sterols and unsaturated fatty compounds. As it happens, trub (hot and cold break material) contains a large proportion of these substances, which are derived from malt. Unfortunately, high trub levels in the wort lead to high levels of fusel alcohols in the finished beer. For this reason, it is important to separate as much of the trub from the wort as possible. Good brewing practice is to rely on oxygen rather than trub for yeast growth. However, yeast do not care where their sterols come from and will gladly accept them ready-made rather than using oxygen to manufacture them.

Respiration is not the simple, single step breakdown implied by the formula given earlier. It is a highly elaborate sequence of steps, each mediated by one or more enzymes. The first step is splitting the 6-carbon glucose molecule into two 3-carbon molecules of *pyruvic acid*. This involves not only breaking a carbon-carbon bond, but also detaching and rearranging many of the hydrogen and oxygen atoms bound to the carbons. Formation of pyruvic acid also means an increase in wort acidity; during fermentation the pH drops about one unit.

In its turn, pyruvic acid is reduced to *activated acetic acid* (acetyl CoA). This is a 2-carbon molecule attached to a complex organic carrier, Co-enzyme A. The third carbon of the pyruvic acid molecule is released as a molecule of carbon dioxide. Finally the acetyl CoA is oxidized via the citric acid cycle, a chain of chemical reactions during which *adenosine triphosphate* (ATP) is created. ATP can be thought of as a biochemical battery: it is a readily tapped power source. Some steps in the initial stage of respiration actually consume ATP, but at the end of the citric acid cycle the net result is a tremendous energy gain for the cell.

If respiration of glucose into $CO_2$ and $H_2O$ were all that went on during the respiratory phase, I would not have bothered to describe it. But I wanted to make it clear that many enzymes are at work, and a lot of energy is available during this stage. It is, therefore, not surprising that several important by-products are created, also. They will be discussed shortly.

# Fermentation

Compared to respiration, fermentation is rather straightforward. Once all the oxygen in the wort has been used up, the citric acid cycle can no longer operate. The yeast continue to cut apart glucose molecules and rearrange them into molecules of pyruvic acid. Then, each molecule of pyruvic acid is reduced in turn: not to acetyl CoA, but to *acetaldehyde*. This is a 2-carbon molecule, and it is at this point — just as in respiration — that the odd molecule of carbon is sloughed off as carbon dioxide. However, no complex cycle follows. The acetaldehyde is reduced (by the addition of hydrogen ions) to ethyl alcohol. The equation is:

$$C_6H_{12}O_6 \rightarrow 2\ CH_3COCOOH \rightarrow 2\ CO_2\ +\ 2\ CH_3CHO \rightarrow 2\ CH_3CH_2OH$$

(glucose)      (pyruvic acid)    (carbon dioxide) (acetaldehyde)        (alcohol)

The first step is complicated, but the rest is simple and the result is only a small gain in energy. The simplicity of fermentation makes it less interesting as a biochemical process than respiration. Of course, for beer lovers, it is the whole point of the exercise. Also, more goes on during fermentation than the reaction outlined here. It is now time to turn our attention to some of the by-products of yeast metabolism and their significance to the flavor of beer.

# By-Products

Two significant by-products of fermentation are the *vicinal diketones* (VDK), *2,3 pentanedione* and *2,3 butanedione*. The latter is usually called "diacetyl."

## Vicinal Diketones

Vicinal diketones have a strong aroma and flavor: pentanedione has a sweet, honey-perfume smell, and diacetyl resembles butter or butterscotch. Of the two, diacetyl is more significant because it has a taste threshold 10 times lower than its partner, and most yeast strains make more of it than pentanedione. For most people, the taste threshold of diacetyl is about .1 ppm. VDK are created when certain precursors are expelled from the cell into the surrounding wort; if these compounds encounter dissolved oxygen, they will oxidize into VDK. This means that diacetyl is formed only when there is oxygen in the wort. It also means that it is, to some extent, inevitable, since the wort must be strongly aerated at pitching.

The other factor affecting VDK formation is temperature. The warmer the environment, the more VDK precursors will be expelled into the wort.

In practice, VDK is formed during the initial aerobic stage of fermentation. During this stage, all the oxygen in the wort is consumed by the yeast, so there should be no further production unless air is reintroduced. However, all yeasts can, to some extent, reduce VDK to flavorless diols. This is one of the key properties of yeast. Given time and the right conditions, most yeast strains can reduce VDK to below the flavor threshold level during the anaerobic (fermentative) phase of their activity.

The reason most commercial beers are essentially free from diacetyl is that fermentation is managed so as to discourage its creation and encourage its reduction. High temperatures assist this reduction, and some German breweries actually raise the temperature of the beer from 48° to 60°F when fermentation is about two-thirds finished, precisely to allow their yeasts to eliminate VDK. However, not all lager breweries do this, and the famous Pilsner Urquell, the granddaddy of all pale lager beers, has a perceptible level of diacetyl. Furthermore, many Belgian and British ales also have the butterscotch note of diacetyl.

As noted above, most commercial breweries scorn diacetyl and bend over backwards to eliminate it from their beer. But in some styles it can be a characteristic — not necessarily a fault — and homebrewers are free to decide for themselves whether they want it.

## Fusel Alcohols

The next group of by-products is the fusel alcohols, sometimes called "higher alcohols." They resemble ethyl alcohol but are made from longer strings of carbon atoms. For example, the formula for butyl alcohol is $C_3H_7CH_2OH$. Fusel alcohols have a sweetness at the front of the mouth combined with a harshness on the back of the tongue. They are formed in the same way as is ethyl alcohol but from different materials. Amino acids in the wort are first broken down and transformed into *keto acids* (pyruvic is the simplest keto acid); these acids are then reduced to *aldehydes* and finally to alcohols. Production of higher alcohols is affected by temperature; just as with diacetyl, low temperatures discourage their formation.

All beers contain some amount of fusel alcohols, and, generally, the stronger the beer, the higher the content will be. As with diacetyl, the usual modern practice is to try to eliminate them as much as possible.

One subtype of higher alcohol of special interest is the phenolic alcohols, which contain a phenolic 6-carbon ring. These alcohols tend to have very strong medicinal flavors. Many wild strains of brewers' yeast *(S. Cerevisiae)* produce phenolic alcohols that are intense and very unpleasant. Such flavors are the signature of a wild yeast infection, which is one of the commonest and worst of fermentation problems. However, there is one phenolic alcohol, 4-vinyl-guaiacol, whose clove-like flavor is part of the taste profile of Bavarian wheat beers, and the ale yeast strains used for these brews produce perceptible amounts of this alcohol. This is another by-product that is considered a flaw in most styles of beer but is acceptable and even expected in certain cases.

## Fatty Acids

Fatty acids are formed when the yeast cuts up amino acids into their component strings. These acids tend to have soapy flavors. Like the other by-products discussed here, they are discouraged by low temperatures. In a strong fermentation, most fatty acids will be reduced by the yeast to aldehydes, then to alcohols. This is considered desirable, and is one of the reasons a strong fermentation is the goal for most brewers.

## Esters

Esters are produced by the combination of an alcohol with an acid. For example, ethyl acetate is the product of a reaction between ethanol and acetic acid (or acetyl CoA, which is called "activated acetic acid"). This particular ester is predominant in beer, but it has a higher sensory threshold than some others. Esters made from longer acids and/or higher alcohols tend to have powerful fruity aromas. Isoamyl acetate is the aroma of banana; ethyl butyrate is the aroma of pineapple. Ethyl acetate, in high concentrations, smells like a solvent and, in fact, has commercial use as a nail polish remover. It can be detected in some strong ales.

Esters are formed when fatty acids combine with fusel alcohols. During the yeast growth stage, these fatty acids are built up into sterols and other compounds that make up the cell wall and other structures. If the wort lacks oxygen, however, this cannot happen and the yeast will, instead, attach these acids to alcohols, making esters. Thus, if we want to keep esters down, the wort must be aerated, especially at the beginning of fermentation. Temperature during this period is also important; like the other reactions described here, ester formation is greater at high temperatures.

Nature has contrived things so that the higher the gravity of the wort, the less oxygen it will hold. This means that high gravity beers always feature a disproportionate amount of esters. To hold them down in high gravity brewing operations, commercial brewers inject oxygen into the wort. This raises the diacetyl level, but they can (hopefully) cope with this later on, when fermentation is essentially over.

Besides temperature, another factor that influences the creation of by-products is the pitching rate. The higher it is, the less the yeast needs to reproduce before fermentation begins; and since most of these by-products are created during the growth phase, a high pitching rate will hold them somewhat in check. On the other hand, too high a pitching rate will result in a large proportion of old, tired yeast cells, especially after several repitchings. As a result, each fermentation is less vigorous than the one before, takes more time, and often yields a higher terminal gravity. For these reasons, very high pitching rates are not a good solution to a problem of unwanted by-products in the finished beer. The best practice is to pitch a proper amount of active yeast into a thoroughly aerated wort. If you get a good fermentation but unacceptable amounts of by-products, change to a "cleaner" strain of yeast.

## Flocculation and Secondary Fermentation

Flocculation is the joining together of yeast cells into large clumps. Yeasts vary greatly in their tendency to flocculate. Many yeast strains do not flocculate at all. Others flocculate strongly, very early in the fermentation. When this happens, the evolving carbon dioxide gas carries the flocs to the surface of the beer, where they form the pancake so typical of top-fermenting yeasts.

Bottom-fermenters flocculate later, when most of the sugar in the yeast has been consumed and much less gas is evolving. As a result, the flocs fall to the bottom of the fermenter.

The slow end stage of fermentation (when all the simple sugars and most of the maltose has been used up and the yeast is left to chew on ends of maltotriose and other complex, hard to ferment sugars) is called "secondary fermentation." In the case of ales it is usually rather brief, because most ale yeasts cannot handle the complex triple sugars very well. Lager yeasts, however, can work their way slowly through the less edible foodstuffs, and so lagers have a rather lengthy secondary fermentation. This is especially true if it is conducted at very low temperatures, as is typically the case.

The long secondary fermentation of lager beers is important because lager yeasts produce large amounts of by-products during the active part of fermentation. On the third day of fermentation, lager beer will reek of diacetyl, acetaldehyde, and a host of other compounds. During the cold secondary fermentation, the yeast reabsorbs and further metabolizes these substances, and the end result is a clean, crisp flavor in the finished beer.

## Yeast Autolysis

During the last part of fermentation, yeast cells sense that food is becoming scarce. They respond by abandoning fermentation and concentrating instead on using the malt sugars to build up glycogen reserves. Then they go dormant and largely live off their stored food supply.

Not every yeast cell will do this, and not all of them do it at the same time. With any given strain, the lower the sugar content of the wort drops, the more cells will start making glycogen. With many yeasts, the end of the glycogen buildup coincides with dropping out of suspension to the bottom of the fermenter.

The problem is that the stored glycogen will not last forever. Eventually it is used up, and the yeast cell faces starvation. Lying there on the bottom of the tank, covered by other cells, it cannot take in more wort sugars even if they are still available.

The danger at this stage is *autolysis.* This is a last-ditch measure in which the yeast cells excrete proteolytic enzymes, breaking down the walls of neighboring cells so that they can ingest their components and hopefully survive. As autolysis goes on, sulfury compounds are released, and the result is a rotten, rubbery stench in the beer. Of course, autolysis does not begin immediately, or all at once. Much depends on the strain of yeast and the temperature. As with all metabolic processes, the warmer the medium, the faster autolysis sets in. This is why commercial breweries either will chill their beer, or will rack it off the yeast layer once fermentation is ended. Because most homebrewers lack refrigeration capability, autolyzed, yeasty flavors are one of the most common defects of homebrew.

## Other By-Products

Mention of the sulfury odor of autolysis leads us to some by-products that generally are not related to yeast activity. These are sulfur compounds such as *dimethyl sulfide* (DMS) and *hydrogen sulfide.* It used to be thought that yeast produce DMS during fermentation, but most experts no longer believe this. In fact, some DMS is eliminated during fermentation as it is flushed out along with evolving carbon dioxide. Brewers' yeast does produce hydrogen sulfide (rotten-egg gas), which is one of the components in the typical stench of beer at the high kraeusen stage. The term *kraeusen* is used here to describe the large head of foam that forms on the surface of the wort during the early stages of fermentation. However, this gas also is flushed out and generally is not present in perceptible amounts when fermentation ends.

Another class of by-products not directly related to fermentation are the so-called staling compounds; these are mostly *aldehydes* of various sorts. They are produced by oxidation of alcohols and various fatty substances. Active yeast is a strong oxygen scavenger, so usually these staling by-products arise in beer that is aerated after fermentation is over. Bottle-conditioned homebrew with active yeast is less susceptible to such oxidation than beers that have the yeast filtered out. However, the other side of the story is that bottle-conditioned beers are very prone to autolyzed flavors. In brewing, there is no ideal solution to every problem; things that help in one way can hurt you in another.

# Practical Implications

As you can see from even this sketchy and incomplete discussion, managing a fermentation to get a clean result is no mean feat! Various demands of the process pull the brewer in different directions. For example, the problem of esters and diacetyl requires contradictory strategies to minimize their production. How this is handled clearly depends on the brewer, the yeast, and the beer being made. Ale brewers expect esters and usually can count on high fermentation temperatures to reduce diacetyl. Lager brewers, on the other hand, usually want to keep both by-products down; hence the practice of starting fermentation cool, which minimizes both by-products, and then, if necessary, raising the temperature to make sure diacetyl is reduced. By this time the raw materials from which esters are formed have been mostly disposed of, so one can get a large reduction in diacetyl in exchange for a small increase in esters.

The many and widely varied fermentation practices employed in breweries around the world are the result of trial and error, using a vast number of yeast strains with markedly different characteristics to brew equally different beers. As noted earlier, yeast makes beer, so a good brewer, while regarding yeast as a servant, also understands what an indispensable and yet temperamental beast it can be. With some strains, a difference of 5°F in fermentation temperature, or 5 points of specific gravity, will drastically change the finished beer; other yeasts, with stronger personalities, are far less affected by the conditions under which they work. In every case, however, the brewer has chosen a yeast that will give the results he wants for his own beers, and, having made the choice, must then learn that yeast's characteristics and be ready to adapt to them.

# 19

# Wort Aeration and Pitching

**T**he key to a successful fermentation is getting the process off to a good start. If an adequate quantity of fresh, active yeast is pitched into a wort that is saturated with air, fermentation will start quickly and go to completion. A slow, feeble fermentation is a bad sign, and almost always means that the beer will have abnormal amounts of fermentation by-products.

It is worth repeating that once you get to the cold side of the brewing process, infection is an ever-present danger. Cold wort is an ideal medium for the cultivation of many types of microorganisms, and most of them will harm the beer's flavor if they are allowed to take hold. Everything that touches cold wort or beer must be clean and sanitized.

## Aerating the Wort

Most microbreweries aerate the cooled wort by using an aeration stone, which is the same as a carbonating stone. These days, commercial aerating stones are usually made of stainless steel, which makes them easy to clean and sanitize. They are often placed in the wort line on the cold (output) side of the heat exchanger (wort cooler). Carbonating stones that are designed for similar use on the output side of a filter are becoming available, and, with a little home engineering, the same stone could be pressed into use for aerating the cooled wort.

It is vital that the cooled wort be saturated with air. While trub can provide lipids that substitute to some extent for oxygen, the yeast always grows better when it gets plenty of air. Furthermore, trub leads to off flavors and can actually harm the fermentation in later stages, and so hot trub should always be separated from the wort prior to fermentation, as much as possible.

In addition to separating hot trub, many commercial breweries, especially lager breweries, also take pains to remove some of the cold trub (cold break) that forms during wort cooling. This can be accomplished in two ways. The cold wort can be allowed to stand for 8 to 12 hours so that the cold trub settles, and then can be racked out of the settling tank, aerated, and pitched. Alternatively, the cold wort can be run into a tall narrow tank, called a flotation tank, fitted with aerating stones at the bottom. The air bubbles carry cold break particles to the surface, where they form a foamy scum. Then the wort is drawn out from the bottom of the tank into the fermenter. Yeast can be pitched either into the settling tank or the fermenter.

Cold trub removal is never complete, but the methods described can eliminate about 50 percent of the material, and, at least with lagers, the resulting beers seem to have a longer shelf life. However, cold trub is not nearly as damaging to beer flavor as is hot trub, and many ale breweries do not bother with it.

For homebrewers who wish to remove cold trub, the flotation tank method is the safest, because you can pitch the yeast into the flotation tank while the wort is running into it. In homebreweries, wort and beer transfers normally involve exposure to air, and with that exposure comes the risk of airborne bacteria. A stray bacterium or two is of little consequence as long as the wort is pitched promptly with yeast, because the yeast, as they grow, will make conditions unfavorable for competing organisms.

The most common sorts of "wort spoiler" bacteria cannot survive once the yeast takes hold. Therefore, the sooner the yeast is pitched after cooling, the better.

Whether or not you decide to employ a flotation step, you should aerate and pitch the cold wort promptly for the reasons given above. It is virtually impossible to maintain wort in a sterile condition, and in practice all brewers must rely on their yeast to knock out stray contaminating bacteria.

If you do not use an in-line aerating stone, the best way to ensure total aeration of the wort is to use an aquarium aerating stone in either the flotation tank or the fermenter. The basic aerating stone setup has already been described in Chapter 17. It is useful to have a valve in the line that will allow you to regulate the flow of air through the stone. Without it, the flow may be too great, quickly forming a large head of foam on the wort. You need to slow down the flow so that air can bubble through the wort for as long as possible — ideally at least 20 minutes. A brief period of bubbling, no matter how vigorous, may not saturate the wort with air.

Various other methods of aeration are used by homebrewers, but most fall short of the goal of saturation. Many are also invitations to disaster, such as shaking a closed fermenter, pouring the wort back and forth, and fanning the wort down the side of the fermenter.

The best way to assess your wort aeration is by checking the lag time. A fully saturated ale wort pitched with a good, viable yeast slurry should be fermenting vigorously in 8 hours or less. Lagers take longer due to the colder temperatures, but should be starting to ferment within 16 hours after pitching.

One commercial brewing practice that can lead to trouble is the use of oxygen rather than air. Pure oxygen seems like the ideal gas to use, since it is what the yeast wants. Nitrogen, which makes up almost 80 percent of air, plays no part in yeast growth. The problem with using pure oxygen, however, is that it is possible to get too much of it into the wort. Wort saturated with air will contain about 8 parts per million (ppm) of dissolved oxygen. It is true that some strains of brewers yeast will grow faster and in greater quantity if they get a little more oxygen than this — perhaps 10 to 15 ppm. However, wort saturated with pure oxygen may contain 40 ppm of the gas. At that level, oxygen is a highly effective sanitizing agent, lethal to all microorganisms including yeast.

Thus, if a little is good, more is not always better. If you have a dissolved oxygen meter, you can experiment with different levels of oxygenation to get the best possible yeast growth. However, few homebrewers possess such an instrument, and, without one, there is a good chance you will kill your yeast rather than help them by using pure oxygen. Air is safe.

## Pitching

When pitching yeast, sanitation must be observed. If you are working with a starter built up from a smack pack of liquid yeast, be sure to wipe the mouth of the jug with alcohol and flame it with a blowtorch or lighter before swirling the contents and emptying them into the fermenter or flotation tank. Take similar measures when recovering yeast from one fermenter to repitch into a subsequent batch. Thoroughly clean and sanitize all jars and implements.

A yeast starter culture should be pitched as soon as it is in active fermentation. That is when the vitality of the cells is highest. Slurries made by rehydrating dry yeast should be pitched as soon as they are ready.

Many methods have been devised for assessing the *viability* (ability to reproduce and ferment) of yeast. In general, the easier the method, the less reliable it is, and even the simpler, quicker methods require a microscope. For homebrewers, the best rule to observe in repitching yeast is the sooner, the better. Yeast that is harvested and repitched within a week of the previous pitching will generally be quite viable, as long as it is stored under refrigeration during the interval between harvesting and reuse.

Top-fermenting yeasts, which throw a pancake layer of yeast on the surface of the fermenter, must be reused within a short time. Normally, in an open fermenter, the crop is skimmed daily. The first skimming is discarded, as it contains a high proportion of dead cells, cold trub, and other extraneous matter. The second crop contains the most viable yeast, and is the one that should be harvested for repitching.

Bottom-fermenting yeast are in some ways more difficult to deal with. If the fermenter has a flat bottom, the yeast can be recovered when the beer is racked for secondary fermentation, but the bottom layer (which corresponds to the first crop of a top-fermenting yeast) will be stirred up and mixed with the more viable layer above it. Tanks with a conical bottom avoid this problem because the layers of yeast can be drawn off through the valve at the base of the cone, and they remain fairly well separated.

Usually it is not possible for a homebrewer to use methylene blue stain or other microscopic techniques to evaluate a yeast slurry, but you can use your senses. The color of yeast depends in part on the color of the wort into which it was pitched, but any yeast, as it gets old and decrepit, will darken and acquire a rusty or reddish tinge. The lighter the color, the better. Good yeast also will have a fresh, clean, yeasty flavor and aroma. Yeast that has a sulfury or rubbery smell has begun to autolyze.

The best way to store yeast is at 33°F under a layer of beer. Under these conditions, yeast can last a week if it was fresh when harvested. Note that, with bottom-fermenting yeasts, the yeast is essentially being stored under beer in the bottom of a fermenter, so that, if you cool the beer as recommended at the end of fermentation, you are also storing the yeast for reuse under refrigeration. However, even under proper conditions, stored yeast will autolyze, and you must always evaluate your slurry before repitching it.

Pitching rate is one of the hardest things for a homebrewer to pin down. The standard laboratory method of determining pitching rate requires, among other things, a microscope, a *hemacytometer* (a special type of microscope slide), and a centrifuge. Without these tools, repitching yeast is a bit of a guessing game. If the yeast is fresh, light, and foamy, 1 cup (half a pint) of slurry is plenty for 5 or 6 gallons of wort. Wet, heavy yeast slurries may contain more cells per unit of volume, so less may be needed.

There are problems with under- and overpitching yeast. Underpitching will result in a long delay before fermentation gets under way, which gives "wort spoiler" organisms a chance to grow, and a lengthy and often incomplete fermentation as shown by a high terminal gravity. Note, however, that weak (low viability) yeast and/or poor wort aeration or nutrition also can cause these symptoms. Overpitching will lead, over a few generations, to slower and slower fermentations with higher terminal gravities. This is because from the beginning there were too many yeast cells in the wort. Too many cells means not enough growth and thus not enough young ones. To repeat: Yeast are like people — only the young can be strong.

If your yeast slurry is old or if sensory evaluation shows it is in poor condition, the best course of action is to *rouse* it before pitching. Rousing is, essentially, making a starter culture in a jug using two quarts of sterile wort and perhaps ⅓ to ¼ of the normal pitching volume of slurry. After making up the starter, shake it several times at hourly intervals to thoroughly aerate the wort, and let it stand at room temperature for 24 hours before use. The shot of wort will wake up the yeast and give the viable cells a chance to grow. That is why the name is so appropriate.

Repitching is universal in commercial breweries, and some ale yeasts have been repitched successfully for hundreds of generations. However, repitching requires frequent brewing sessions in order that there will always be a slurry of fresh yeast available. This makes it more problematic for homebrewing. As a rule, it is better to err on the side of caution and use a fresh yeast culture — whether grown from a homemade slant or a newly purchased smack pack — after 3 or 4 repitchings. Also, when you are repitching, the purity of your yeast depends on your sanitation, not only in yeast handling, but also in the entire brewing operation. The technique therefore requires a lot of commitment to cleanliness, as well as confidence.

# 20

# Running the Fermentation

**F**ermentation is the most complicated part of brewing, chemically, but it is the easiest for the brewer in that it does not require much effort. The yeast does the work, and your job is to monitor the process, make adjustments to temperature, and transfer from one vessel to another as required.

## The Lag Period

After boiling, wort should be cooled to fermentation temperature, aerated, and pitched with yeast as soon as possible. If these steps are carried out correctly, an ale wort should be showing signs of fermentation — evolution of $CO_2$ and formation of foam on the surface — within 6 to 8 hours. Lager yeasts can take 12 to 18 hours, depending on the temperature.

One controversial practice is to pitch yeast at a relatively warm temperature — say 75°F for an ale — and then lower the temperature as soon as the wort begins to ferment. The idea is to reduce the lag time, and it works. However, you have to consider why a short lag period is desirable. Basically, the lag period is when the wort spoiler bacteria have the best opportunity to play havoc with the beer. Once the yeast takes over, it eradicates them. Since bacteria, as well as yeast, are more active and grow faster at higher temperatures, it is questionable whether a warm temperature during lag period will do much good. The key to defeating the wort spoilers is not a short lag time *per se*, but rather impeccable sanitation plus pitching a sufficient quantity of fresh, active yeast into a fully aerated wort. A long lag time is a symptom, and pitching warm often only masks a problem. It does not eliminate it.

## Fermentation Temperature

One of the most asked questions about homebrewing is the proper pitching and primary fermentation temperatures. Generally accepted wisdom is around 65° to 68°F for ales and around 46° to 50°F for lagers. These guidelines work for most yeasts, but the brewer must consider the style of beer being made and the particular strain being used. Some Belgian strong ales are fermented at temperatures up to 75°F in order to encourage the production of esters and diacetyl, both of which are considered desirable in these beers. On the other hand, for a normal gravity ale, such a high fermentation temperature may produce a more intense flavor profile than you want. Similarly, yeasts differ in their response to temperature. Some yeasts are rather insensitive and will give you pretty much the same result whether you run them at 60°F or 70°F; others act like a different animal entirely if you alter the temperature.

With lager beers, where a clean flavor profile is generally desired, the yeast strain is equally important. Some strains, such as the famous Weihenstephan 308 (Wyeast Labs #2308), are very prone to diacetyl. They must be started and run cool (46° to 48°F) to minimize the butterscotch flavor in the finished beer. Similarly, Wyeast #2206 is prone to esters and must be run cool to minimize those by-products. On the other hand, Weihenstephan 34/70 (Wyeast Labs #2124) is temperature tolerant and can be run as warm as 55°F without changing its snappy, malty character. Most American breweries now ferment their lagers at about 54°F, and, as you would expect, careful selection of an agreeable yeast strain is what has allowed them to do this.

# Primary Fermentation

In addition to having a longer lag period, lager yeasts take longer to build up a head of steam and reach maximum fermentation activity — the so-called high kraeusen stage, named after the head of foam that crowns the beer. A true top-fermenting ale yeast may reach this point within 24 hours and begin throwing its typical pancake layer of grayish-tan yeast cells to the surface. A lager may not reach this point for 48 to 72 hours after pitching, and of course it will never form the sort of dense, yeasty head that a top-fermenter will. Bottom yeasts may put only a few inches of fluffy white foam on the surface.

Top yeasts should be skimmed from the surface of an open fermenter daily until fermentation subsides. If this is not done, the yeast crop with all its associated "garbage" — hop resins, trub, and so on — will fall back into the beer when primary fermentation ends. The head can collapse in a matter of a few hours. Furthermore, this load of yeast and other material may not settle to the bottom very readily. It is best to get rid of it while it's right there.

If you use a closed fermenter with a top yeast, be sure the vessel is sized so that there is very little headspace. Affix a large diameter "blowoff tube" and immerse the other end of the tube in a bucket of sanitizer. When the fermentation starts, all the yeast will be ejected from the vessel and will not drop into the beer. This blowoff method is wasteful because you lose a couple of quarts of beer, but it is the best way to reconcile the sanitation advantages of a closed fermenter with the behavior of top cropping yeast strains.

To recover yeast from a top fermentation, select the second day's crop. The first day's crop contains a lot of garbage, while the third day's is not usually as viable — it is all worn out. Store the yeast in a closed, sterile jar in the refrigerator under a layer of beer, and repitch it within a week.

Closed fermentation is recommended for bottom-fermenting yeasts, whether making ale or lager. The container should be considerably oversized (about ⅓, e.g., 13⅓-gallons for 10 gallons of wort) so there is plenty of headspace for the foam. Since bottom-fermenters do not throw yeast up with the foam, there is no need to worry about allowing the head to collapse when primary fermentation ends.

Unless your fermenter has a conical bottom that is fitted with a valve, recovering the best yeast (the middle layer) is problematic. Also, since the yeast does not drop out until fermentation is just about finished, you may not be able to recover it until a week or more has passed. Since it is older when it is recovered, it should be stored for as short a time as possible before repitching; ideally, 24 hours or less.

## Racking

*Racking* is the procedure of transferring beer from the primary fermentation vessel into another container for secondary fermentation. All transfers involve some exposure to air and some risk of contamination, and modern brewing practice is to conduct the entire fermentation in a single vessel. However, this practice virtually requires the ability to chill the beer as soon as fermentation is ended. Otherwise, the yeast accumulating at the bottom of the fermenter will start to autolyze. In other words, if you can cool your beer when fermentation is over, single stage fermentation is a good option; however, if you lack refrigeration, you should rack your beer off the dregs at the end of primary fermentation into a vessel of the same volume as the batch size. For most homebrewers, this means a 5-gallon carboy for a 5-gallon batch.

Racking beer is a simple procedure, and the only real trick is to maintain sanitation. You may prefer to use a hand vacuum pump to start the siphon, rather than relying on your mouth, which is a convenient but highly unsanitary suction device.

# Secondary Fermentation

With ales, secondary fermentation is normally conducted at the same temperature as primary fermentation, and it usually lasts only 1 to 2 days. By the end of this time a normal strength ale is finished, and, except for the yeasty taint and cloudiness, it is ready to drink. Subsequent storage is mainly to allow the beer to clear somewhat before being packaged and/or filtered.

Lagers, on the other hand, go through significant flavor changes during secondary fermentation, and the process takes considerably longer. Normally, the beer is cooled at a rate of 2° to 4°F per day until it is at 32° to 34°F. This is why lager brewing virtually requires a refrigerator. Even if your basement is cool enough for primary fermentation, you must be able to cool the beer down gradually starting about 24 hours after primary fermentation ends.

It is considerably more difficult to mark the transition from primary to secondary fermentation with lagers. Rather than dropping off rather abruptly, fermentation gradually slows down as the yeast consumes the wort sugars. The most reliable way to judge the fermentation of lagers is by the specific gravity. Unfortunately, this requires taking a sample, which is inherently risky. You may choose just to observe the bubbling of the fermentation lock and make a judgment call that when bubbling slows to, say, once every 2 seconds, primary fermentation is over.

If you do take a sample, the most practical method is to use a sanitized baster to withdraw it from the carboy, about 1 ounce at a time. Be sure to stir the beer thoroughly to de-gas it before taking a reading with the hydrometer. Never return a sample to the fermenter after reading. Either drink the sample or discard it.

# The Diacetyl Rest

Some lager breweries, especially those that use Weihenstephan 308 or similar yeasts, employ a "diacetyl rest" in order to minimize this by-product in the finished beer. Basically, the procedure is to allow the beer to rise from primary temperature (around

48°F) to 60°F or 65°F when the primary fermentation is coming to an end. Normally, the time is determined by the attenuation of the beer. If, for example, the wort original gravity was 1.050, and the expected terminal gravity is 1.010, then the diacetyl rest would be commenced when the beer has attenuated to about 1.023, when about ⅔ of the total fermentable material in the wort has been consumed. The diacetyl rest normally lasts for 24 to 48 hours, until primary fermentation is over and secondary fermentation is under way; then the temperature is lowered in the usual way, probably 4°F per day, until the lager temperature of 34° to 32°F is reached.

# 21

# Maturation and Lagering

**M**aturation is the time between active fermentation and filtration, or, in the case of unfiltered beers, consumption, during which the beer loses its "green beer" character and reaches its best flavor. *Maturation* is due mainly to two factors: first, the continued slow working of the yeast, reabsorbing and metabolizing by-products such as acetaldehyde and diacetyl that were excreted earlier; and second, the flocculation and dropout of suspended yeast cells, so that the beer loses its yeasty taint and the flavor of malt and hops comes through.

The first part of the process — the slow metabolizing of by-products — takes place during secondary fermentation. Depending upon the temperature and the strain of yeast, a good deal of flocculation may take place during this period, as well. With most yeasts, however, flocculation is very slow and must be helped along in various ways, such as "fining," in order to achieve the clarity desired in the finished beer. *Fining* is used here as a general term meaning a clarifying process that adds organic or mineral

settling agents during secondary fermentation to precipitate colloidal matter through coagulation or adsorption. A more complete
discussion of types of finings is found in Chapter 23.

Lagering is the slow, cold maturation normally given to
lager beers. Ordinarily, the maturation of ales is fairly rapid. The
exceptions are the high gravity, bottle-conditioned ales, which
continue to change and improve in the bottle for several months.

## Maturation of Ales

Ales of normal gravity (original gravity of 1.055 or lower) usually
do not require much maturing. Secondary fermentation lasts only
a day or two with most ale yeasts, and at the end of this time, the
flavor is fine except that the beer probably is loaded with yeast.
To assist yeast dropout and forestall autolysis, the best procedure
is to cool the beer as rapidly as possible, a procedure known as
"crash cooling." In practice, this means moving the carboy or other
secondary fermenter into a refrigerator set at 32° to 34°F. Seven
to 10 days of cold storage will give as much yeast dropout as possible, and at this point the beer will be ready to be clarified and
packaged.

Crash cooling will usually give a cleaner flavored beer than
allowing the yeast to drop out at fermentation temperature. If the
beer is to be carbonated artificially there are no drawbacks to the
process. If the beer is going to be carbonated naturally by priming with sugar and then undergoing a second fermentation either in a cask or bottles, then there is a chance that the yeast may
be stunned by the cold, or, if the beer falls very clear, that there
may not be enough live yeast in suspension to bring about the
second fermentation. However, both of these possibilities are re-
mote with most strains of yeast. Cold does not kill yeast cells — it
only puts them to sleep — and if you warm them up and feed
them some sugar, they will wake up and go to work. Similarly, very
few yeasts will drop out completely during ten days of cold storage. Usually there are plenty of yeast cells left. However, if you
have experienced trouble with the bottle or cask fermentation,
you may want to add 1 or 2 tablespoons of yeast from the bottom

of the secondary fermenter just before racking or bottling the primed beer.

One complication that can be introduced in the maturation of ales is a "conditioning rest" of about 4 days at 55° to 60°F. This requires a secondary fermenter that can withstand pressure, such as a soda keg. As soon as primary fermentation is over, transfer the beer into the soda keg, close it up, and lower the temperature as required. By deliberately slowing down the secondary fermentation, you allow the beer to absorb the $CO_2$ and carbonate naturally. This procedure is especially useful if you plan to serve the beer unfiltered, either from a cask or bottles, as it makes priming unnecessary. The carbonated cold beer can simply be transferred under counterpressure into the package. However, if you wish to filter the beer, then be advised that filtration is much more difficult with carbonated beer, and you will have an easier time of it if you give up the idea of natural carbonation and just carbonate the beer artificially after filtering it.

# Lagering

The traditional method of maturing a lager beer is to lower the temperature slowly over a period of about a week, from primary fermentation temperature to around 32°F. This procedure gives the lager yeast time to adapt gradually to the lower temperatures and slowly continue to work. Lagering requires a refrigerator, and you must remember to set the temperature down 3 or 4 degrees a day until the final point is reached. After this, 2 to 3 weeks will generally bring most lager beers to the peak of flavor, although up to 6 weeks may help with strong bock beers.

The lager periods recommended here depend upon using the modern fermentation methods described in the previous chapter, specifically, a primary fermentation temperature of 50° to 55°F, and, if required, a diacetyl rest at the end of primary fermentation. If you follow the old lager brewing practices of fermenting very cold (42° to 46°F), with no diacetyl rest, then you may have to lager the beer for months to bring down the "green beer" flavor notes. Pilsner Urquell, which is still made the old-fashioned way, requires 9 or 10 weeks of lagering, and it still has discernible amounts of diacetyl in the finished product.

Some American lager breweries do not find it necessary to go through a cold lagering. They allow the secondary fermentation to go on at primary fermentation temperature, and crash cool the beer only 24 to 48 hours before filtration. This procedure saves energy costs and can produce excellent, fully mature beers in less time than the traditional method, but requires a cooperative strain of yeast in order to get good dropout and avoid autolysis. If, like most homebrewers, you work mainly with the European lager yeast strains, you will get better (if slower) results using the modern German method of lagering.

# Beer Clarification

**F**or centuries beer drinkers and brewers alike have considered clarity to be a desirable trait in their favorite beverage. With a few notable exceptions, such as the Bavarian hefeweizen or the Belgian wit (white) beers, most styles of beer are expected to be clear when they are served. There are several reasons for this preference.

First, there is the aesthetic factor. Beers come in a range of colors. The darkest styles, such as stout, are virtually opaque, but most have a color that is intrinsically pleasing to the eye. That color is most appreciated when the light passing through the beer is not scattered by suspended particles (haze).

Second, haze is generally associated with instability and off flavors. An infected beer is almost always hazy. Bacteria and wild yeasts do not fall out of suspension as do most brewers' yeasts, and a clear beer that throws a haze in the package may be exhibiting symptoms of contamination.

Finally, even if it is not contaminated, a beer that is hazy often will be judged inferior in flavor to a clear beer of the same style. There are two factors that account for this judgment. Yeast is the main cause of permanent haze in uninfected beers, and yeast has a flavor that is — well — yeasty. The taste is not unpleasant as such, but to most drinkers it is not as appealing as the malt and hop flavors of beer. Also, yeast adsorbs hop resins during fermentation; consequently, it imparts an unpleasant bitterness called "yeast bite." Note that the traditionally cloudy styles of beer mentioned above are both very lightly hopped. The additional bitterness of the yeast does not overwhelm the malty flavors of these brews.

## What Causes Haze?

Haze is caused by suspended particles in beer that scatter light passing through it. The suspended particles may be of several kinds. They may be an infecting microorganism — wild yeast or bacteria, as mentioned above — or they may be a non-infecting microorganism — in other words, the yeast you deliberately introduced into the wort. There is, however, a third possibility.

Beer contains proteins and tannins in solution. These are both highly complex and varied classes of organic matter. The solubility of many proteins and tannins depends upon the temperature of the solution. As the liquid is cooled, some of them will become insoluble, and, as they come out of solution, they will form colloidal particles that are too small to precipitate but are large enough to scatter light, thus clouding the beer. This is the well-known phenomenon called *chill haze*. Chill haze is reversible: it appears when the beer is chilled, and, after the beer returns to room temperature, it will disappear again. Chill haze is unimportant from a flavor standpoint, but the aesthetic expectations of consumers make it a major bugaboo for commercial brewers, who often must go to elaborate lengths to chillproof their products.

# Dealing with Haze

The homebrewer has several options for coping with the haze in his or her beer. The first and easiest is to ignore it, and this is still the most commonly chosen method especially for beginners. However, more and more advanced homebrewers are looking critically at their beers and concluding that, in some cases at least, clarity is more than an aesthetic issue. With the exception of chill haze, the things that cloud beer also affect its flavor. Even if you could not care less what your beer looks like, you may find that clear beer in many cases will taste better.

Assuming that the issue is flavor, the kind of haze with which you need to concern yourself is caused by suspended microorganisms. If they are wild yeasts or bacteria, there is little you can do about them in the finished beer. These bugs do not easily drop out of suspension. They can be removed by filtration, which will restore the optical clarity of the beer; however, the metabolic by-products they leave behind cannot be removed, and so the beer will still taste as bad as ever. The only thing a brewer can do about infected beer is to dump it, institute a major sanitation effort, and try again.

Yeast haze from brewers' yeast can usually be removed. There are two general techniques that can be employed. One is to encourage the suspended yeast to flocculate and drop out of suspension. How easy this is depends greatly on the yeast strain with which you are working. Cold temperatures will assist the drop-out of many brewers' yeasts, and are one of two reasons (the other is avoiding autolysis) why beer should be cooled after fermentation. However, with many strains that will not be enough. Adding finings to the beer will often produce dramatic results, turning a muddy beer bright in a matter of days. If you have no means of refrigerating your beers in bulk, and if you are not concerned about chill haze, finings may be the only clarification technique you need.

The other method of yeast removal is filtration. This method has three advantages. First, it is instantaneous and certain, whereas finings can take days to work and may not be 100 percent effective. Second, depending on the type and grade of filter material, filters can also remove chill haze along with the yeast. Third, finings do not actually remove yeast — they only move it to the bottom of the carboy, keg, or bottle. The yeast is still there, and, if the yeast layer is disturbed by movement of the container, then yeast can still end up in the beer. That makes careful serving or racking important.

Just as there are two major means of removing yeast, there are two major means of removing chill haze from beer. One is to filter it through a suitable grade of material while the beer is cold. Remember that the haze particles must be present in the beer before they can be filtered out! Therefore, the beer must be at or below serving temperature when it is filtered, and, ideally, between 32° and 34°F.

The other method of chillproofing beer does not depend so much on temperature. Certain powdered compounds that adsorb protein or tannin molecules can be added to the beer, and they will remove a proportion of these substances, which are the precursors of chill haze. If you remove the precursors, you eliminate or reduce the end product. The disadvantage to using these substances is that many of them are not adequately selective. Proteins and tannins are responsible for body, head retention, and some of the flavor of beer. Ideally, you want an agent that will adsorb only those proteins and tannins that contribute to chill haze. Some clarifiers are better than others, but all of them will, to some extent, remove desirable as well as undesirable proteins or tannins from beer, removing a certain amount of body, head retention, flavor, and even color.

The same, by the way, can be said of filtration. Depending on the type of filter and the "tightness" of the filter element or material, filters will remove some of the color, flavor, foam retention, and body from beer along with the yeast and chill haze. The trick is to find the most selective and effective clarifier or filter medium that you can, and to filter only enough to get the results you want, while minimizing the undesirable side effects.

# Flavor Stability of Clarified Beer

It is often said that clarified beer is more stable in flavor than cloudy (yeasty) beer, but that depends on exactly how it was clarified and how it was handled before and after the treatment. It would be more accurate to say that, depending on how it is clarified, the process may trade one set of problems for another.

Yeast makes finished beer unstable because sooner or later it will begin to autolyze, creating sulfury, yeasty, or even rotten flavor notes. How prone yeasty beer is to autolysis depends on several factors, including storage temperature, the amount of yeast, and the beer's alcohol content. Strong bottle-conditioned beers of 8 percent alcohol or more often seem to hold up for months, even when they are not stored cold. On the other hand, bottle-conditioned beers of normal strength will often show signs of autolysis after only a few weeks if they are not refrigerated.

This makes it seem that yeast causes spoilage and should be removed from the finished beer. Well, maybe, but yeast is also an oxygen scavenger, just about the only one available that actually works in beer. As long as there are live yeast cells in the beer, they will consume any free oxygen that becomes available, whether it comes from air dissolved during bottling or transfer, or from tannins or melanoidins that were oxidized during the hot side of the brewing process. As a result, live yeast makes a beer much less prone to the stale, cardboard, or sherry-like flavors so common in old filtered beer.

The moral of this story is that you never get something for nothing, at least not in a brewery. If you filter your beer to remove yeast, you had better be very careful about hot-side aeration and dissolving air during transfers and bottling. You also had better store the beer cold and move it around as little as possible, because both agitation and high temperatures accelerate oxidation. On the other hand, if you choose to clarify your beer by fining and/or using haze preventing agents, then your beer may be prone to autolysis, and, again, the best way to forestall it is to store the beer cold and drink it soon.

# 23

# Clarifiers, Filters, and Filtration Equipment

**B**eer clarification can be as expensive as your budget allows; it also can be as complicated as your ingenuity can make it. Filtration for homebrew, in particular, is only beginning to become popular, and much work remains to be done. This chapter looks at the current state of the art, but also points to some likely future developments.

## Clarifiers

The simplest and easiest methods of clarifying beer do not involve filtration. Instead, they involve the addition of various substances that will remove one of the haze-causing agents found in unfiltered beer.

The first and most effective step you can take to clarify a beer is to remove the yeast. Most yeasts will flocculate and settle out eventually, especially at cold temperatures, but the process can take many weeks in the case of some yeast strains. Finings will often drop a beer bright in 2 or 3 days. There is no question that the most effective type of finings is isinglass.

Isinglass finings are made from the swim bladder of the sturgeon. They are almost pure collagen, a protein material that possesses a strong electrical attraction to brewers' yeast. It can accelerate greatly the flocculation of many yeasts, and it also causes the yeast to settle down more firmly so that it is easier to draw off the clear beer without disturbing the yeast layer at the bottom of the vessel.

Isinglass requires particular conditions in order to work. It must be dissolved in a mildly acidic solution, at a temperature between 50° and 60°F. These days, isinglass usually is packaged in a mixture that includes the proper amount of tartaric acid, so that you don't need to worry about adding acid to the solution or fiddling with pH measurements. Commercial finings also include some sodium metabisulfite as a preservative. Many homebrew supply stores sell finings prepackaged in the correct amount for a 5-gallon batch. You should be aware, however, that the amount needed will depend on the amount of yeast in your beer. You may need to do some experimenting to find the proper dosage. If your isinglass comes in a large package, start with about ½ gram per gallon of beer and increase this dose, if necessary, for subsequent batches. The isinglass can be dissolved in a cup of cool (50° to 60°F) boiled water. The isinglass solution must be allowed to rest for 24 to 48 hours prior to being added to the beer. Under no circumstances must the temperature be allowed to rise above 65°F — the finings will go "slack" and become useless.

Finings can be added to beer in the secondary fermenter, or they can be added at a later stage. For bottle-conditioned or cask-conditioned beers, they can be added just before the primings, at packaging time. They work best at 50° to 60°F, which is the right temperature for carbonation of these beers.

There is some dispute about the effectiveness of finings with lager yeasts. However, many lager brewers have used them successfully. Since many lager yeasts are somewhat powdery (they settle out slowly and incompletely), finings are certainly worth a try. Even if you are filtering your beer, they may help by decreasing the amount of yeast the filter has to handle.

Another type of yeast-removing finings is gelatin, which is made from animal protein. Gelatin is less particular about its working conditions than isinglass but it does not work as well, and many brewers report that it has not helped them much, if at all. The protein molecules are smaller than those of isinglass, and, therefore, the clumps it forms are not as large and do not settle out as well.

Other clarifiers are used to remove the precursors of chill haze. These agents are similar to filter media and have the same disadvantage that they may remove color, flavor, and body from the finished beer. On the positive side, they not only reduce or eliminate chill haze, but also may improve the flavor stability of the beer by removing certain precursors of oxidation compounds.

The haze fighters attack one of the two main precursors of chill haze, tannins and proteins. Some are more selective than others in removing only that fraction of the material that causes haze, while leaving alone the desirable fraction, which lends body and flavor.

The two agents that are used to remove haze-forming proteins are silica gel and tannins of various kinds. Both of these substances will bind with proteins and form a precipitate that can then be filtered out or allowed to settle out naturally. If you do not plan to filter, silica gel is more effective, but it is less discriminating in protein removal. Some tannins — especially gallotannins — are reported to be highly selective in their action. However, the precipitates formed by tannins are relatively light in weight, and tannins are best used as a pretreatment prior to filtration.

There is another method of attacking protein in beer, which is to add protein-degrading enzymes such as papain (derived from the papaya, and also used in meat tenderizers). This method is not favored generally by homebrewers, as it thins the body considerably. It is only appropriate for light-bodied beers.

The agents used to remove tannins from beer include polyvinyl pyrrolidone (PVP), often sold under the brand name Polyclar, and other synthetic polymers, such as *Nylon 66*. These are all plastics ground up into a fine powder. They can be effective, and may work better in conjunction with silica gel.

# Filter Types

There are two main types of filter that can be used for beer: the barrier filter and the depth filter. These filter types are fundamentally different in their action.

A barrier filter consists of a sheet of some type of material — often a plastic compound — which is perforated with millions of tiny holes. Such filters are graded according to the size of these holes, or pores, and also according to the degree of uniformity in the pore size. This uniformity is called the "delta rating." Basically, the higher the delta rating, the more uniform are the filter holes in size. The highest grade is called "absolute," because it will remove all suspended particles of the stated size or larger.

A depth filter consists of a layer of adsorbent particles that either are held in place against a screen or are formed into a solid piece of material. One type of depth filter that is familiar to most people is the sand filter commonly used to clean swimming pool water. The layer of particles forms a multitude of twisting passageways through which the beer must flow, and as it flows, the suspended matter — yeast cells and chill haze particles — are adsorbed by the filter media and held tight.

In general, depth filtration is more selective, and more appropriate for beer. It is more selective because the filter media adsorbs only those particles that carry an electrical charge opposite to itself, which are the ones responsible for haze. This obviously makes it more appropriate for beer, since the object of the exercise is to clarify the product while removing as little of its desirable characteristics (body, color, and flavor) as possible.

A barrier filter must be very "tight" (small pore size) in order to filter a beer optically clear. Many homebrewers have found that a pleated cartridge filter must have a rating of 0.5 microns to remove chill haze from their beers. On the other hand, a depth filter using diatomaceous earth with a nominal rating of 5 microns

— 10 times larger — will filter beer bright. Obviously, the depth filter is able to remove haze particles far smaller than its nominal rating size. This is practical evidence of the depth filter's selectivity. It also points to a major problem with barrier filtration, the phenomenon known as "stripping." The term *stripping* is used because a barrier filter removes almost everything bigger than its rated pore size, including a good deal of color and flavor along with the yeast and chill haze. Keep in mind that this is a matter of degree. A depth filter will perform a small amount of stripping. But a barrier filter capable of producing beer of the same clarity will strip far more.

The disadvantage of depth filtration is that it is never 100 percent effective. Since the passageways through the filter bed are bigger than the nominal rating, even though many smaller particles are removed, some larger ones get through. A 5-micron depth filter will produce a clear beer, as stated above, but the filtered beer will contain a few yeast cells. If there are any bacteria in the beer, some of those will get through, too.

This is why beer that has been depth filtered cannot be considered microbiologically stable. The big commercial breweries, knowing the time and conditions their products must survive, always take additional measures with their bottled and canned beer. (Draft beer in kegs is kept cold and drunk quickly, so it sometimes does not get these additional treatments.) The two methods available are pasteurization and sterile filtration. Pasteurization kills any surviving yeast and bacteria with heat. Sterile filtration uses a barrier filter with a very small pore size — often .22 microns — to ensure total sterility of the filtered product. Sterile filtration is well known for stripping, while pasteurization accelerates oxidation. Homebrewers are fortunate that they do not need to use such methods with their beer.

# Filtration Equipment

The first thing to remember about filtration is that it requires a substantial investment in equipment. You will need not only the filter itself, but also an entire homebrew draft beer system, including

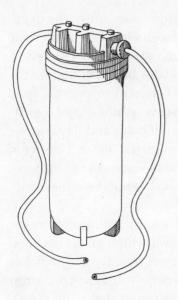

*The cartridge filter contains a filter element through which the beer is forced under pressure.*

at least two soda kegs, a $CO_2$ tank with regulator, and various hoses and fittings. The benefits of filtration are major, but so is the cost.

There are three main types of filters that can be used for homebrewing. The first is the cartridge type, which contains a filter element through which the beer is forced under pressure. Several different types of elements are available. Some consist of a length of string wrapped around the core. These are more or less depth filters. However, the more usual type is the pleated filter element, which is a large sheet folded to fit in the cartridge. This is a barrier filter,

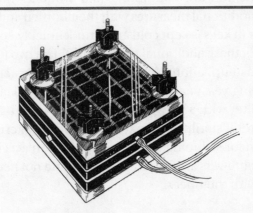

*The Macron filter, designed for use by homebrewers, consists of a frame that holds a stack of sheets made of cellulose fibers impregnated with diatomaceous earth. Beer is forced under pressure through the sheets, which removes the yeast and haze particles.*

and has all the drawbacks discussed earlier in this chapter. However, it is relatively economical to buy and use, and is easy to clean.

The second type of filter is a miniature version of the plate-and-frame sheet filter used by many commercial breweries as a secondary or polish filter, and by many microbreweries as the sole filter. This type consists of a plastic or metal frame that holds a stack of sheets that are made of cellulose fibers impregnated with diatomaceous earth. The combination is quite effective in clarifying beer. In use, the beer is forced under pressure through the sheets, which removes the yeast and haze particles.

A sheet filter is basically a depth filter. However, any filter sheet has a surface layer, and, if enough large particles accumulate on that surface layer, it will become impermeable, so no more beer can flow through the filter. This condition is called "blinding." Sheet filters, though they have many of the advantages of a depth filter, have the disadvantage (shared with barrier filters) that they are prone to blinding, especially if the beer is very cloudy or if a tight grade of filter sheet is used. They may need to be backflushed with water several times during a filter run in order to unblind them and allow more beer to pass through. Another minor disadvantage is that sheet filters "weep" slightly because the edges of the sheets are open. Losses are negligible, but, depending on where you are working, you may need to take precautions to prevent making a mess. A more significant drawback is that the filter sheets must be flushed out with lots of water prior to filtration, in order to remove loose cellulose fibers that would impart a paper taste to the filtered beer. Another drawback is the cost of the sheets themselves, which must be replaced after every run. The advantages of a plate-and-frame sheet filter are its simplicity of operation, its effectiveness, and the basic depth filtration advantages discussed earlier.

The last type of filter is a pressure filter that uses diatomaceous earth (D.E.). D.E. pressure filters are the most efficient available, which is why they are used almost exclusively by large breweries for rough filtration. Commercial pressure D.E. filters have large leaves consisting of a "sandwich," with a sheet of stainless steel on the bottom, a very coarse screen on top of that, and a very fine mesh screen as the top layer. A number of these leaves are enclosed in a pressure chamber that is first filled with beer or water. The liquid is recirculated through the leaves, and a dose of D.E. slurry is injected into the liquid during recirculation. As this continues, the D.E. accumulates on the mesh screen and forms a filter bed. When the bed is set, the beer running out of the filter will be clear, and can then be run into the receiving or bright beer tank. Fresh cloudy beer is then used to feed the filter, and D.E. is injected continuously as the filter run progresses. The advantage of this system, compared with a sheet filter, is that the beer constantly flows through a fresh surface layer of D.E. This greatly reduces the tendency of the filter to blind, and pressure D.E. filters have the largest capacity for their size of any filter type.

The disadvantages of D.E. pressure filters are that they are more complex in construction and operation than other types of filters. In practice, a pump is required so that the beer can be recirculated. So far, only a handful of homebrewers have accepted the challenge of building their own pressure D.E. filters, and no commercial examples have come on the market. However, as more homebrewers get into large batch brewing, the advantages of this filtration method will become more compelling, and ready-made units are bound to appear. The homebrew units that have been built thus far are of the "candle" type, which is a far simpler and less costly design than the leaf type described above.

# 24

# Clarification and Filtration Techniques

**I**f you want a clear finished beer, you need to make some decisions about how to accomplish this goal. While some methods can be implemented at the last minute, others require more time and must be done at an earlier stage in the brewing process. Planning is important. This chapter gives practical information on when and how to use the various materials and methods discussed in the last chapter.

## Finings

Finings must be made up 24 to 48 hours before they are used. The amount depends on the type of yeast and the amount of yeast in suspension. These factors make it impossible to set a general formula for all cases. With well-behaved bottom-fermenting yeasts, 2 to 4 grams of isinglass finings per 5-gallon batch should be enough. However, other strains that are more powdery may need more. You should start by following the manufacturer's instructions and see how that works with your beer; if it fails to clear completely after a week of cool storage (50° to 60°F), double the dose for the next batch.

Finings should be added after secondary fermentation is over. If added earlier, they can arrest the fermentation by pulling the yeast out of suspension. Whether you choose open or closed fermentation, and whether you use a separate secondary fermenter or not, the beer must be racked into a clean, sanitized vessel before adding finings. During racking, take care not to pick up any sediment from the bottom of the fermenter.

Use of finings varies according to the way you package your beer. For bottle-conditioned beers or cask ales (see Chapter 27), the best time to add finings is right at bottling or casking. Just stir them into the cask or bottling tank of beer, then add your priming syrup (if used) and proceed as usual.

For beers that are to be filtered or artificially carbonated, the goal of fining is not only to drop the yeast out of the beer, but also to remove the yeast prior to packaging or filtration. This requires allowing the fined beer to stand for a few days or a week to clear before the final transfer. There is some debate among brewers as to the usefulness of finings for beer that is going to be filtered anyway. Obviously, the more yeast you remove prior to filtration, the more beer you can run through the filter before it blinds. If your filter clogs up repeatedly during a typical run, you may find that fining will make your brewing easier. However, if your filter has no trouble coping with a batch of beer, there is no reason to fine it beforehand.

## Clarifiers

Clarifiers are used in a manner similar to finings. However, while finings can be added at bottling or casking time, clarifiers such as silica gel or PVP are always added earlier and allowed to settle out for a day or two.

One of the biggest problems with clarifiers is that they cause a great deal of foaming. When added to the beer, the fine particles become nucleation sites for the formation of gas bubbles that then rise to the surface, creating an impressive layer of foam. Since clarifiers are added after fermentation ends, the beer is usually in a carboy or other vessel of the same size as the batch of beer (no headspace), so the foaming causes a messy overflow and loss of precious homebrew. Even beer at room temperature will contain enough dissolved $CO_2$ to create these difficulties.

Foaming can be alleviated somewhat by first mixing the dry clarifier with a quart or two of beer in an open container, then adding the slurry to the bulk of the beer. This may not be enough to prevent an overflow, but it sometimes helps. Using an oversized container (7-gallon carboy for 5 gallons of beer) for the mixing and settling vessel is the best remedy. As soon as you have stirred in the clarifier slurry, pop an airlock on so that the escaping $CO_2$ will form a layer over the beer.

The usual recommended dose of Polyclar (PVP) is up to one gram per gallon. This is about 4 level teaspoons per 5-gallon batch. More may be needed for beers with a high tannin content. For silica gel, up to 3 grams per gallon may be used. Dosage of clarifiers, as with finings, must be determined by experiment. Often, silica gel and PVP in combination will be more effective in removing chill haze than either one by itself. You should try to determine the minimum amount necessary for your own beers.

# Filtering with a Cartridge or Sheet Filter

The first step to take in preparing to filter beer is something you should not do — that is, carbonate the beer. While it is possible to filter a carbonated beer under counterpressure, the flatter the beer the less trouble you will have filtering it. Do nothing to expose the brew to air or risk contamination, but make sure the beer sits under an airlock during secondary fermentation (and lagering for lager beers) to keep the $CO_2$ level to a minimum.

Filtration requires a basic homebrew draft beer system, including at least 2 soda kegs (Cornelius kegs), a $CO_2$ tank and regulator, plus an assortment of hoses and fittings. The first step is to rack the beer into one of the soda kegs and let it sit in a refrigerator at 32°F for at least 24 hours prior to filtering. This is necessary

so that chill haze will form; remember, you cannot filter out particles that are not in suspension.

When it is time to filter, the first step is to assemble the filter
and flush it with tap water. Attach the filter inlet to a hose attached
to your tap water supply and the filter outlet to your receiving tank
(spear or drawoff tube fitting). Hold the gas fitting open and fill
the receiving tank with water.

If you are using a sheet filter, you should not fill the receiving tank until you have flushed the filter for a while first. You have
to wash out the loose paper fiber. It is easy to tell when you have
flushed enough: the water coming out of the filter will gradually
lose its papery taste.

After filling the receiving keg with water, you must purge the
water from the filter, lines, and keg with $CO_2$. To do this, disconnect the hose from the receiving tank, disconnect the inlet hose
from the filter, and attach a hose from the gas tank to the filter
inlet. Set the gas pressure to about 12 pounds per square inch
(psi), and blow the water out of the filter. Then attach the gas hose
to the gas fitting of the receiving tank. Attach a clean beer tapping hose to the spear fitting and open the tap. Blow the water
out of the keg, close the tap, and let the keg pressurize to 12 psi.
Then you can disconnect the gas from the receiving tank.

To begin filtration, attach 2 beer hoses to the filter inlet and
outlet. The other end of each hose should have a spear (draw-off

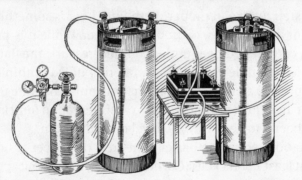

*A basic filtration setup. Gas pressure is applied to the keg of
unfiltered beer (left), and the beer is pushed through the filter
into the empty keg (right).*

tube) fitting. Attach these fittings to the beer keg and the pressurized receiving keg. Finally, attach your gas line to the keg of cold beer and pressurize to 12 pounds per square inch. Leave the gas line attached to the beer keg with the gas on. Start bleeding pressure off the receiving tank until beer flows. You will have to continue to bleed off gas from the receiving tank from time to time to keep the beer flowing. The best way to gauge the progress of the filter run is to shake the beer keg from time to time — when it is empty, you're finished.

Normally, as filtration goes on, the pressure differential will have to be raised because the filter will clog with trapped yeast cells and haze particles. If you reach a point where the beer will not flow even though the pressure in the receiving tank has been completely released (i.e., zero), then the filter is blinded and will have to be flushed out before you can continue. To do this, disconnect the hoses from the kegs, and, using whatever fittings and adapters are required, attach the outlet hose from the filter to your tap water supply. Run tap water backwards through the filter (backflush it) until the water runs clear. Then push the water out of the filter with $CO_2$ pressure before continuing with filtration.

If you cannot trust your local water supply, filtration is much more difficult. You must have a supply of water treated with chlorine or another biocidal agent at hand, plus a spare soda keg to use for pushing the water through the filter. All in all, pressure filtration with diatomaceous earth may be more practical under these conditions.

## Diatomaceous Earth Filtration

The basic process of D.E. pressure filtration was described in the last chapter. However, the details of the procedure for operating this type of filter vary considerably from one unit to another. Since no commercial examples are available as of this writing and many basic questions remain to be settled concerning the best design for a practical homebrew D.E. filter, the intrepid homebrewer who chooses to construct and use one of these units is best advised to follow the advice of the designer.

# 25

# Carbonation

**T**he process of dissolving carbon dioxide gas in beer or other liquids is called *carbonation*. Because $CO_2$ is released by the yeast cells during fermentation, all beers will contain dissolved $CO_2$. Carbon dioxide enhances the flavor of many types of beer; drinkers often use terms such as "lively" to describe a well-carbonated brew. However, the degree of carbonation that is desired in a particular beer depends on the flavor of the beer, the brewing tradition behind the style, and the expectations of the consumer. Beers with a light to moderate body and hop rate benefit most from high carbonation. With such beers, carbonation is an important flavor component that helps to balance the rather bland sweetness of pale malt.

## Carbonation Basics

The amount of $CO_2$ gas dissolved in a liquid is usually measured in *volumes*. If a liter of gas is dissolved in a liter of beer, its carbonation level is one volume. This measurement is independent of temperature.

The amount of gas that *can* be dissolved in beer, on the other hand, depends greatly on temperature. When a beer has as much gas dissolved in it as it can hold, it is said to be saturated with gas. If you bubble more gas through a saturated liquid, you will not increase its carbonation. The gas will simply rise through the liquid and escape. However, if you lower the temperature of the beer, the saturation point will rise, so that more gas can be dissolved in it. Conversely, if you raise the temperature of a saturated liquid, some of the dissolved gas will bubble out.

The other factor that affects the solubility of gas in beer is pressure. Suppose you put beer into a sealed container and apply a given amount of $CO_2$ pressure to the headspace, say 10 psi. The pressure will raise the saturation point of the beer. If you increase the pressure, the saturation point will rise further. If you release some of the head pressure, the saturation point will be lowered. If you look at the carbonation chart (see pages 332 and 333), you can see how these things are related. The saturation point (in volumes) increases with every pound of pressure. It also increases with every drop in temperature.

Now, let's assume you apply 10 psi of head pressure to your keg of beer and then disconnect the gas, but leave a pressure gauge attached to the keg. Let's also assume the temperature does not change and that there are no leaks (two enormous assumptions). Now, you walk away and leave the keg for a week. When you come back to check it, you will find that the head pressure has dropped! Where did the gas go? Remember, we are assuming that there are no leaks. The answer is that some of the gas in the headspace dissolved into the beer. The pressure in the headspace went down because the carbonation level of the beer went up.

The key to understanding the dynamics of carbonation is this: given time, a container of beer with a layer of gas above the surface of the liquid will reach an equilibrium. If the head pressure is such that the beer is not saturated with $CO_2$, the beer will absorb $CO_2$ from the headspace until saturation is achieved. Conversely, if the head pressure is such that the beer is supersaturated, then gas will come out of solution and bubble into the headspace until the head pressure is high enough to maintain the remaining carbonation of the beer.

To further illustrate what happens in practical brewing, let us now look at two kegs of beer held in a cooler at a constant temperature. Both beers are kegged in an absolutely flat condition (no carbonation, zero volume of $CO_2$). Both are pressurized to 12 psi and held until they reach equilibrium. However, the gas hose is left attached to one keg and not to the other. What will we find at the end of our experiment? The tank with no gas attached will

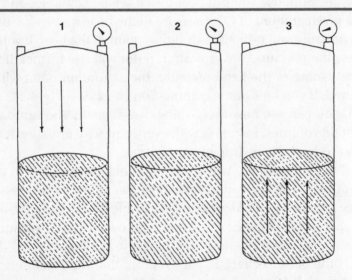

*Carbonation dynamics. The temperature of all kegs is 38°F, and the beer has been carbonated to 2.5 volumes $CO_2$. 2.5 volumes requires 11 PSI head pressure. Keg 1 (left): With 14 PSI head pressure, beer will absorb gas from headspace until it reaches equilibrium at 2.75 volumes of carbonation. Keg 2 (center): With 11 PSI head pressure, there is equilibrium between the gas in the headspace and the carbonation in the beer. Beer is saturated with gas. Keg 3 (right): With 8 PSI head pressure, beer is super-saturated with gas. $CO_2$ will "gas out" into the headspace until equilibrium is achieved at 2.2 volumes. Note: A similar illustration could be done with constant head pressure and different temperatures.*

show what was described above: the head pressure will be down because much of the headspace gas has been dissolved into the beer. The other keg, however, will have the same head pressure as when we left it. This is because it is attached to a gas supply, so that as gas dissolved into the beer, more flowed into the headspace to maintain the pressure. And the carbonation level of that beer is of course considerably higher. The two kegs have reached different points of equilibrium because we set them up differently.

Now let us make a further experiment with these two kegs of beer. What will happen if we alter the temperature of the cooler we are holding them in, say by lowering the temperature 10 degrees? Again the answers are different. Remember that by lowering the temperature of the beer we have raised its saturation point. However, the one keg is sealed, with no external source of gas. The carbonation level of that beer will change very little, because the temperature drop will lower the pressure in the headspace. Equilibrium will be maintained, even though the beer is no longer saturated with $CO_2$. However, the other kegful of beer, with its steady supply of gas, will absorb a good deal of $CO_2$ and eventually reach equilibrium at a much higher level of carbonation than it had to begin with.

## Practical Implications

These two contrasting sets of results correlate with the very different dynamics of bottled versus draft beer. Bottled beer is sealed in a pressure-tight container with no external source of $CO_2$. Thus, its carbonation level remains relatively constant once the bottle is capped. Draft beer, on the other hand, is normally put on line and served with an external gas source attached to maintain head pressure (and thus carbonation) and push the beer through the lines and out the tap. The implications of this arrangement will be further considered in Chapter 29.

For brewing purposes, the important thing to understand is that carbonation — the dissolving of $CO_2$ in beer — follows physical laws whose practical results are summarized in this chapter. The relationship between temperature, pressure, and carbonation level is fixed and cannot be changed. You have to work with the conditions you face. However, you also need to remember that any carbonation chart is based on the assumption that the beer is in fact saturated with gas. In practice, saturation is not always easy to achieve. For example, with bottle-conditioned beer, the priming sugar will ferment in 24 hours or less. At the end of that time, all of the gas is in the bottle. However, most of it is in the headspace, because it just rises through the beer as it is produced. It can take weeks for the headspace gas to dissolve into the beer until, finally, equilibrium is achieved and the beer is saturated.

The same is true with artificial carbonation methods as would be used for flat, filtered beer. It is not usually practical to just apply head pressure to a keg of beer and wait for it to reach saturation. The most common method of carbonating beer artificially is to use a carbonation stone. Nonetheless, the process is far from being efficient. A good deal of gas is wasted, which explains why most commercial breweries prefer to carbonate beer naturally and only use artificial carbonation for "touch-up" purposes, that is, to make final adjustments right before packaging. Unfortunately, the types of filters used by homebrewers tend to cause a lot of gas break-out during filtration, so usually it is more practical to filter homebrew flat and rely on artificial carbonation.

## Natural versus Artificial Carbonation

Natural carbonation is done by yeast. $CO_2$ gas that is released during fermentation will maintain the beer in a saturated condition from very early in the process. However, unless pressure is applied to the headspace of a closed fermenter, the actual level of carbonation will be low because beer in an open vessel cannot hold much gas at 50° to 75°F (the normal range of temperatures for primary fermentation of lager and ale). When brewers use the term *natural carbonation,* they are referring to fermentation in a closed container so that head pressure can build up and thus raise the saturation point.

There are a number of methods for naturally carbonating beer, and they are described in the next chapter. The point that needs to be addressed here is the controversy over the merits of natural versus artificial carbonation. Among homebrewers and beer aficionados, there is a widespread feeling that artificial carbonation produces inferior results. Sometimes it is claimed that naturally carbonated beers have a "finer bead" — that is, they produce a multitude of tiny bubbles when poured rather than a smaller number of larger bubbles, as would be produced by artificially carbonated beer.

The fact is that carbon dioxide is carbon dioxide, whether it is released by a fermenting yeast cell or a pressurized container that was filled at the local welding supply store. The size and number of bubbles produced when pouring a beer depend on a host of variables including the cleanliness of the glass, the viscosity of the beer, the temperature of the beer and the glass, and the level of carbonation. None of these is directly related to the method by which the gas was put in the beer.

However, it is also true that any of the methods used for natural carbonation will affect the flavor of the finished beer. This is because they all involve doing part of the fermentation in a sealed container under pressure, which traps not only $CO_2$, but also a host of fermentation by-products, many of which would otherwise be carried out of the beer along with the escaping gas. Thus, an artificially carbonated beer will always taste different from a naturally carbonated brew, even if both are made from identical recipes in the same brewery using otherwise identical methods.

Another factor that may help to explain the perceived difference between natural and artificial carbonation is that artificially carbonated beers are almost always filtered, whereas naturally carbonated beers (especially homebrews) often are not. Filtration removes many small, suspended particles from the beer, and these particles, besides affecting clarity, also provide nucleation sites for the formation of gas bubbles. When a beer is poured, the head pressure is suddenly reduced to zero, which means that the liquid is now super-saturated with gas. Naturally, gas starts coming out of solution. This effect is accelerated by the agitation and warming which accompany the release of head pressure.

Therefore, it is easy to understand why an unfiltered beer, with its abundance of haze particles, would yield up its $CO_2$ more quickly, and why the bubbles formed would tend to be smaller than those formed in a filtered beer, which would not present as many nucleation sites. The observable differences are easy to equate with some sort of qualitative difference in the carbonation.

# 26

# Beer Carbonation Methods

**There are numerous ways** to carbonate beer. The most fundamental distinction is between artificial and natural carbonation, but, within those categories, there are many alternatives. In general, the brewer faces the same sort of choices as with other aspects of brewing. Simple, inexpensive equipment usually requires a time-consuming or labor-intensive method of carbonation, whereas the quickest, easiest methods require a considerable outlay of cash.

## Natural Carbonation

The most common method of carbonating homebrew is to use natural carbonation. For beginners, it is usually the only practical choice, since carbonating beer requires some kind of container that can be sealed and can withstand considerable gas pressure. The only item in a beginner's kit that meets this description is a beer bottle.

Actually, there are several ways to carbonate beer in the bottle. The beer can be primed with wort or sugar syrup right before bottling. The bottle fermentation then produces pressure in the headspace, from which the gas eventually dissolves into the beer until equilibrium is reached. Depending on the pressure and headspace size, this can require 2 to 4 weeks.

These same methods can be employed for carbonating beer in a draft container, such as the 5-gallon soda keg favored by many homebrewers. Essentially, the keg is treated like a big bottle. The priming sugar or wort is added after racking the beer out of the secondary fermenter.

The problems with this carbonation method mostly revolve around subsequent difficulties with dispensing the beer. Bottle-conditioned beer must be decanted for serving, and the layer of yeast in the bottom of the bottle makes it difficult to transport without clouding the beer. This is a source of continuous frustration for homebrewers, who often wait weeks for their beer to clear in the bottle, only to see it clouded again if they misjudge the pouring or try to carry it in a car or airplane. Similarly, naturally carbonated beer in a keg will have a layer of yeast at the bottom, right where the pick-up spear will draw it into the first few pints. Subsequent glasses will become progressively clearer, but usually it takes a gallon or so before the beer loses its yeasty appearance and flavor.

One possible cure for kegs is to store the carbonating tank on its side. Then, after carbonation, turn it upright and transfer the beer to another keg under gas pressure. This may help but it is an iffy proposition, because usually there is sufficient yeast in the keg so that some of it will slide down to the bottom and be drawn out the spear.

Priming is the usual method of natural carbonation for homebrewers because it is the easiest to implement and control. Glucose priming is especially attractive because the sugar is 100 percent fermentable, which usually makes it possible to repeat or adjust the level of carbonation to suit your personal taste. However, even with glucose, there can be surprises. Depending on the health of your yeast and other factors, you may still have some residual malt sugars in your beer when you bottle or keg, and those residuals can lead to higher-than-expected carbonation. The situation is more complicated with wort priming, because wort (whether from malt extract or grain) can vary so much in its fermentability. For most homebrewers, the only way to determine the fermentability of a wort is actually to ferment it, so getting repeatable results takes some experience.

One way to cut down the risk of over-carbonation is to test the sugar content of the wort with a sugar test kit. These kits are marketed by drug companies for use by diabetics. The kits are far from foolproof, and they need recalibration in order to give accurate results with beer. If you experience problems with carbonation in bottle-conditioned beer, it may be worth your while to start using one of these kits. Many homebrew supply shops now carry them, or they can be obtained at most pharmacies. The bibliography lists an excellent article that details the test procedure.

The problem of over-carbonation is less serious with kegs, because the excess carbonation can be lowered by blowing the pressure off the headspace — repeatedly, if necessary — thus forcing some of the gas out of solution. With bottles, over-carbonation is just something you have to live with, but once you experience it you will want to make doubly sure that you get a rapid, complete fermentation with future batches; that is the best way to avoid the problem.

Besides the uncertain fermentability, another minor problem with wort priming is that usually it will result in more yeast in the bottle or keg, and possibly a ring of protein scum at the fill level. If you enter such beer in a competition, the judges may attribute the ring to a bacterial infection, which sometimes produces the same symptom. The reason you get more yeast is that wort is a well-balanced product with all the nutrients needed for growth. Glucose, on the other hand, will induce the Crabtree effect, so that the yeast does not multiply but goes straight into fermentation. Glucose fermentation in the bottle is also more rapid (often 24 hours or less), for the same reason.

In addition to priming with sugar or wort, there are two other methods of natural carbonation that may be used. Both produce much more yeast in the keg or bottle. For this reason they are not as popular with homebrewers, and are most practical when natural carbonation is accomplished in a dedicated keg, after which the beer is perhaps fined and then transferred under counter-pressure into another keg or bottles for serving.

The two carbonation methods are: (1) Krausening, which is priming the finished beer with about 10 percent of fresh fermenting wort in the high kraeusen stage; and, (2) Spunding, which is transferring the beer to a closed pressure vessel during secondary fermentation, when there is about 0.5 to 1 percent by weight (2 to 4 points S.G.) of fermentable sugar remaining in the beer. In either case, carbonation takes place in exactly the same way as with primed beer. However, as noted in the last chapter, the fermentations create different by-products, so the flavor of the beer is affected by the method chosen. Usually, beer that has been carbonated by kraeusening will have a fresh, snappy flavor associated with rather high amounts of acetaldehyde and other "green beer" constituents.

Kraeusening is a very difficult process for most homebrewers. It requires ongoing production of the same beer, so that fresh kraeusen wort from one batch is always on hand to carbonate a previous batch. Alternatively, if you have enough equipment, you can brew up a special batch and use that to kraeusen several different brews at the same time. If you try this, just remember that your batches will all be diluted with about 10 percent of kraeusen beer, which should be a pale, lightly hopped brew.

The problem with the spunding (secondary fermentation in a closed fermenter) is, of course, knowing exactly when to seal up the keg. In practice, the best procedure (if you are not sure of the residual sugar level in the beer) is to transfer the beer to a closed keg as soon as primary fermentation ends, which is easy to judge by the bubbling of the airlock. Attach a pressure gauge to the gas outlet of the keg and watch it. Release gas if necessary to hold the head pressure to the required value for the desired level of carbonation.

In practice, the range of sugar quoted above will give the range of carbonation desired in most styles of beer if the beer is at 55° to 70°F at the start of the process. However, beers that have been given cold storage will contain a lot more dissolved gas, so the amount of sugar required would be less.

Because there are so many variables, it is best to regard the carbonation specifications in homebrew recipes as rules of thumb rather than absolute and immutable laws. For instance, most recipes will suggest ½ cup of corn sugar for priming a 5-gallon batch of English style ale. Three-quarters of a cup is suggested for most lagers and German style ales. Assuming that the beer has fermented out, and is saturated with as much gas as it will hold at atmospheric pressure, these quantities will give proper carbonation (2 to 3 volumes of $CO_2$) for bottle-conditioned beer. However, if you want precise, repeatable results, you will find it easier to use draft kegs, which will allow you to increase or reduce the carbonation level if necessary, as described above.

One final note on natural carbonation. Most homebrewers find it easier to filter flat beer, which is why artificial carbonation is usually recommended with filtration. The equipment required is needed for filtration anyway, and the beer is carbonated quickly after it is run through the filter. However, it is quite possible to filter carbonated beer, and almost all commercial breweries do it routinely. The major requirement is that the beer be filtered cold, under counterpressure. The ideal arrangement is to use gravity or a pump to move the beer, rather than relying on differential pressure. This arrangement causes less gas breakout. You start the filter run with the beer keg and the receiving keg both pressurized to the same level, and with a hose connected between the gas inlets of the two kegs. As beer is moved out of one keg and fills the other, gas moves in the opposite direction to the beer flow so that counterpressure is maintained. This technique, while not yet common in homebrewing, makes it possible to create a naturally carbonated yet filtered brew.

## Artificial Carbonation

Because of all the variables involved — beer temperature, residual sugar, and so on — purely natural carbonation, while it looks far simpler at first, is, in fact, far more difficult to work consistently. The easiest way to get repeatable results is to saturate your homebrew with gas under the counterpressure required for the temperature and degree of carbonation you want.

The procedure for doing this is pretty simple. Chill the beer, then rack it into the soda keg or other draft container. Take the temperature of the beer before closing it up. Now apply counterpressure to the level suggested by the carbonation chart (see pages 332 and 333). Release the gas pressure, apply it again, then release it again. This will purge most of the air from the headspace. Finally, apply pressure for a third time. Set the gas tank on a shelf or table above the beer keg, then agitate the tank to help dissolve the gas. One fairly easy method of agitation is to set the keg on its side on a fulcrum of some sort and rock it back and forth.

The reason you need the gas tank and regulator above the keg is so that if, heaven forbid, beer should back up into the gas line, it will not reach the regulator. When you first start agitating, you will hear the regulator working to admit more gas and maintain head pressure as the gas dissolves. As agitation continues and carbonation approaches the saturation point (equilibrium) the regulator will work less. Probably the most difficult part of the process is judging when the beer is saturated. You have to listen carefully to the regulator to try to judge when it has stopped working.

Commercial breweries normally use tank or in-line carbonators (usually stones) that eliminate the need for agitation. In-line carbonators are placed in the beer line during transfer from one vessel to another. The transfer is done either with a pump or by gravity, under counterpressure sufficient to give the right degree of carbonation. The in-line carbonator is under exactly the same pressure as the vessels. If the beer is not saturated with $CO_2$, gas will be released into the beer stream and dissolve. The system is quick and efficient. In-line carbonating devices are now becoming available for homebrewers, and they offer the ultimate in convenience and consistency.

The in-tank method requires a carbonating stone, or several stones, mounted in the wall of the tank near the bottom. Gas at several psi over the desired value is forced through the stone. A valve at the top of the tank is opened to allow surplus gas to bleed off while maintaining the proper head pressure. This method is wasteful but rapid and is especially useful for touching up the carbonation level of naturally carbonated beers. For home-brewers, a carbonating tank might be constructed by fitting a stone in the wall of a quarter- or half-barrel keg.

# 27

# Bottle- and Cask- Conditioned Beers

**C**onditioning — that is, maturation and carbonation — in the final package is the oldest and in some ways the simplest way to deal with beer after it has fermented out. The by-products of the conditioning fermentation are trapped in the package, so such beer always has a lot of "fermentation character" such as esters. It is, therefore, especially appropriate for ales, where fermentation character is a big part of the flavor profile. For beers with a clean flavor, where malt and/or hops are expected to predominate and fermentation characteristics are a minor component, other, more complex methods of treatment will give better results.

The problem with conditioning in the bottle or cask is yeast. The "bite" that suspended yeast adds to a beer is not appreciated by all drinkers, and it can be very harsh, especially with highly hopped beers. Therefore most bottle- or cask-conditioned beers must be handled very gently to avoid stirring up the yeast sediment when the beer is served. There are a few exceptions — most

notably, the Bavarian hefeweizens and Belgian white ales, which
are lightly hopped and are meant to be drunk in a cloudy state,
yeast and all — but as a general rule, the yeast should stay in the
package.

Another problem with yeast is autolysis. Eventually, the
sedimented yeast will begin to feed off of itself (see Chapter 18
for details) and impart a nasty, sulfur or rubber odor and flavor
to the beer. The more yeast there is, the worse it will get. Therefore, you want to remove most of the yeast before packaging, leaving only enough to do the conditioning. The rate at which yeast
autolyzes depends on a number of factors, including the particular strain, the condition of the yeast (yeast from a slow, weak fermentation will be in poor health and not capable of holding up
under the near-starvation conditions of storage), the temperature,
and the alcohol content. This last factor is important. The bottle-
conditioned beers that keep well are the high alcohol types such
as Trappist ales and barley wines. Naturally conditioned beers of
normal gravity and alcohol are intended to be drunk young. Cask
ale, called "real ale" in Britain, is almost always consumed within
4 weeks of brewing.

This requirement runs headlong into the need to let the yeast
settle out. Most homebrewers find that they have to wait several
weeks for their beer to clear in the bottle. With many strains of
yeast, isinglass finings will speed up the dropout dramatically, allowing beers to be drunk sooner, while they are at their best.

The other factor that requires time in the bottle or cask is
carbonation. This depends on the rate and type of priming used.
Glucose (corn sugar) priming gives a rapid fermentation, but it
takes a couple of weeks for the $CO_2$ to dissolve into the beer from
the headspace. The dissolution will go faster if the beer can be
stored cool (serving temperature, about 50° to 55°F for ales) once
the fermentation is over.

One advantage that unfiltered beers, including cask- and
bottle-conditioned ones, possess is that they are relatively resistant to oxidation. Live yeast is a great oxygen scavenger, and, as
long as there are healthy yeast cells in the beer, any stray oxygen
that might be picked up — during transfers, for example — will

be utilized by the yeast before it can produce the stale flavor notes typical of oxidized beer. However, this is not a justification for sloppy techniques. Carelessly handled beer can pick up enough air to overwhelm the oxygen scavenging capabilities of yeast.

The fact is that bottle- or cask-conditioning is a trade-off. What you gain in resistance to oxidation, you lose in the risk of autolysis. And since both processes, autolysis and oxidation, depend on time and temperature, the best advice for any type of packaged beer is to store it cold (once conditioning is complete), and drink it soon after. Beer, with the exception of a few very strong types, is not like wine: it does not improve with age.

## Bottle-Conditioned Beer

There are two ways to prime beer for bottle-conditioning. One is to put a bit of sugar in each bottle; this method is called "dry priming." The other, and more common, method is to make up a syrup with a pint or so of boiling water, and dissolve the priming sugar in the beer before filling the bottles. Both methods have advantages. Dry priming can, in theory, produce less oxidation because you do not need to stir the beer. On the other hand, it is also considered riskier because the sugar is not sterilized by boiling. In practice, neither of these consequences seems to rear its head very often, and, as long as the materials (including the beer) are handled carefully, either method will work well.

The primary source of oxygen in bottle-conditioned beer is the headspace. For this reason, the best bottling method for such beer is to fill the bottle right to the rim. Many homebrewers are reluctant to bottle without leaving a headspace, but the practice causes no difficulties as long as the beer is kept at temperatures below 100°F, as it should be in any case.

Finings are definitely recommended for bottle-conditioned beers. Be sure to follow the instructions for making up the finings — the method varies depending on their form. These days, most finings are prepackaged with a measured amount of dry tartaric acid, which will give the correct pH when the solution is made up with tap water. The finings must be made up 24 to 48 hours before use, and they must not be allowed to rise above 65°F or they will "go slack" (the protein will denature) and become useless.

Bottle filling is a simple procedure. The main disadvantage is that it is boring and repetitive. Caps should be placed on the bottles as soon as they are filled, but crimping can be done after all bottles are filled.

## Cask-Conditioned Ale

In principle, a cask of real ale is no different from a bottle-conditioned ale. In both cases, the finished beer is primed, finings are added, and the container is filled and sealed. Then the beer is allowed to carbonate and clear before being served.

The differences are dictated largely by the serving, because you do not drink up an entire cask at a sitting as you do a bottle. Since cask ale was developed before the advent of compressed gas, there was no choice but to tap the cask and use either a hand pump (beer engine) or gravity to get the beer out of its container. This meant opening the cask to allow air to enter as the beer was drawn: after all, something had to displace the liquid that was being removed.

Once a cask is tapped in this manner, carbonation quickly drops to whatever the beer can hold at atmospheric pressure, given its temperature. Cask ale is normally served at 50° to 55°F, which means its carbonation level is about one volume. For comparison, lager beers usually have about 2.5 volumes. Most drinkers cannot taste carbonation at this level, and will describe the beer as "flat." The amazing thing is that a well-formulated ale will taste quite wonderful this way. By getting the numbing cold and the tingle of $CO_2$ out of the way, the malt and hop flavors come through as never before.

Traditional casks have two openings: a large bung in the side and a smaller tap opening in one end. A plug, called a "keystone" is driven first into the tap opening, then the beer is racked into the cask through the bunghole. Finings, primings, and sometimes dry hops are added, then the hole is plugged with a large wooden bung. The cask is rolled around for a bit, then allowed to condition at cool room temperature for a week or so. During the early part of the fermentation, the bung is fitted with a porous wooden plug (the soft spile), which allows most of the $CO_2$ to escape. When the hissing slows down, the soft spile is removed and a gas-tight, hard spile is fitted in its place. This allows the buildup of a slight amount of pressure. When the fermentation is ended and the beer is clear (10 to 14 days after casking), the tap is driven into the end opening. It knocks the keystone center into the cask, and, hopefully, forms a tight seal. This is the toughest part of cellarmanship, because you only get one whack, and the blow has to be hard enough to knock out the keystone and seat the tap, but not so hard as to smash it. Finally, the hard spile is yanked out and the beer is ready to serve.

While it is possible to go the whole route to cask ale, using authentic British casks (the 5.4 gallon "pin" is the most practical size for homebrewers), there is a big drawback to the traditional service method. Once the hard spile is removed, you have about 3 to 5 days to drink up all the beer. After that, it will almost certainly begin to spoil, as airborne bacteria, including the notorious acetic acid bugs, will find their way into the cask.

To get around this shelf-life problem, many casks nowadays are dispensed using a cask breather. This is just a little piece of stainless steel tubing that fits into the bung in place of the hard spile. The breather is attached to a gas hose and ultimately to a tank of $CO_2$ or nitrogen that is regulated to 1 psi. This is not enough pressure to push beer out the tap; it still has to be drawn out by gravity or a beer engine. All the breather does is to allow the beer to be displaced with a sterile gas that will not allow spoilage or oxidation. One psi of $CO_2$ will not increase the carbonation level perceptibly.

Real ale fanatics denounce the cask breather as a terrible desecration of the old methodology, but, for homebrewers who take weeks to go through a batch of beer, it is the only practical way to maintain the character of the beer over such an extended service time.

An alternative to a traditional cask is to adapt another container, such as a quarter-barrel beer keg. The older style kegs with a bulbous cross section and openings in both the middle and the bottom (the Golden Gate type) are the easiest to adapt. While it is possible to set up a full home system with a beer engine pump, these items are very expensive. Also, with the wide fluctuations of temperature that occur in most parts of North America, the most practical way to maintain the British "cellar temperature" of 50° to 55°F is to fit a refrigerator with a high temperature thermostat. The cask can be stored upright in this refrigerator and the beer can be drawn by gravity from the bottom.

An inexpensive way to try your hand with cask ale is to use a collapsible plastic container in a cardboard box. Because this container collapses as it empties, air will not be drawn into it. The main drawback to these "cubitainers," as they are sometimes called, is that the plastic often is gas-permeable, so that over time some oxygen may get into the beer. However, it is an inexpensive way to get into real ale.

The priming rate for cask ale can be very low — about ¼ cup of glucose for 5 gallons. Remember, the beer has low carbonation anyway. For cubitainers, even less should be used, perhaps 1 or 2 tablespoons.

Dry hops are an excellent way to enhance the aroma of cask-conditioned pale ale. One to 2 ounces of whole hops per 5 gallons usually gives good results. If dry hops are used, the tap must be fitted with a screen to keep hop seeds and other bits from being drawn into the glass. Because of this problem, pelletized hops are not suitable. Pressed whole hop plugs, usually ½ ounce each, are a convenient form to use as the plugs are small enough to drop into the bunghole. The plugs swell and release their aroma once they get wet.

# 28

# Draft Beer Equipment

**B**y far the most efficient way to handle homebrewed beers is to use a draft beer system. Bottling is a time-consuming and tedious job, and bottle maintenance is an ongoing chore. Bottles are convenient for transportation to social gatherings, but, with the use of a counterpressure bottle filler, it is possible to bottle off draft beer as needed. Also, clear draft beer can stand agitation during shipment, whereas bottle-conditioned beer will need a few days to settle if the yeast layer is disturbed. Finally, the only practical stainless steel pressure vessels that are widely available are draft kegs, so, if you are going to artificially carbonate your beer or filter it, you must have a draft system.

## Kegs

The 5-gallon stainless soda keg is the universal choice of advanced homebrewers. It is the right size for a batch, or, if you are doing 10-gallon batches, they can be split between 2 kegs. Each keg weighs about 50 pounds when filled, which is as much weight as you probably want to handle. They are made to withstand very high pressures, far in excess of anything a homebrewer needs. Fittings and spare parts are easily available.

The drawbacks of soda kegs are rather minor. They can be tough to clean thoroughly if they get grungy inside; you may have to remove the poppet fittings and spear and clean them separately. However, if you wash them out on a regular basis, kegs are fairly easy to keep clean and sanitary. Sometimes the lids do not want to form a seal; you will have to do occasional maintenance and check for leaks. The only substantial drawback, however, is cost. A home draft system with several kegs, a small gas cylinder and regulator, and fittings and hoses to make it operable represents an investment of $200 or more.

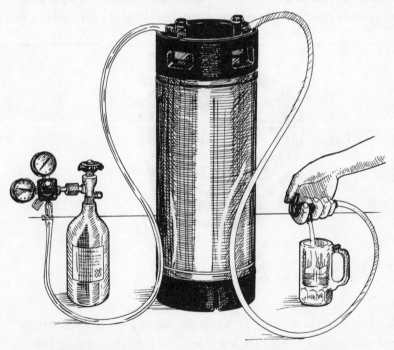

*A basic draft beer setup, consisting of (left to right): $CO_2$ cylinder with regulator and gauges, gas line, soda keg, beer line, and serving tap.*

Soda kegs come with two types of fittings, the so-called ball-lock, and pin-lock or bayonet. Both work well. With the ball-lock fittings, the gas and spear (product) valves are distinguished only by size, so as to avoid confusion they should be labeled. The pin-locks have a different pin arrangement, two pins for gas and three for product, so there is no possibility of connecting them incorrectly.

If you are buying new kegs, or new lids for old kegs, the lids with a safety valve that can be opened to release pressure are convenient. Without this feature, you can release pressure only through the gas fitting, and, if the tank is full, you may get a faceful of beer when you do it.

If soda kegs are beyond your budget, several systems based on various plastic vessels are available. The problems with plastic draft vessels are, first of all, difficulty in sanitation; the situation is similar to that for plastic fermenters. Also, plastic is inherently more fragile and prone to breakage if dropped or over-

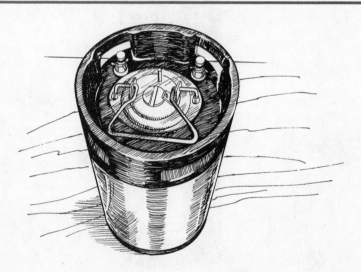

*Top view of a soda keg. This is a pin-style keg: The gas fitting has two pins, the beer fitting three. On a ball-lock keg, the fittings are of different diameters, and connections must be made carefully. Marking the style of keg you're using avoids confusion.*

pressurized. Nonetheless, for beer dispense only, they represent a viable alternative. They do not have the hardware options and flexibility to make them useful for filtering or counterpressure bottling.

In theory, regular stainless steel kegs as used for commercial beer are another option. These kegs are expensive and the most common type in use — the single-valve keg with the Sanke well-type coupling — is difficult and dangerous to work on without special tools. These kegs are almost impossible to clean without a dedicated piece of equipment that can pump cleaning solution into the keg while it stands upside down. Couplers and other fittings are more expensive than for other containers.

## Gas Tanks and Regulators

Carbon dioxide tanks are available in all sizes. The smallest — 2½- and 5-pound cylinders — are the easiest to handle and best for homebrewers. They are the single most expensive item in the draft beer system, but they last forever and can be refilled cheaply at any welding or other gas supply shop.

Some plastic draft systems offer gas dispensers that utilize the small $CO_2$ bulbs used in seltzer bottles. This is cheap to begin with, but the cost of the bulbs quickly eats up the savings in initial outlay.

Regulators are usually bought at the same time as a new gas cylinder. If you manage to find an old gas cylinder it will probably be tight (though you should check it by spraying some soap solution around the valve after having it filled), but the regulator may be in rough shape and need replacing. Even if the regulator looks all right, at least get a new secondary gauge. For most purposes, a $CO_2$ regulator with a secondary pressure gauge reading from zero to 30 psi is ideal. If the regulator has two gauges, the second one is to read the primary pressure — the pressure in the gas cylinder — which is useful as it gives an indication of when a refill is needed.

When using a regulator, it is important to set the pressure correctly. Carbonation and beer flow depend on it. Gauges are not always accurate, and it is worthwhile to swap gauges with a friend and compare readings. This is especially useful if you are experiencing problems that seem to be caused by high or low gas pressure. Another point to remember is that, whenever you set the pressure, the adjusting screw must first be turned all the way counterclockwise so that the pressure drops to zero, then retightened until the correct setting is reached.

Regulators and gas lines and fittings need to be checked with soap spray occasionally. A good time to do this is when you reconnect a cylinder to the regulator after having it filled.

## Dispense Fittings

There are two common means of drawing beer from a draft keg. One is the permanently mounted, tavern-style draft faucet or tap. The other is the simple plastic "cobra head" that attaches directly to the beer line. For use in a home system with a dedicated refrigerator, the regular tap is convenient — it allows you to pour beer without opening the door. The tap can be mounted either in the door or side of the refrigerator.

Regular draft taps attach to the beer hose with a standard threaded fitting called a beer nut. Various nipples of different sizes are available to match the beer nut connection to the size of hose you are using.

If you have a refrigerator you can dedicate to draft beer, it is possible to dispense several types of beer simultaneously just by adding more beer taps, lines, and kegs. One gas cylinder and regulator can serve all the kegs. To get more space for beer, you can put the gas cylinder outside the refrigerator and run the gas line in through a hole drilled in the wall.

## Beer and Gas Hoses

Gas hose is usually 5/16 inside diameter (i.d.) vinyl. Vinyl is flexible and comes in colors as well as clear. Beer hose may be either vinyl or polyethylene; polyethylene is semiopaque and rather stiff. For most homebrew installations, the flexibility of vinyl makes it a better choice. Clear hose makes it easy to spot deposits in the lines and decide when cleaning is required.

Be sure that the nipples you buy match the inside diameter of your hoses. This is especially important with polyethylene, which is unyielding. Stainless steel hose clamps are best because they will not corrode in the often dank environs of a draft beer system.

# 29

# Draft System Design and Operation

**D**raft beer systems are relatively common among home-brewers. Unfortunately, many of these systems do not work very well, and the bad experience of their friends keeps many homebrewers from taking the plunge. Some people have become so frustrated with their systems that they have sworn off them and returned to bottling. All this misery is due to bad system design and a lack of knowledge. With a little understanding of the mechanics of draft beer, you can set up a system that is as elaborate as your taste and budget allows, and that works every time.

## How a Draft System Works

A draft beer system consists of a few basic components. First is a gas tank and regulator, which delivers $CO_2$ to the keg to maintain beer carbonation and push it through the lines to the tap. The second component is the keg and delivery system, which is just a beer line and tap. Many commercial draft systems have a third component, a refrigeration system that is used to maintain the beer temperature as it travels through the line to the tap. For a simple homebrew system, where the tap is mounted directly on the door or wall of the keg refrigerator, this component is not needed.

The gas system simply applies pressure to the headspace above the beer in the keg. If you recall the theory of carbonation, $CO_2$ will always try to reach equilibrium, with the head pressure in the keg balancing the carbonation level of the beer. In a bottle, equilibrium is reached automatically over a period of time. This is because a bottle is a closed system, and the bottle, once opened, is immediately consumed. A keg of beer, on the other hand, is an open system, fitted with a tap precisely in order to allow the beer to be withdrawn from it over a period of time. This is why an outside source of gas is needed. If beer is drawn from a keg without pressure, some of the $CO_2$ in the beer will come out of solution after each serving is dispensed, until equilibrium is restored. Thus, as the keg is emptied, the beer will gradually lose its carbonation. To prevent this, we have to apply $CO_2$ pressure to the keg from a gas source.

Head pressure also serves another function. The draft beer line and the tap have a certain amount of restriction, just as any pipe or hose does. It takes a certain amount of pressure to overcome that restriction and push the beer through the line and out the tap. Ideally, draft beer should flow at a rate of about 1 gallon per minute, or 10 seconds for a 12-ounce glass. If the beer flows any faster, it will splash in the glass, creating excessive foam.

## Draft System Design

The object in designing a draft beer system is to balance the variables so that the beer carbonation in the keg is maintained and so that the beer pours at the proper rate when the tap is opened. Some of the variables are fixed by the brewer; for example, the correct degree of carbonation. Most ales need about 2.0 to 2.2 volumes of carbonation; most lagers, 2.5 to 2.7. Serving temperature is also pretty standard, although (as with carbonation) there is room for individual taste. British ales are usually served at 45° to 55°F; most lagers and German ales at 40° to 50°F.

Once you have decided on the temperature and carbonation you desire for your beer, it is easy to carbonate it to that level and to maintain that carbonation by applying the correct gas pressure to the keg. Just read the number off the carbonation chart. The only trick is to make the beer flow correctly. This requires that the total restriction imposed by your beer line be just equal to the head pressure in the keg. For example, if your beer requires 10 psi of head pressure, your beer line should impose 10 psi of restriction to balance it.

Restriction is imposed in two ways. One is the actual resistance of the beer hose walls, as mentioned earlier. The other is the force of gravity. If the beer has to flow up from the keg to the tap, then each foot of lift imposes .5 psi of restriction. Restriction of the beer hose depends on the inside diameter, the material, and the length of the run. The most restrictive material in common use is ³⁄₁₆-inch vinyl, which has a restriction of 3 psi per foot. This material is a good choice for most homebrew setups because you can get the proper amount of restriction with a short length of hose. If you want to make a longer run, larger hose, such as ³⁄₈-inch polyethylene, should be used. It has a restriction of only .07 psi per foot.

Draft beer systems with a long run require some way of cooling the lines so that the beer does not warm up as it flows. It is best to avoid this complication and put the tap on the refrigerator.

## System Design Example

If you prefer to dispense your beer at 48°F with 2.2 volumes of carbonation, the carbonation chart says that you will need 13 psi of head pressure on your keg. You need to set up your beer line with 13 psi of total restriction. First, measure the lift from the middle of the keg to the tap. For this example, the tap is mounted on the side of the refrigerator, 2 feet above the middle of the keg. Two feet of lift equals one psi of restriction. Therefore, the line needs to provide 12 psi. Using ³⁄₁₆-inch vinyl beer hose, that means

4 feet. This is a reasonable length, and, since it is all inside the refrigerator, it does not need a separate cooling system.

## Operating a Draft System

The only problem with operating a balanced system is that you need a couple of extra pounds of pressure to push the beer through the tap at about 1 gallon per minute. This pressure is necessary because the beer tap itself imposes some restriction. However, there is an exception: the so-called cobra head plastic taps that are often fitted directly to the end of the beer hose impose almost no restriction, and so extra pressure is not required.

If you are using a regular draft beer tap that has some restriction, the correct way to operate it is to set the head pressure a couple of psi above the balance point — in our example, 15 psi — in order to get the correct rate of flow. Remember, though, that if you leave the gas set at 15 psi, eventually the carbonation of the beer will increase. To avoid this, reset the head pressure to the balance point whenever you are finished dispensing beer for the day, and turn it up just before you use the system again.

## Draft System Troubleshooting

There are two common problems caused by unbalanced systems. They are a rapid flow rate, and gas break-out in the line. Both can cause messy, uncontrollable foaming.

If beer pours too rapidly, pouring can be nearly impossible. The condition can be caused by excessive head pressure, or by too little restriction in the beer line. Either way, the cure is to balance the system, which will require adding more restriction.

With gas break-out, the beer flows at a normal rate, but because $CO_2$ is coming out of solution, it pours as foam rather than beer. This can be caused by a rise in temperature as the beer flows through the line: remember that gas is less soluble at higher temperatures. It can also be caused by low head pressure, relative to the level of carbonation. Low head pressure will cause gas to break out of solution until equilibrium is reestablished.

A temporary solution to gas break-out is to increase the head pressure a few pounds. This will often cure the condition for a while; however, over time the high head pressure will increase the carbonation level of the beer, making it even more prone to gas break-out. If the beer is over-carbonated, the only cure is to take the keg off line and release the head pressure. After several hours, check the pressure in the keg and if necessary release head pressure again. After a day, you can recarbonate the beer to the correct level and put the keg back in service.

The permanent cure for gas break-out is the same as for rapid flow rates: balance the system. If you have done this, but still encounter repeated bouts of gas break-out, your pressure gauge on the regulator may be off. Check it by comparing readings with several other gauges.

# 30

# Bottled Beer and Bottling

**O**ne advantage of bottled beer is portability. It is also some-what easier to store in a refrigerator because bottles can share space easily. A draft keg, even a small one, generally requires a separate refrigerator in order to avoid domestic friction. For homebrewers, however, the biggest advantage of bottled beer is cost. This is somewhat ironic. Commercial breweries find bottles and cans to be the most expensive form of packaging, because of the price of the containers and the costs in machinery and labor required to fill those containers. By comparison, draft kegs are reusable almost without limit and require relatively little time and equipment to clean and refill.

The situation is different for homebrewers, largely because bottles are far less expensive than kegs. However, the labor required to clean and fill bottles is considerable, and mind-numbing. There is excitement and pleasure in brewing beer, but very little of either in packaging it. Even the most ardent homebrewers generally want to eliminate bottling and bottle washing from their routine as soon as they can afford it.

Nonetheless, all homebrewers find reasons to bottle beer sometimes, for picnics or parties or gifts, or for entry in competitions. Every homebrewer needs a bottle filler for such uses.

The chief dangers associated with bottling are infection and oxidation. Cleaning and sanitizing a large number of small containers is a dreary job, but it must be done well. Also, the smaller the package, the easier it is for the beer to pick up air while filling it. Commercial breweries use complicated machinery with heart-stopping price tags in order to get the lowest possible level of "package air." Homebrewers cannot afford to buy their way out of this difficulty, but, even with a simple counterpressure filler, careful technique can make a big difference in the outcome. Another fact to keep in mind is that filtered beer is much more susceptible to oxidation than unfiltered beer. Care in filling will be repaid with longer shelf life.

Finally, remember that all beer, whether filtered or not, whether in kegs or in bottles, will keep better cold. When you filter beer you trade off the risk of yeast autolysis for a greatly increased rate of oxidation, but the best way to forestall both of these problems is to store the beer cold.

# Bottling

The procedures for bottling bottle-conditioned beers have been covered in Chapter 27. They require no special equipment and the technique is basically the same as any other siphoning operation. Beers that are not going to be bottle-conditioned must be carbonated prior to bottling. This requires a homebrew draft system, including a gas cylinder and regulator, and at least one keg. The basic procedure for artificial carbonation is explained in Chapter 26. Beers that are destined for bottling should be carbonated to a slightly higher level than draft beers because some carbonation will be lost during the filling operation.

Counterpressure bottle fillers are simple and can be built at home or purchased ready-made. The bibliography includes an article that gives plans and construction details. Alternatively, you can buy a filler from your homebrew supplier. If your supplier does not stock them, they can order one for you.

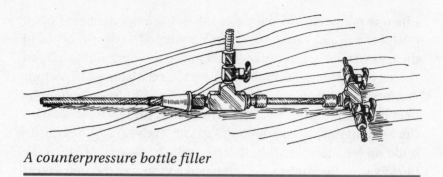

*A counterpressure bottle filler*

A counterpressure filler basically is two tubes, one inside the other. The inner tube is long enough to reach the bottom of the bottle. The outer tube is short, just reaching the bottom of the drilled rubber stopper into which it fits. The stopper is sized to seal the mouth of the bottle when the tubes are inserted. The outer tube is attached to a single valve, while the long fill tube terminates in a tee with a valve on each branch. There are two ways it can be used, depending on how it is set up and your layout. In both methods, counterpressure is applied to the bottle during filling in order to prevent loss of carbonation.

In the first method, gas pressure on the beer in the keg and inside the bottle are equal, and beer flows into the bottle by force of gravity. In the second method, the pressures are equal at first, but then the pressure in the bottle is lowered just enough to allow the beer to flow. The advantage of this second method is that the keg does not have to be elevated above the level of the bottles. The disadvantage is that there is more foaming, and more loss of carbonation. However, with practice, both of these difficulties can be minimized.

The preliminary steps are the same for both methods: first, chill the beer down to 32°F. Unless the beer is very cold, foaming is liable to be unmanageable. If possible, wrap the keg in an insulating blanket during bottling, or keep the keg in the refrigerator. Clean and sanitize all equipment.

To fill by gravity flow, first close all the valves on the filler device. Then hook up your lines as shown in the illustration, with the gas connected to the keg and to the lower valve of the filler (the one connected to the outer tube). Connect the beer line to one of the upper valves (the ones connected to the branches of the tee). Set the keg a couple of feet above the work surface. Open the valve on the gas cylinder and set the regulator to 15 pounds of pressure. Then place the filler in the first bottle, and open the beer line valve briefly to allow beer to flow into the line, shut off the beer line valve, and open the gas line valve. Let the pressure build up for a few seconds, then shut the gas valve and open the bleed valve (the other valve attached to the tee, the one that is not connected to the beer hose). Release the pressure in the bottle, then repressurize it by first closing the bleed valve and then

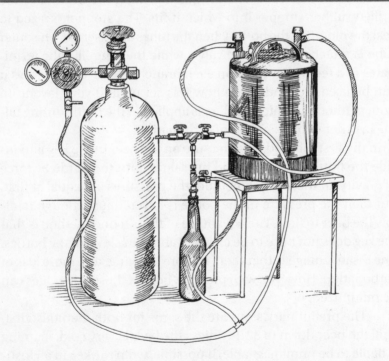

*Counterpressure filling setup for bottling by the gravity-flow method. The gas line is attached to the lower valve of the filler, the beer line to one of the two upper valves. The T connector allows you to apply gas pressure to both the beer keg and the filler.*

reopening the gas valve. The objective is to purge air from the bottle before filling it. Then open the beer valve and let the beer flow into the bottle. When the bottle is filled to half an inch below the rim, shut off the beer, then shut off the gas, remove the filler, and place it in the next bottle. Immediately cap the first bottle. Warning: As soon as you remove the filler, the bottle will start to foam over. Move quickly.

To fill successive bottles, repeat the sequence above. Purge air by pressurizing and then releasing pressure in the bottle, then open the gas line, open the beer line, fill the bottle, close the beer line, close the gas line, remove the filler, and cap the bottle. It sounds a little complicated, but after you do it a few times, it's no more complicated than anything else in brewing.

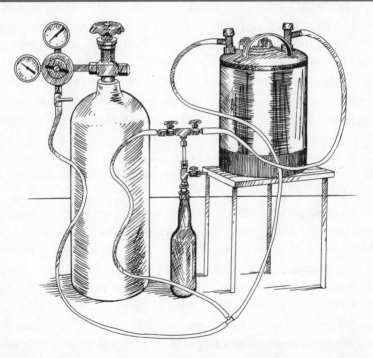

*Counterpressure filling setup for bottling beer by the second method described in the text. The gas line and beer line are attached to the two valves at the top of the filler. The gas line is also connected (by a T fitting) to the beer keg.*

The second method of using the counterpressure filler requires a different arrangement of the lines. The beer line and gas line are both attached to the upper fitting, which leads to the small inner tube. The outer tube is used to bleed pressure from the bottle so that beer can flow (see illustration).

To use this method, first turn off all the valves on the filler, and connect the lines to the filler and keg as shown. Next, open the valve on the gas cylinder and set the regulator to 15 pounds of pressure. Insert the filler into the first bottle. Purge the bottle by pressurizing it with gas, then close the gas valve and open the bleed valve to release the pressure. Close the bleed valve. Open the gas valve for a few seconds to allow the bottle to repressurize. Close the gas valve. Then open the beer valve, and open the bleed valve slightly — just enough to allow the beer to flow smoothly into the bottle. It takes some experimenting to find the optimum setting that will give minimum foaming during the fill. Toward the end of filling, allow excess foam, if present, to escape through the bleed valve.

When the bottle is full to within ½-inch of the rim, close the bleed valve, then close the beer valve. Remove the filler and cap the bottle immediately. Proceed to the next bottle and repeat the same sequence of steps: purge the bottle, repressurize the bottle, close the gas valve, open the beer valve, open the bleed valve and fill the bottle, close the bleed valve, close the beer valve, remove the filler, and cap the bottle.

The key to avoiding excessive loss of beer and carbonation, especially with the second method, is to fill the bottle slowly so that foaming is kept to a minimum. There is a natural tendency to hurry, especially if you have a lot of bottles to fill, but the inevitable result is lots of foam and even more time spent trying to purge it from the bottle to get a good fill level. On the other hand, some foam is all right and even desirable. Since foam bubbles are full of $CO_2$, it is actually better to have the neck space of the bottle full of foam right to the rim. This will practically eliminate headspace air. Many commercial bottling machines give the bottles a little shake after filling, in order to make sure they are foaming when the cap is put on.

# 31

# Cleaning and Sanitation

**C**leaning and sanitation are the most important aspects of brewing technique. You can spend a lot of money on a state-of-the-art homebrewing system, but, if you neglect cleaning and sanitation (which have been aptly called the janitorial side of the craft), your beer and your money will both go down the drain. The brewing process has some latitude; for example, variations of up to one degree F during the mash will usually not affect the finished beer perceptibly. The same goes for minor variations in the fermentation conditions. With sanitation and cleanliness, however, no such latitude exists. If you neglect or inadequately clean even the smallest piece of brewing equipment, it will soon become a reservoir of infection and ruin every batch of beer it touches.

At this point, a distinction must be made between the cold side and the hot side of the brewing process. The hot side is everything through the boil. The cold side starts when the wort is cooled to a point where microbes can survive in it (around 140°F, depending on the microbe in question). On the hot side of the process, cleaning is all that is required, and the standard need not be terribly high. A buildup of tannin "varnish" on the walls of a kettle or lauter tun does no particular harm until it gets bad enough to impede heat transfer or darken the wort. You can clean such vessels the same way you clean other cooking equipment.

The cold side is a totally different story. Wort and beer are full of particles that tend to precipitate. They are also sticky, and will adhere to any surface they happen to strike. These precipitated particles are mostly organic matter, and that means they can be utilized as nutrients by certain microorganisms. Sooner or later, any bit of organic scum that remains in a piece of brewing equipment will become a site of infection. A microbe will find its way there and start to multiply.

This is not important on the hot side because boiling the wort kills any living organisms that might be growing in it. It is a good thing this is true, because malt itself is far from a sterile material. It contains a multitude of microorganisms, including thermophilic bacteria that will survive even mash-out temperatures. These bugs are killed only when the wort is boiled. (If you are skeptical about this, store some spent grains from a mash for a few days in a closed container at room temperature. Then take off the lid and take a whiff. What you are smelling is the typical stench of a full-blown lactobacillus fermentation.)

Wort must be cooled so that yeast can survive and multiply in it. But wort is an excellent medium for the growth of many other things besides brewers' yeast. Once the wort is cooled, all equipment that touches it must be clean and sanitary. This remains true for the finished beer as well. If sanitation is not maintained, the wort or beer will be contaminated and an infection will take hold. What happens from that point on depends on the stage of the process, the degree of contamination, and the nature of the contaminating microorganism. Sometimes the yeast is able to suppress its competitor. Some infections (such as wild yeast) grow relatively slowly, and may need several repitchings before they reach sufficient numbers to damage the beer. Other bugs grow like wildfire.

If your cleaning and sanitation are not up to par, you may get away with it for a while, especially with new equipment, but sooner or later your luck will run out.

## Clean versus Sanitary

Clean and sanitary are not divergent conditions. One depends on the other. Sanitary basically means germ-free, and nothing can be germ-free unless it is also clean. Think about it. If you have a fermenter, for example, with deposits of scum on the walls, microbes are going to find those deposits and multiply in them. Sanitizers are basically poisons, and, like any poison, they have to make contact with the intended victim in order to kill it. But the scum deposits, which serve as a source of nutrients for an infecting organism, also serve as a hiding place because the sanitizer cannot get through the scum to reach the microbes. No piece of brewing equipment can be sanitized unless it is first cleaned.

## Brewing Equipment

The first criterion in selecting a piece of brewing equipment is whether it will work. The second, not far behind, is whether it can be cleaned. Commercial breweries pay a lot of attention to the grinding and polishing of welds in their stainless steel pipes and tanks. The brewmasters know that their ability to make good beer largely depends on the cleansability of their equipment.

In order to be clean, a surface must be smooth. If it is not smooth, then the scratches or pits will become lodging places for deposits, with the inevitable result. This is one reason why stainless steel has become the universal choice for commercial brewing vessels. The material is resilient, soft enough to be shaped and polished, yet hard enough to resist scratching. In addition, it resists corrosion by most common cleaners and sanitizers, so that repeated treatments will not cause pitting of the smooth, polished surfaces. Glass, which used to be common in breweries (it was applied as a lining to mild steel), fell out of favor because it is brittle and prone to cracking. For small vessels, though, it is almost as good as stainless steel. However, no material is perfect, and the next two chapters will discuss the precautions that need to be taken in cleaning and sanitizing stainless steel as well as glass fermenters and other equipment.

Plastic has acquired a bad reputation among homebrewers, because it scratches so easily. Nonetheless, it is almost the only practical choice for transfer hoses and certain other pieces of equipment. The best course for homebrewers is to avoid plastic fermenters, which always pick up a layer of tough, sticky soil during fermentation. Repeated scrubbings always lead to bad scratches and, eventually, bad beer. However, plastic can be used for transfers of wort and beer provided it is cleaned properly and replaced periodically.

The cleansability of equipment depends on its design as well as its material. There are two common trouble spots. First, beware of any piece of equipment in which the surface that touches the wort or beer is hidden and cannot be visually inspected. Typical counterflow wort coolers fall in this category, as do some filters. These pieces of equipment require scrupulous cleaning using powerful chemicals. The other trouble spot is a blind alley or dead end in the path of flow of wort or beer. Most transfer lines — whether rigid metal tubing or flexible hose — must be cleaned by circulating cleaning solution through them. This sweeps the dirt deposits away. In a blind alley, there is little turbulence or flow, and deposits will tend to accumulate and not be washed away. The only effective way to clean such spots is to disassemble the fitting where the blind alley is located, and clean it by hand.

# 32

# Cleaners, Sanitizers, and Cleaning Equipment

**C**leaning and sanitizing are indispensable. Putting these procedures into practice starts with choosing the right weapons for the job. There is a surprising variety of cleaning materials available. In making your choices, you must first consider the material you have to clean; then the method to be used (manual or clean in place); and finally, safety and cost. All these factors will be discussed in the sections that follow.

## Cleaners

The mildest cleaners generally used to clean brewing equipment are the liquid, hand-dishwashing detergents. They are very safe to handle and fairly effective. However, they require a lot of elbow grease to remove heavy deposits on kettles or fermenters, and are not strong enough to be effective in hands-off cleaning (e.g., clean in place, or CIP, of counterflow wort coolers).

Up the line is trisodium phosphate, or TSP, a much stronger cleaning agent. Plain TSP is available at paint and hardware stores. This compound is a good choice for heavy duty hand cleaning. Two tablespoons per gallon of water is more than adequate. Rubber gloves should be worn when using it.

Still more powerful are the combination products sold for automatic dishwashers. They are more alkaline than TSP and definitely require gloves. They usually contain a phosphate (either TSP or sodium tripolyphosphate), a water softener such as sodium carbonate, and a silicate (often sodium metasilicate). Silicates are mild abrasives and enhance the scrubbing ability of the compounds in hands-off cleaning, such as their intended use in automatic dishwashers. However, silicates can etch glass, so automatic dishwasher detergents are not a good choice for cleaning carboys. Also, many of these products are chlorinated, and chlorine can both etch glass and corrode stainless steel. Therefore, you must read the label carefully and select a product that is oxygenated rather than chlorinated (that is, it contains an oxygen-yielding compound rather than a chlorine-yielding compound). This is probably the best choice for cleaning metal surfaces. A concentration of 2 tablespoons of powder per gallon of hot water is recommended for heavy-duty cleaning.

The most powerful cleaners used in breweries are based on caustic, either caustic soda (sodium hydroxide) or caustic potash (potassium hydroxide). Caustic soda is the best protein solvent known, and it is the universal choice for CIP operations in commercial breweries. Unfortunately, human skin is also protein, and caustic poses a serious danger of severe chemical burns, or, if it gets into the eye, of blindness. It should never be used for hand cleaning, and should be handled only by experienced personnel wearing proper protective clothing, including a rubber suit or apron, boots and gloves, goggles and dust mask, and a face shield. Eyewash stations and showers should be nearby in case of an accident. In addition to its other propensities, caustic will etch glass and literally eat up aluminum. This is one reason why modern brewery vessels are not made of those materials.

Those homebrewers who are trained in working with hazardous chemicals may elect to use caustic solutions for CIP cleaning of difficult metal or plastic pieces, such as hoses and counterflow wort coolers. The correct concentration is about 2½ percent by weight, or 3.4 ounces per gallon of water.

Homebrewers can usually substitute automatic dishwasher detergents, which are far less dangerous, for caustic soda in CIP operations. However, for cleaning draft beer lines, caustic potash liquid compounds are available, and these, while still dangerous, are suitable for line cleaning operations in homebreweries. Be sure to strictly observe all precautions and use the recommended safety equipment as directed by the manufacturer.

## Sanitizers

The old homebrewing standby is chlorine, most commonly available as bleach, which is a liquid solution of sodium hypochlorite. It yields free chlorine, which is an excellent biocide. Chlorine at high pH values (as in hypochlorite) is very corrosive, and will not only etch glass, but will also cause pitting in stainless steel and most other metals. Obviously, time and concentration play a part in how rapidly the corrosion occurs, but hypochlorite has fallen out of favor in commercial breweries because of its corrosive character. If you wish to use it, limit the dose to 2 tablespoons of bleach per gallon of water, which should give 100 to 200 ppm free chlorine, an effective dose. Also limit contact time to 10 minutes, and rinse with plenty of water. Hypochlorite is definitely not recommended for no-rinse applications (see discussion of rinsing in the next chapter), even in very weak solutions.

Another chlorine compound, widely used in homebrewing, is chlorinated TSP, which is a cleaner-sanitizer. Uses of these combined products is discussed in the next chapter. Chlorinated TSP is alkaline and corrosive, and its use should be limited in the same ways as hypochlorite solutions.

A more recent development in chlorine sanitizers involves various organic chlorine products that yield free chlorine at a lower pH. Such compounds have been used in the dairy industry for many years and are considered to be safe when used at the recommended concentration. (Check the manufacturer's instructions.) Some microbreweries have used them also, with no observable pitting of stainless steel equipment. However, their reaction with glass has not been tested. These products often contain sodium phosphate and have some cleaning ability.

One problem with using any chlorine-based sanitizer in a no-rinse situation is that chlorine reacts with tannins in beer to form chlorophenols, which are a very harsh, nasty-tasting class of compounds. How badly this affects the beer depends on several factors, including the amount of chlorine that is mixed into the beer. But the chlorophenol problem has led most homebrewers to seek out alternatives if they feel they must go the no-rinse route.

Iodine-based acid sanitizers (iodophors) are safe for glass and stainless, and will kill microbes at a much lower concentration than chlorine will (25 ppm iodine as opposed to 100 to 200 ppm chlorine). They are usually a mixture of phosphoric acid, iodine, and a surfactant, and the surfactant is the key. It makes the cell wall permeable so that the iodine can penetrate it and thus poison the microbe. Another advantage of iodophor is that it gives a visual indication of its effectiveness. When the working solution loses its amber color, it has also lost its killing power. Unfortunately, the surfactant can also cause problems when iodophor is used as a no-rinse sanitizer. Once the killing power has gone (a matter of a few days), molds can grow on the surfactant if moisture and oxygen are available. Also, the surfactant may reduce the head retention of beer. Iodine can also react with beer tannins just as chlorine can. Nonetheless, many homebrewers have successfully used iodophor as a no-rinse sanitizer.

The two newest compounds for sanitizing are chlorine dioxide and peroxyacetic acid. Both are oxygen-based, non-corrosive sanitizers. They are highly regarded for no-rinse sanitizing and are quickly gaining favor with the large commercial breweries. There have been criticisms, however. Peroxyacetic acid has been criticized because one of its breakdown products is acetic acid, which in a 5 percent solution is vinegar. Nonetheless, in actual tests using the proper dilution of peroxyacetic acid, the increase in acetic acid level of beer was not detectable, even when the solution was not rinsed off before filling the test vessel with beer. Chlorine dioxide has been criticized for its instability, but new stabilized formulations have appeared that are safe and effective. It should be noted that peroxyacetic acid and chlorine dioxide are strictly sanitizers: they have no cleaning ability. Therefore they depend on proper cleaning in order to work.

## Cleaning Equipment

The most common piece of cleaning equipment in a home-brewery is an ordinary dishwashing sponge. This is the only implement that can be used on plastic and other soft materials. The so-called green pads (sold by 3M under the trade name Scotchbrite) are more effective at removing baked-on deposits in kettles and are preferable for scrubbing metal.

For cleaning glass carboys, twisted-wire-handled nylon brushes are available from homebrew supply stores. The bristles should be soft, as a combination of hard bristles and an inappropriate cleaning agent can easily scratch glass. Smaller brushes are available for cleaning bottles by hand. Still smaller brushes are useful for cleaning small metal pieces such as the fittings on soda kegs and beer lines.

For cleaning hoses and counterflow wort coolers, as well as some types of filters, a small pump is required. These are available from several sources, including W.W. Grainger. The best design for cleaning is probably a small plastic-bodied centrifugal pump with a magnetic impeller coupling and an integral motor. A look at the Grainger catalog will show several suitable models. If those are too expensive, even a small plastic pump attached to an electric drill with suitable hose adapters may work satisfactorily for CIP cleaning. The key requirement for any pump is that it must be able to develop sufficient pressure. The best way to judge this, without a pressure gauge, is to check the flow rate it can deliver. For example, for cleaning a counterflow wort cooler, if it takes 20 minutes to siphon 5 gallons of wort through the cooler, then the cleaning pump should be capable of pushing 5 gallons of water through in 10 minutes or less.

# 33

# Cleaning and Sanitizing Procedures

**C**leaning and sanitizing are the janitorial parts of brewing. Although very simple and familiar to anyone who has washed dishes, they are also tedious and repetitive, but represent the most important part of the whole brewing process. You do not have to understand enzymic degradation of carbohydrates or the metabolic pathways of yeast in order to make good beer, but you have to know how to clean and sanitize. This is worth repeating because many new homebrewers spend a fair amount of money getting started in this hobby, and meet with some success initially, only to find subsequent brews getting worse, rather than better. In almost every case, this happens because cleaning and sanitizing have not been given sufficient attention.

## Hot-Side Cleaning

Equipment used on the hot side of the process can usually be cleaned like any other cooking utensils. Sanitation is not an issue, and therefore it is not necessary to clean equipment to "sparkling like new" standards. For metal vessels, a green scrub pad (Scotchbrite) works quite well with dishwashing liquid; for plastic vessels such as bucket-style lauter tuns, a soft sponge is better.

In spite of routine cleaning, you may find a layer of "varnish" building up on the surfaces of your lauter tun and kettle. This varnish is mostly tannin material and can be scrubbed off with a lot of elbow grease if you feel it is worth the trouble. It is not a problem, except that, if it gets too thick, it can interfere with heat transfer. The best way to remove it is to soak the equipment in a strong cleaning solution (non-chlorinated TSP at ¼-cup per gallon is recommended) overnight to soften the varnish. Then it should come off easily with hand cleaning.

Varnish and protein deposits can cause a problem with transfer hoses if the same hoses are used on the hot and cold sides of the process. The easiest way to deal with this is simply to maintain separate sets of hoses. However, most vinyl and other small diameter hoses used by homebrewers are not made to withstand temperatures near the boiling point. Keep a close eye on hoses you use for moving hot wort, and replace them frequently.

## Cold-Side Cleaning

All equipment that contacts wort or beer on the cold side of the process must be cleaned scrupulously. However, it is important not to scratch the surface being cleaned, as every scratch forms a trench where deposits of scum — and eventually microbes — can hide, unreachable by cleaners and sanitizers. For this reason, the rule is always to use the softest cleaning implement that will do the job, and avoid cleaning and sanitizing agents that can corrode or etch the material.

The toughest items to clean are counterflow wort coolers, wort and beer lines, cartridge type filters, and carboys. Carboys are hard primarily because they have to be cleaned with a brush. Fill the carboy with a strong TSP solution and let it soak for several hours before attacking it.

Carboys are a critical component of most homebreweries, and it is worthwhile checking the efficacy of your cleaning. When you think you are finished, rinse out the carboy and spray in a little hot water. The steam will condense on the walls. If you can see patterns in the droplets, then either there is still scum on the walls, or the glass has been scratched. Try further cleaning. If that does not clear up the problem, you should replace the fermenter.

Hoses, racking tubes, bottle fillers, and counterflow coolers are best cleaned by a CIP (clean in place) procedure similar to that used in commercial breweries. CIP is basically using a pump to circulate cleaning solution through the equipment for a fixed period of time. The procedure requires a pump, as well as a vessel that serves as a reservoir for the cleaning solution. The easiest sort of reservoir to make is a bucket fitted with a tap, to which a piece of transfer hose is attached. Other items to be cleaned are connected in series to this hose, and the last piece is another length of hose that returns the solution to the reservoir.

The basic CIP procedure, then, is to make a loop beginning and ending at the reservoir, with the pump stationed as near as possible to the reservoir. With most pumps, the reservoir must be above the pump; however, some types of pump will work with their intake above the reservoir. A self-priming pump is advantageous, as other pumps require priming — that is, the pump body and intake line must be filled with fluid — before the pump will work. If your pump is not self-priming, it is easier and safer to fill the reservoir with water first, then connect your loop together and start the water flowing to the pump. Make sure the pump is primed before adding your cleaning chemical. Sometimes the only way to get the pump primed is to start a siphon by sucking on a hose downstream from the pump outlet, then quickly completing the loop and turning on the pump. Naturally, you don't want to do this after you have added dishwasher detergent or line cleaner.

One principle to observe when cleaning a counterflow cooler or filter body is backflushing. This means simply connecting the piece of equipment so that the cleaner flows through it in the opposite direction of the wort or beer. Backflushing is much more effective in lifting and removing deposits than frontflushing. Equally important is that the pump has to deliver sufficient pressure. The flow rate should be several times faster than the flow rate of wort or beer through the lines and equipment.

For CIP of hoses and other items, probably the most effective cleaner is a liquid sold commercially for cleaning draft beer lines and based on caustic potash. This is dangerous, but less so than caustic soda. Be sure to read and follow all safety precautions. For cleaning cold wort lines and wort coolers, you may need to increase the strength of the cleaning solution, as wort is dirtier than finished beer. Automatic dishwasher detergent solutions are also effective.

Be sure to check all joints where hoses are clamped to pieces of tubing or adapters. This is an area where deposits can be hard to remove. Once in a while you should disassemble these joints and inspect them for buildup. If found, either cut off the hose end or replace it.

A good CIP regimen is:

1. Make your loop and backflush with tap water until it runs clean.
2. Put the pump into the loop, fill the reservoir (1 gallon of cleaning solution is enough), and get the pump primed.
3. Stir in the cleaner and circulate it for 40 minutes (wort lines) or 15 minutes (beer lines).
4. Dump the cleaning solution, rinse out the reservoir and fill with tap water, and pump the tap water through to rinse. This may take more than 1 gallon. The water should smell and taste like water at the end of the rinse.
5. Make up your sanitizer and recirculate it through the loop for 10 minutes. Unless you are using chlorine sanitizer, leave the loop closed up and full of sanitizer until the next use.

## Cleaning Bottles

The chore of cleaning bottles is one of the main motivations for moving into draft beer. However, if you wash out your bottles right after emptying them, the ongoing chore of bottle cleaning and sanitizing is much less burdensome. Cleaning a set of bottles for the first time, however, is a lot of work.

The best way to clean "new" (to you, that is) bottles is to soak them for several hours or overnight in a TSP solution in a large tub, then scrape off the labels with a windshield scraper and a nylon scouring pad. Some homebrewers leave the labels on, but this is dangerous. The labels and glue are a perfect incubating site for microbes, and if you normally sanitize your bottles in a batch process (for example, in a large tub or a dishwasher) the huge number of bugs will overwhelm the sanitizer and spread from the labels to the inside of the bottles. After de-labeling, attack the interiors with the bottle brush. After cleaning, inspect each bottle by holding it up to the light so you can see through the bottle mouth to the bottom. When you are satisfied that the bottles are clean, rinse them thoroughly before sanitizing and filling.

# Keg Cleaning

There are two ways to clean a soda keg. Hand cleaning is one, and it can be difficult because of both the small size of the opening and the spear and gas fittings, which are hard to clean around. You will have to disassemble these fittings at least for every third or fourth cleaning. Fortunately, kegs are normally not very dirty inside and a thorough rinse will get rid of most of the yeast, so that hand cleaning with a cleaner-sanitizer will do the job.

The other way to clean kegs is by CIP, taking advantage of the spear. The keg is set open upside down over a bucket of cleaning solution, with a pump in line between the bucket and the spear (draw-off tube). The keg is first flushed out with tap water, either using the pump or water pressure, then the bucket is emptied and cleaner-sanitizer is mixed up in the bucket and recirculated for a few minutes. Then the keg is rinsed out with tap water, the lid is cleaned and rinsed by hand, and the keg is pressurized with $CO_2$ to seat the lid. The keg is ready to refill. There are just two precautions with this method: first, you still should disassemble the fittings and clean them by hand once in a while; second, be sure your pump has enough power to deliver a good strong flush of cleaner-sanitizer that shoots out the spear and flows down the walls of the keg.

## Cleaner-Sanitizers and No-Rinse Sanitizing

The question is, how is your water — and air. If you are on a municipal water supply, you probably can use it for rinsing with little fear. On the other hand, if you have well water or if your local water has a questionable reputation, you probably can't. If you can't, then you should consider going to a no-rinse sanitizing procedure. Another indication is if the air in your region is likely to be loaded with wild yeast spores, as is the case in wine districts. In these areas, you may need to go with no-rinse sanitizing unless your home is equipped with an electrostatic air filter in its HVAC system.

The biggest problem with no-rinse sanitizing is that the best no-rinse sanitizers have no cleaning ability. That is a nuisance because vessels that are lightly soiled can usually be cleaned and sanitized in a single step. However, the chlorine-based cleaner-sanitizers must be rinsed off after use, for the reasons discussed in the previous chapter. In practice, no-rinse sanitizing will probably require you to do a preliminary rinse, then a separate cleaning step, followed by a second rinse before applying sanitizer.

## Principles of Sanitizing

Whether you rinse or not, the most basic precaution to follow is to use sanitizers according to the manufacturer's directions. Most are formulated so that a contact time of 10 minutes will give a kill rate close to 100 percent. However, doubling the concentration will not necessarily allow you to cut the contact time in half. Stick to the recommended dilution and be patient.

Even if you use a no-rinse procedure, it is best to re-sanitize any vessel, hose, or other item that has been empty for more than a couple of days before putting wort or beer into it. The only exception is items that have been left completely full of sanitizer.

The only effective alternative to chemical sanitizers is heat. Boiling water is an excellent sanitizer. However, it cannot be used in plastic hoses or vessels. Also, it is dangerous to use it on glass because the stresses of expansion may cause the material to crack.

One practical use of heat is in the sanitizing of clean bottles. These can be run through a short cycle in a dishwasher using plain water — no detergent, no rinse agent — followed by a "heat dry" cycle. Because the bottles are heated and cooled slowly, there is little danger of cracking, and they will be sanitized and ready to fill as soon as they are cool.

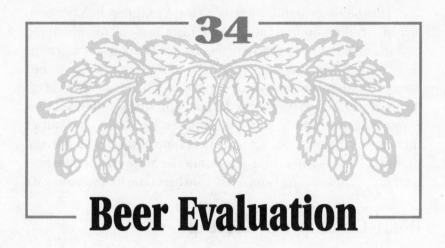

# 34

# Beer Evaluation

**O**ne of the key requirements for improving your homebrew is being able to evaluate it objectively. The typical homebrewer has no way to routinely subject samples to even a rudimentary lab analysis. Your own nose and taste buds must be your instruments.

You should understand, though, that all the scientific apparatus at the disposal of the big commercial breweries does not allow them to dispense with the kind of analysis you should be doing. The major breweries spend a lot of time and money on sensory training and taste panel evaluations. Think about it. The only reason any number is important is that it refers to something that consumers can taste when they drink the beer. What continues to drive the development of more and better analytical procedures is that the ones already in existence do not fully explain the findings of the tasters. In other words, the human senses are the ultimate instrument for beer evaluation, and will remain so. Learn to use yours.

On the other hand, there is a world of difference between sensory evaluation and the kind of "taste testing" for which the patrons of most brewpubs, or neighborhood saloons for that matter, are so anxious to "volunteer." They seem to think that sensory evaluation is a wonderful opportunity to guzzle beer all afternoon without paying for it. In fact, you drink very little beer when you evaluate it, and you have to be stone cold sober throughout the exercise. Also, the best time to taste beer is in the morning. That is when your senses are sharpest. It is not the best time of day for drinking beer, but it's the best time for evaluating it.

## Basic Concepts of Tasting

There are only four tastes that are distinctly discernible by the taste buds of the tongue. These are sweet, sour, salty, and bitter. Each of these tastes is picked up by different types of taste buds, which are found on different areas of the tongue. The basic

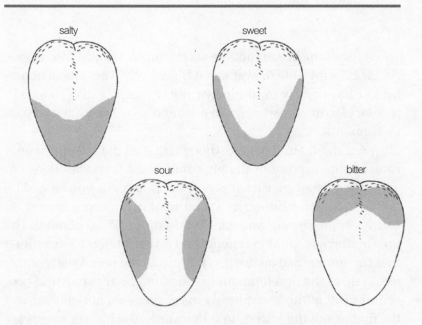

*There are only four tastes that are distinctly discernible by the taste buds of the tongue: sweet, sour, salty, and bitter.*

tastes of beer are sweet and bitter. Sweetness is tasted at the tip of the tongue, while bitterness is tasted at the back. This, incidentally, explains why, to taste beer properly, you must swallow it. If you spit it out (as wine tasters do) it will not flow over the back of the tongue and you will not get a true impression of its bitterness.

The only one of the four basic tastes that is intrinsically pleasant is sweet. This is probably because sweet-tasting substances are good to eat, and so natural selection would favor the survival of species and individuals with a predilection for sweet foods. All other tastes, but especially bitter, are less reliable as indicators of whether something should be ingested. In fact, most natural poisons (as found, for example, in toxic plants) are alkaloids and intensely bitter. This probably explains why bitter is the least tolerated of the four basic tastes.

On the other hand, sweetness alone is not enough to satisfy the human craving for sensory delight. Sweetness alone quickly becomes cloying. Even the sweetest foods need some other taste to balance them and make them more palatable. For wine, what offsets the sweetness of the drink is the natural acids found in the fruit. Wine tastes sweet-and-sour. For beer, what offsets the sweetness is the presence of isohumulones derived from the hops. *Isohumulone* is a chemical term synonymous with iso-alpha acid, a compound formed during the boiling of wort. Isohomulones account for 60 to 90 percent of beer bitterness, depending on the style. Beer is, therefore, bittersweet.

Thus, the first thing to be appreciated about any beer is its balance. When you taste beer, you experience the bitter and the sweet together, in different proportions according to the brewer's design. It is important to understand that the perception of these two basic tastes is relative. A high gravity, intensely sweet beer may carry a very high amount of bitterness — 40 to 50 IBU — yet taste less bitter than a lighter beer that has 30 or even 25 IBU.

One of the first and most critical steps you should take in learning to evaluate beers is to understand your own tastes. Not all beers have, or should have, the same balance, but most brewers will find that their own preferences lie within a certain range.

This often will explain a preference for certain styles or a dislike for others. For example, bock beers, especially dark bocks, are balanced toward the sweet end of the scale. Many American pale ales, on the other hand, are balanced toward the bitter end. If you would rather drink a bottle of Sierra Nevada pale ale than a bottle of Spaten Optimator doppelbock, then your personal preference is clearly for beers balanced toward the bitter rather than the sweet. If the opposite is true, then your tastes lean the opposite way.

There are, of course, a host of other factors that influence a beer's flavor and influence our judgment and appreciation. Balance is primary, however, because all beers have it.

# Flavor

Flavor involves the sense of taste, as discussed above, but is equally dependent on the sense of smell. Whenever we eat or drink anything, we taste and smell it at the same time. Since there are only four basic tastes, it is easy to understand that the myriad of aromas found in beer are, in fact, largely responsible for its flavor.

The three primary sources of beer aroma are the malt, hops, and yeast. Malty aromas come primarily from the various caramelized products created during the malt kilning; they are a result of the Maillard reactions in which sugars and amino acids combine to create caramel-type compounds which often have a deep color as well as a strong aroma. Other malty aromas come from various sulfur compounds, such as DMS. Hop aromas, of course, derive from the aromatic oil contained in the lupulin glands of the hop cone; they contain hydrocarbons (primarily myrcene and humulene) and other, more complex, organic substances, such as higher alcohols (e.g., geraniol), many of which have intense aromas. The primary classes of fermentation by-products have already been discussed in Chapter 18. They include higher alcohols, including phenolic alcohols, as well as fatty acids, the vicinal diketones, and esters.

With all the major ingredients — and many aspects of the process — influencing the variety of flavor components in the finished beer, it is no wonder that no two beers taste the same, or that replicability is the stiffest challenge faced by the big commercial breweries. For the sort of sensory evaluation with which most homebrewers are concerned though, it is usually possible to sort out these components into their major categories and just make note of those that are clearly and distinctly recognizable in the finished beer.

## First Steps in Evaluation

The way to start learning about beer is to evaluate a number of beers, both commercial and homebrew. Usually it is best to evaluate two at a time. Both beers should be the same style, and one should be a well-known commercial example. This system usually works well because most homebrewers, especially when they start out, have a particular beer in mind that they regard as a model for their own effort.

Have some plain white bread on hand to clear the palate between samplings. The beers should be poured and evaluated one at a time — in other words, run down the entire form, assessing all characteristics of the first beer before moving on to the second beer. Normally, you would taste the commercial beer first, though you can try it both ways to see whether the order affects your judgment.

It is usually best to take one slow swallow and base your impression on that. You can take another if needed to refresh your memory, but let some time pass and eat a little bread first.

The proper order is that given on the evaluation form. The aroma is clearest when the beer is freshly poured, so always get your impressions of this down immediately. Then you can hold up the glass at leisure to evaluate appearance. Tasting comes last, because it is the best part of the procedure.

As you can see, not all the qualities are rated numerically. This is because the purpose of your evaluation is not judgment, but comparison. The numbers are not intended to correlate with whether the flavor or aroma in question is good or bad, but only its intensity. In a direct comparison, all you are really interested

## A Sample Evaluation Sheet

|  | BEER 1 | BEER 2 |
|---|---|---|
| **I. AROMA** | | |
| Hops (0–3) | | |
| Malt (0–3) | | |
| Other | | |
| | | |
| **II. APPEARANCE** | | |
| Color | | |
| Clarity | | |
| Foam | | |
| | | |
| **III. FLAVOR** | | |
| Sweetness (1–5) | | |
| Bitterness (1–5) | | |
| Caramel (0–3) | | |
| Roasted Grain (0–3) | | |
| Body (0–5) | | |
| Graininess | | |
| Maltiness (1–5) | | |
| Carbonation (1–5) | | |
| Defects | | |

in is which beer has more of a certain property, and how much. Do not let assigning numbers get in the way of your basic objective.

As a guideline to using the numbers: the hop aroma of most mainstream American beers is 1; a fresh Continental Pilsner would get a 3, as would most American pale ales. The malt aroma of most American beers is 1. ("Lite" beers get a 0.) Again, these are not value judgments; they just reflect the fact that some beers have a more intense aroma than others. Similarly, the sweetness of most bock beers is 4 or 5; American lagers are usually 1 or 2.

In evaluating a beer, you should not limit yourself to numbers. Try to describe what you are tasting, too. Hop aroma is a place, for example, where with experience you can often pin down the type of finish hops, and this is an important part of the style in some cases. For example, a Continental Pilsner not only requires a strong hop aroma, but the hop must be Saaz.

Some lines require explanation. Under *Other* in the *Aroma* section would go such important but unquantifiable qualities as fruity, buttery, honey, perfume/flowery, nutty, solvent, medicinal/phenolic, rotten eggs, and skunky. Many of these are, or may be, defects and are discussed in the following chapter. Others reflect the fermentation characteristics or the types of malts used in the grist. In any case, one reason for comparing homebrews with commercial examples is to get an idea of the desired aroma. For example, the clove-like phenolic character of a Bavarian weizenbier would be considered a defect in most other styles. But if you want that style of beer, then you want that aroma.

Under *Appearance* comes color, which is surprisingly complicated. We all see color a little differently, and different malts produce different tints. You can try to describe color by a set of terms like pale yellow, deep yellow, golden, light amber, dark amber, copper, reddish brown, deep brown, and so on. Whatever the color, most beers should appear clear when held up to the light; but stouts are so dark that you cannot see through them, so lack of clarity is a desirable trait in these beers. The heading quality can be described in relation to the size of the bubbles, and the depth and staying power of the head formed.

Under *Flavor,* the first two properties are the most important. As explained earlier, balance probably is the most fundamental characteristic of any beer. The expected balance differs from style to style, and in some styles it can be quite variable. For example, British pale ales vary all over the lot. Also, the presence of other flavors (for example the deep "roasted grain" of a dry stout) affect one's perception. Body or palate fullness is almost as important in defining a beer. It is the thick feeling on the tongue that distinguishes heavy from light beers. The *caramel* taste of crystal malt is almost unmistakable. *Roasted grain* is a property that should be described verbally as well as numerically; the dry acrid bitterness of roasted barley is quite distinct from the smoother quality of chocolate malt, for example. *Graininess* refers to grain flavors that are not malty in character. Beers brewed with wheat, unmalted barley, or corn will show a definite taste of these grains. The astringent or dry mouth sensation produced by malt tannins is another aspect of this attribute. *Maltiness* is an attempt to separate the intensity of malt flavor from the sweetness of the beer. Some pilsner-style beers, for example, are relatively dry (no more than 2 on a 5-point scale) yet have a very deep malt quality in their flavor.

Under taste defects would come such things as metallic, salty, or papery undertones; also, usually, any noticeable sourness. The butterscotch flavor of diacetyl is considered a flaw in many beer styles. Likewise an astringent or harsh note in the bitterness. Most of these problems are discussed in the next chapter.

## The Beer Judge Certification Program

Many homebrewers enjoy entering their beers in local, regional, or national competitions. In these competitions the beers are scored according to a 50-point system, and the higher the score, the better the beer, with scores of 40 and above being awarded to beers of similar quality to well-regarded commercial brews of the same style. Many homebrewers seem afraid to enter their beer in a competition because they think they have no chance of winning, but the prospect of glory is not the only reason to enter. Entering beer in a competition is an excellent way to get feedback from experienced judges who can often give valuable insight into your efforts and point you in the right direction in your quest for the ultimate brew.

On the other side of the equation, every homebrewer should consider joining the Beer Judge Certification Program and serving as a steward or judge in competitions. The program provides a framework for study of beer styles and brewing and offers an opportunity to learn from experienced judges (who are also experienced homebrewers). Information on the program is available from the American Homebrewers Association, which is listed in the bibliography under their magazine, *Zymurgy*.

# 35

# Troubleshooting

**F**ew homebrewers have the time or equipment to do extensive lab testing on their beer. It is possible to do a few routine tests using simple equipment and user-friendly culture media to keep tabs on some of the more common causes of bacterial infection. These tests have been well explained in the specialized homebrewing literature, and the references are listed in the bibliography. However, many problems cannot be diagnosed by simple tests, including two that are among the most common in homebrew: wild yeast and oxidation.

In practice, the foundation of a homebrew quality control program must be the brewer's own senses. Using your eyes, nose, and palate, you can pretty well identify any off flavors in your brews, and a little understanding of the cause will enable you to formulate a strategy for corrective action.

The troubleshooting chart that is found in this chapter lists discrete symptoms along with causes and remedies. Remember that a problem often involves more than one symptom, and the

# Common Brewing Problems, Causes, and Remedies

## Beer Faults

| Off Flavor/ Aroma | Agent Responsible | Cause(s) | Remedy |
|---|---|---|---|
| Astringent (puckering) | Tannins | High-pH or hot sparge water<br>Overagitation of mash<br>Poor quality malt | Correct temperature & pH of sparge water<br>Less stirring<br>Better malt |
| Butter, butterscotch | Diacetyl | High pitching temperature, high fermentation temperature<br>Aeration during fermentation<br>Cooling beer at end of fermentation<br>Infection *(Pediococcus)*<br>Yeast strain | Pitch and ferment at lower temperature<br>Careful racking<br>Diacetyl rest before cooling<br>Sanitation<br>Change yeast |
| Cardboard, paper | 2-trans-nonenal (an aldehyde) | Oxidation | Keep air out<br>Reduce headspace in bottles<br>Do not aerate hot wort |
| Catty (tomato plants) Cooked vegetable | Mercaptopentanones dimethyl sulfide (DMS) | Oxidation<br>Infection (wort bacteria)<br>Pale lager malt | See *Cardboard*<br>Sanitation, forced wort cooling, replace yeast<br>Forced wort cooling |
| Fruity (banana, pineapple, pear, etc.) | Esters | Yeast strain<br>Low-oxygen wort | Use a neutral yeast<br>Aerate wort at pitching |
| Harshness, clinging bitterness | Fusel alcohols Iso-alpha acids & derivatives | High fermentation temperature<br>High hop rate<br>High wort pH<br>Overboiling hops | Ferment cool<br>Change recipe<br>Adjust pH<br>Shorten hop boil |
|  | Ions in water/ wort (magnesium, sodium plus sulfate) | Poor water supply<br>Poor water treatment | Change water<br>Change treatment |
| Meaty, brothlike | Methional | Low fermentation temperature<br>Malt variety | Ferment at 55°F<br>Change malt |

| Off Flavor/ Aroma | Agent Responsible | Cause(s) | Remedy |
|---|---|---|---|
| Medicinal, phenolic | Chlorophenols | Chlorine Chlorinated water | Rinse thoroughly Filter or boil water |
| | Other phenolic compounds | Yeast mutation Wild yeast | Change culture Sanitation |
| Metallic | Ions in water/ wort (iron, zinc, etc.) | Poor water supply Brewing implements | Change water Change equipment |
| Musty | Malt spoilage | Damp malt | Proper storage |
| Rotten eggs | Hydrogen sulfide | Infection Metabisulfites | Sanitation Omit Campden tablets |
| Soapy, rancid | Fatty acids | Same as fruity | |
| Solvent | Ethyl acetate | Same as fruity | |
| Sour | Acetic or lactic acid | Infection | Sanitation, closed fermentation |
| Spicy, clove | 4-vinyl guaiacol | Yeast strain Mutant yeast Wild yeast | Change yeast Replace culture Sanitation |
| Sulfur (rubbery) | Various sulfur compounds | Yeast autolysis | Rack beer promptly Minimize bottle yeast Store beer cool |
| Sweetness, high terminal gravity | Maltotriose | Incomplete fermentation | Wort aeration Strong pitching yeast |
| Toffee- or sherrylike flavor | Furfurals (aldehydes) | Oxidation | See *Cardboard* |

# Other Faults

| Off Flavor/ Aroma | Agent Responsible | Cause(s) | Remedy |
|---|---|---|---|
| Gushing | High carbonation | Overpriming | Lower priming rate |
| | | Wild yeast | Sanitation |
| | Nitrogen | Infection plus nitrate | Sanitation |
| | Other gases | Infection | Sanitation |
| Haze (stable) | Starch particles | Incomplete starch conversion | Lengthen mash, lower temperature |
| | | High sparge water temperature | Sparge below 168°F |
| | Non-flocculating microorganisms | Wild yeast, bacteria | Sanitation |
| Lack of body | Low protein | Low-malt grist | Change recipe |
| | | Overcleaving proteins in mash | Reduce time/raise temperature of protein |
| | Infection (with off flavors) | Wild yeast, bacteria | Sanitation |
| Poor head formation | Low or missing carbonation | Bad seal on caps | Replace capper/caps |
| | | Chipped bottle mouth | Replace bottle |
| | | Forgot to prime | Get more sleep |
| | | Insufficient carbonation | |
| Poor head retention | High surface tension | Overcleaving protein | See *Lack of body* |
| | | Grease, detergent | Careful wash and rinse of bottles and glasses |
| | | Low-protein grist | Increase malt content, use wheat malt or heading compound |
| Ring around bottle neck | Microorganisms | Infection | Sanitation |
| | Break material | Wort priming | Glucose priming |
| Rope (jellylike strands in bottles) | Complex sugar and protein polymers | Infection (lactic or acetic acid bacteria, most often lactic) | Sanitation |

combination of symptoms will often point to one cause rather than another. For example, high diacetyl with no other symptoms would lead one to suspect the yeast, or the fermentation method; however, high diacetyl in combination with sourness and a thin body would point to a bacterial infection. The remaining text of this chapter covers the most common causes of the various symptoms.

If you are having trouble deciding what your symptoms are — if you know the beer tastes wrong but cannot identify what you are tasting — the best course of action is to consult more experienced homebrewers. Local homebrew clubs are a good way to meet fellow homebrewers and the "old hands" are almost always glad to help. Another way of educating yourself is to get into the Beer Judge Certification Program, as mentioned in the last chapter. The practical tasting experience you gain in the program will expose you to almost every possible defect a beer can have: many more (unless you are under some sort of curse) than you will likely encounter in your own beers.

## Bacterial Infections

There are a number of types of bacteria that can adversely affect beer at different stages of the process. The most widespread, because they are ubiquitous, are the "wort spoilers," so called because they grow like wildfire in wort. These bugs can produce a number of off flavors, the most common being a strong dimethyl sulfide (DMS) odor, which is usually described as cooked corn. Some people identify it with tomato juice. Wort spoilers are different species of enterobacteria that live, naturally and usually harmlessly, in the intestines of humans and other animals. As a result, they are common contaminants of water supplies. While these bugs can live in wort, they generally do not survive fermentation. Once the yeast gets to work, it drops the pH and the spoilers cannot survive. There is, however, one exception to this rule: the *Hafnia protea* or "short fat rod," which, while it does not like low pH values, can survive them. This ability is important because it means that this bug can be carried from one brew to another when the yeast is repitched.

The best line of defense against wort spoilers is good sanitation practice and proper yeast handling and pitching, so that the fermentation gets off to a rapid start. Treated well, yeast is capable of defending itself against this competitor. If in spite of good fermentations you have chronic problems, suspect your water supply. Clean scrupulously and consider going to a no-rinse sanitizer, such as peroxyacetic acid, for all equipment on the cold side of the brewing process. Also, since *Hafnia* is the most common wort spoiler in breweries, consider replacing your yeast culture.

Aerobic bacteria, as their name implies, require oxygen to do their dirty work. The main culprits are two types of acetic acid bacteria, *acetobacter* and *acetomonas*. Both oxidize alcohol into acetic acid, which is vinegar. A distinct odor and taste of vinegar is a positive indicator of infection by these bugs. Many "vinegar bugs" also produce other symptoms, including haze and/or "rope," which is long, thick, mucus-like strands.

Aerobic bacteria are among the easiest to control. Since they require both alcohol (produced by fermentation) and oxygen to metabolize, they are never a problem except when fermenting or fermented beer is exposed to air. Thus, they can be controlled by (1) using a fermentation system that keeps the beer under $CO_2$; and (2) being careful to exclude air during transfers and packaging. With good cleaning and sanitation practices, open primary fermenters can be used, but they must be kept covered and the beer must be transferred to a closed container as soon as fermentation abates. Avoid air in the headspace of bottled and kegged beer. If you have vinegar problems with your cask-conditioned ale, consider using a "cask breather" (a fitting in the bung attached to a $CO_2$ line fed with 1 psi of pressure) to avoid pulling oxygen into the cask during dispense.

Another major class of beer infections is the lactic acid bacteria genera *lactobacillus* and *pediococcus*. These are very different in many respects but are classified together because both are anaerobic (do not require oxygen), are capable of surviving at the low pH of beer, and produce lactic acid as a primary product of their fermentation. Because of these abilities, lactic bacteria are among the most feared infections in a brewery. They can produce a wide variety of by-products, including diacetyl and other, less pleasant, odors. Beers with a bad lactic infection may be hazy because the bugs do not flocculate. Rope is also possible.

Most lactic bacteria are sensitive to hop resins, which inhibit their growth. Unfortunately, many strains have adapted and, in fact, are rarely found anywhere except in breweries. You can count on the fact that, if you have been brewing for a while, you could "plate out" lactic bugs from your floor, tables, and other surfaces. The only sure defense against them is diligent cleaning and sanitizing of all equipment on the cold side of the process. Also, be careful not to let a hose end touch anything except another sanitized surface, and if you put racking hose down inside a carboy, for example, clean and sanitize the outside of the hose just as carefully as you do the inside.

Other bacteria sometimes cause trouble, especially in beers that have been primed. *Zymomonas* and *Pectinatus* are the usual culprits. While rare compared with lactic bacteria, they produce hydrogen sulfide, acetaldehyde, and other things that give a truly rotten stench to an infected beer. Be especially wary in the vicinity of new construction, as these bacteria live in the soil and are spread into the air with digging.

With any bacterial infection, the symptoms are likely to include haze and gushing (owing to the production of gas by the bacterial fermentation), in addition to off flavors and odors. Sometimes a ring will be noted at the fill line in the neck of a bottle, but, in all cases (regardless of which bacteria is causing the problem), the remedy will include the following: (1) dump the beer — there is no cure for beer infection, and all cases are terminal; (2) carefully clean and sanitize all equipment; (3) replace the yeast culture, since repitching is the primary means of spreading the infection. Replacement of plastic brewing equipment, including fermenters, is often necessary. If you elect not to do this, accept that you are gambling. One thing you should not do is attempt to make up for inadequate cleaning with large doses of sanitizer. It won't work, and you will probably corrode your equipment, making future infections more likely and more difficult to eradicate.

# Wild Yeast

A wild yeast is any yeast other than the specific pure strain that you intended to introduce into your fermenter. Many belong to other species and even genera, but some of the nastiest off flavors are produced by wild strains of *Saccharomyces cerevisiae*. The typical character of a wild yeast infection is the phenolic or medicinal flavor and odor resembling some old-fashioned patent medicines. It is often described as "smelling like a bandage." A few types of commercial beer, such as the Bavarian weizenbier, have a phenolic character, usually described as "clove-like." The flavor of a typical wild yeast infection is similar, but unpleasantly pungent and harsh.

Since wild yeasts are often close relatives of good brewers' yeast, they can be controlled only by good sanitation practices. They grow slowly, and so a wild yeast that gets into your homebrew may take several repitchings before it reaches sufficient numbers to noticeably taint the beer. However, a yeast packet — especially dry yeast — may sometimes be grossly contaminated with wild yeast, and if you encounter this, your first batch will be full-blown.

One of the nastiest traits of wild yeast is that it not only grows slowly, but also will continue to work, pumping out its by-products, in the keg or bottle. A beer that tasted all right when you kegged it may be undrinkable a few weeks later. This, of course, increases the chances that you will have re-used the yeast before discovering the problem. In any case, the cure is the same as for a bacterial infection: dump the beer, dump the yeast, clean and sanitize everything you can, and replace any equipment you don't feel can be thoroughly cleaned.

# Oxidation

Oxidation is the reason that beer drinkers like fresh beer, and also why draft beer is considered better than bottled. Most bottled beer is pasteurized, and the high temperatures used for this process greatly speed up oxidation.

Two factors account for oxidation of finished beer: oxygen dissolved in the beer during transfers (especially packaging, hence the term "package air"), and the oxidation of various wort compounds on the hot side of the process. These oxidized compounds can later act as donors, giving up their oxygen. Whether from package air or hot-side aeration, oxygen typically combines with various higher alcohols to produce aldehydes that have very strong flavors and are known collectively as staling compounds.

Oxidation produces other bad changes. In fact, the first symptom of oxidation is usually the loss of hop aroma and flavor in a beer. It is only later that the definite stale flavors emerge. Oxidation has different effects, depending on the type of beer. In more lightly colored beers, the dominant note is often a wet-paper or cardboard flavor. In darker beers, a sherry-like flavor is very common. Sometimes other off flavors, including one described as "rotten pineapple" or "garbage-like," are found. Sometimes a sharp bite on the back of the tongue will be noticed, particularly in lightly hopped brews.

To slow down oxidation of your beer, be careful to avoid air pickup both on the hot and cold sides of the brewing process. Specifics are discussed in the relevant chapters. Also refer to Chapter 22 for a discussion of the role of yeast as an antioxidant in naturally conditioned beers. Some breweries used to use ascorbic acid as a preservative, but it has not proven effective. To work, it must be used in combination with sulfur dioxide (from sodium metabisulfite, sold as Campden tablets), which unfortunately gives a sulfury taint to the aroma of the beer. The only practical thing you can do to help finished beer is to store it cold, as heat greatly speeds up oxidative reactions.

## Autolysis

Yeast is an antioxidant, but it brings its own problems to a finished beer. The sulfury, rubbery smell of autolysis is easy to identify in the bottom of a fermenter that is not cleaned out promptly. A less distinct, yeasty flavor is often noted in unfiltered beers, especially those where finings have not been used to help the yeast drop out of suspension, and the yeasty character will eventually become harsh and unpleasant as the beer gets older.

The best way to learn about yeasty notes in beer is to store a six-pack of bottle-conditioned homebrew in a warm place for a couple of weeks, then sample a bottle each week and note the changes. The best ways to avoid yeasty flavors in unfiltered beer are, first, to carry over as little yeast as possible into the package, or only enough for the bottle fermentation in the case of bottle-conditioned beers, and second, to store the beer cold, once carbonation has been achieved.

# Haze

Haze is caused by colloidal particles suspended in the beer. They scatter light that shines through the beer, and thus make it appear hazy.

Permanent hazes (visible regardless of temperature) can be caused by bacteria, wild yeast, starch, or other substances. However, the most common type of haze in beer is chill haze, which appears when the beer is cooled. The phenomenon is explained in Chapter 22.

The easiest way to remove haze from beer is to filter it using a filter element that is tight enough to remove the offending particles. Note that to remove chill haze, the beer must be chilled below the serving temperature and allowed to stand for 24 hours (so that haze will form) before being filtered. Also, some beers are less stable than others, and wheat beers, for example, may throw a haze after sitting in the keg or bottle for several weeks, even though they were filtered bright before going into the package. With other beers, it may take months for haze to redevelop.

# Gushing

Bottle-conditioned beers may gush if they were overprimed. Many infections will also cause gushing, as the infecting bacterium or yeast metabolizes substances that brewers' yeast cannot. Another common cause is that the priming rate was correct, but the beer had a good deal of residual malt sugar when it was bottled. This is usually a sign of a slow, incomplete fermentation due to a weak yeast. The fermentation seemed to have petered out, but in fact it was not finished.

It is important to keep a record of terminal gravities in your brews to get an idea of what to expect from a given yeast with a wort of a certain gravity. Until you get some experience, look for a terminal gravity about one-fourth the original gravity for ale, about one-fifth for lagers. If your beer does not ferment out to such a value, try raising the fermentation temperature in the secondary for a few days. If that does not have any effect, and you cannot filter and artificially carbonate the beer, then be conservative with priming, or, if possible, keg the beer. If kegged beer gets over-carbonated, you can release head pressure and let the beer sit for a day or so before tapping, which should drop the carbonation level. However, in bad cases, you may have to repeat this procedure several times.

With draft beer, excess foam can be caused by over-carbonation, just as with bottled beer. This could be caused by the same factors as with bottled beer, or the beer may pick up carbonation as it sits in the keg under $CO_2$ pressure. To avoid this, lower the pressure on the keg when it is not going to be tapped for a while. Turn the pressure back up before pouring beer. High flow rates, caused by too little restriction in the beer line, also will create a lot of foam in the glass. Another cause, if flow rate is normal, is that the head pressure may be too low. In this case, the gas will break out as it flows through the line. Raise the pressure a few pounds, wait a half hour or so, and the foaming will disappear.

# Skunky

When an isohumulone molecule is struck by light of a certain wave length, one branch of it will vibrate and, eventually, break off. The broken piece will then combine with a molecule of hydrogen sulfide (of which beer always contains a trace) to form a *mercaptan* (organic compound with an -SH group) that is exactly the same molecule that the skunk manufactures in that famous gland under its tail. That is why light-struck beers smell skunky. Imported beers are notorious for this fault, because they often sit on shelves for weeks or months in bottles that offer little or no protection from the offending ultraviolet light. Brown bottles offer the most protection, but they are not perfect. Any beer made with natural hops will get skunky if exposed to too much light. Some commercial brewers get away with clear bottles by using specially treated stabilized hop extracts.

As with infections, there is no cure for a skunky beer. You have to prevent the reaction from occurring. Keep your bottles and carboys out of direct sunlight or fluorescent light.

## Weak Body

Body is the sensation of palate fullness created by dextrins and proteins in the beer. Thin beers often have a low specific gravity. Some malt extracts give a thin-bodied beer because they are low in proteins and unfermentable carbohydrates. Also, infections often produce a thin-bodied beer.

How much body is enough depends on the style of beer. If you feel your beer is too thin for the style, use more grain, or try using some dextrin malt in the grist. Higher mash temperatures and eliminating the protein rest will also help.

## Harshness

Harshness is a clinging, unpleasant bitterness on the back of the tongue. There are several causes, including infection by wild yeast. In uninfected beers, the mineral content of the water can be a factor, as it can lend a harsh character to the hop bitterness. Sodium and sulfate, in combination, have this effect, and so does magnesium. With waters containing these ions, hop rates will have to be reduced. Also, some types of hops, especially the high alpha varieties, can give an "edge" to the beer. A high proportion of dark roasted malts in dark beers such as porters can also lead to harshness. Boiling the hops too long is yet another factor.

In addition, serving temperature and carbonation both play a large part in the perception of bitterness. Any beer will taste smoother if it is served warmer and with lower carbonation. This is undoubtedly why so many Britons prefer "real ale" (cask-conditioned) to the chilled, highly carbonated "keg bitters." Even German lagers are normally served warmer than Americans would expect, and the famous "ten minute pour" greatly reduces the carbonation in the glass.

# 36

# Beer Styles

**For purposes of judging** in competitions, and also for other formal evaluations, beers are classified according to their style. The classification makes it possible to compare beers objectively. With a clear, fairly precise description of what a beer's flavor, aroma, and color should be, a group of experienced judges can assess how well the various samples meet the criteria for the style.

Some old-time homebrewers do not feel comfortable with the style classification system, because it seems to turn a homebrew competition into a look-alike contest, where beers are judged by how closely they resemble a commercial exemplar. However, the alternative to stylistic criteria is chaos, with the judges arguing as much about their own tastes and preferences as about the beers in front of them.

Nonetheless, it is true that the beers come first, and stylistic descriptions are possible only because brewers have, over the centuries, tended to imitate one another (especially within a geographic region) and produced similar beers. You should not feel limited by a stylistic description; rather, these criteria, and the commercial examples cited, should serve as a guide that, combined with firsthand experience, will make it possible to learn what you like and decide what recipes you want to try.

Over the past few years, a body of literature on beer styles has sprung up. The seminal works are those of Michael Jackson (see bibliography); for those who want to enter competitions, the stylistic descriptions published by the American Homebrewers Association are quite detailed and precise. They are constantly in a state of revision as experience in competitions shows the need for small (or occasionally sweeping) reclassifications. The descriptions given here are more general.

# British Ales

Pale ale is one of the most famous, and diverse, of all beer styles. It is brewed throughout the British Isles. The common elements to all Pale ales are: amber to copper color, moderate to high bitterness, and low to moderate carbonation. A definite estery character is almost always noted. Use of some dark sugar and/or adjuncts is accepted in these styles and contributes to the complexity of many brands. The preferred method of presentation is as cask-conditioned draft beer. Draft pale ale is often called "bitter." However, pale ale is also bottled, and traditionalists prefer it bottle-conditioned. Classic commercial examples, available in this country, include Bass and Whitbread Ale.

Two famous sub-styles of Pale ale are India Pale Ale (IPA) and Extra Special Bitter (ESB). IPA was originally created to withstand the rigors of long sea voyages from Britain to India during the Raj. It was very highly hopped and quite strong (Original gravity [OG] from the 1060s to 1080s). These days it is much weaker, but still on the strong side for a pale ale (ordinary pale ale usually has an OG in the mid- to high 30s these days). The hop character remains. Young's Ram Rod is a good example. ESB is maltier and sweeter than ordinary pale ale, with an OG around 1045–1050. Hops are restrained (at least compared with IPA). Fuller's is a classic example.

Another classic British ale style is stout and porter. The dividing line between these two beers is fuzzy at best. Both are thick and black with bitterness from roasted grains as well as hops. Stout was originally a high-gravity porter called "stout porter," which soon became simply "stout." These days, porters are usually distinguished by a slightly lighter color and a roasted-grain flavor derived from chocolate or black malt, as opposed to roasted barley, which is typical of stout. Stouts are divided between dry (or Irish) stouts typified by Guinness, and sweet stouts, which often have some caramel malt flavor and a sweeter flavor. Some sweet stouts, such as Mackeson, are very sweet indeed, though the roasted grain bitterness is also in evidence. A sub-style of sweet stout is oatmeal stout, which uses flaked oats for added body and smoothness. Samuel Smith makes a good example.

Brown and mild ale are similar in color, falling between pale ale and porter. Brown is bottled and somewhat stronger (mid-40s), whereas mild is a draft beer of very low gravity, often in the low 30s. These beers often feature the flavor of dark sugars. Hop bitterness is low compared to pale ale.

Old ale is a high-gravity relative of brown ale. Its most distinctive trait is a strong flavor of molasses. Old Peculier is the pre-eminent example.

Scotch ale in general resembles brown ale in its low hop rate and sweetness. It is made in a variety of gravities, and the color is variable from amber to brown. The higher gravity versions can be very sweet indeed.

The strongest of British beers are Barley wine and Imperial Stout. Both are strictly bottled beers. The latter was brewed for export to the Russian court at St. Petersburg in the nineteenth century. Imperial stout is not necessarily black, but it is very strong, approaching wine in alcohol content. The same goes for barley wine, which is amber to copper in color. Both beers pack a huge estery character, with little discernible hop aroma. Unlike conventional beers, they are intended to keep several years in the bottle before being drunk.

# Belgian Ales

Belgium produces a greater variety of beers than any other nation. The famous Belgian specialty ales are so different from any other beers, and from each other, that a complete account requires an entire book. Fortunately, Michael Jackson has written it.

Many Belgian ales require a mixed or spontaneous fermentation. Basically, a mixed fermentation includes the action of lactic acid bacteria as well as yeast, resulting in a sour character. Examples of these styles include the red copper ales such as Rodenbach or Bios, and the Flanders Brown ale. Spontaneous fermentation means that a pitching culture is not used—instead, the indigenous microflora that float in the air are allowed to take hold in the wort and produce a long, slow fermentation characterized by a definite progression, as first one, then another, microorganism dominates, each leaving its distinctive flavor signature in the finished product. Lambic beers from the Senne valley near Brussels are the only spontaneously fermented beers that are still being made commercially. Blending old and young lambic makes gueze, a tart beer that is sometimes available in this country. Saint-Louis is an example, rather sweeter than most. Also available are the fruit beers made by racking Lambic over crushed fruit in large wooden barrels.

Production of mixed and spontaneous fermentation beers is outside the scope of this book. Besides being difficult, they are dangerous because many homebrewers have found that it is much easier to introduce a wild yeast or bacterium into a brewery than it is to get rid of it; in other words, a deliberate lambic may be followed by a series of accidental lambics. It is best to use a separate set of equipment—and, if possible, a separate brewing area—for making these beers.

Other Belgian ales are easier to do at home. The Belgian Wit (White) beer, made with unmalted wheat and flavored with coriander and orange peel as well as hops, has become very popular and is now being brewed in the United States by Celis Brewing Company of Austin, Texas. A stronger version, Grand Cru, is also available. The strong ales produced by various Trappist abbeys in

Belgium have also acquired a following. These enormously complex beers, with hints of diacetyl, phenolics, and other fermentation by-products, are widely imitated by commercial Belgian breweries. They are made in several styles including Double, which is brown, sweet, and about 1.070 gravity; and Triple, which is paler, dryer, and even stronger (about 1.080).

Special strains of yeast are now offered by laboratories that allow the homebrewer to approach the fermentation characteristics of these Belgian beers. Bottle-conditioning is the preferred method of packaging.

## German Ales

There are four distinct styles of German ale. Two are brewed in the Rhine valley, one in the Northeast, and one in Bavaria.

The beers of the Rhine country are Alt and Kolsch. Alt is an amber to brown beer, moderately hopped, with the malty character typical of most German brews. Kolsch is a light-colored beer with a lighter body than alt, mildly hopped, and often slightly tart. Both are best made with yeast strains that impart the aroma characteristics required.

The other two ales are made with malted wheat. (Kolsch and Alt may also be made with wheat, but it is not definitive). The Berliner weissbier is a brew made with 25 percent wheat malt. It is very low in gravity (low 30s), lightly hopped, and quite tart. It is made using a mixed fermentation including lactic acid bacteria as well as yeast. It is often served with raspberry or green woodruff syrup, whose sweetness balances the acidic flavor.

Bavarian weizen (wheat) bier is entirely different. Unfortunately, many commercial examples are labeled as "Weiss," but a glance at the label will identify the Bavarian origin. Commercial examples are widely available, brewed by all the major Bavarian breweries and many smaller ones. This style is normal in gravity (around 1045–1050), brewed with 40 to 75 percent malted wheat. Its distinguishing feature is a strong clove-like spicy flavor and aroma, produced by the special strains of yeast used to ferment the wort. There are several sub-styles of weizenbier. The clear filter version is sometimes called kristallweizen. The unfiltered, which is more popular, is called hefeweizen (hefe means yeast). The dark version is known as dunkelweizen; it is usually brown in color. Finally, there is a strong version called weizenbock, which is similar to dunkelweizen but brewed to a high gravity (1064–1068).

Berliner weiss and the Bavarian weizenbiers both resemble Belgian ales in that much of their character comes from the fermentation. They are often a love-it-or-hate-it proposition. As with the Belgian beers, the special yeast used for German wheat ales is an absolute requirement for making an authentic version.

## American Ales

The craft brewing movement in America has fostered the development of a number of beer styles. Most of these are based on European models, but they have a distinct personality of their own and in some cases have even been recognized as distinct styles for purposes of judging.

The lightest American ale style is called "cream ale." It resembles American light lager, but usually has a fuller body and sometimes a more prominent hop character. Similar is the American wheat ale, which unlike the German versions, is brewed using a conventional, often fairly neutral ale yeast. American wheat ale may be found in both filtered and unfiltered versions, the latter sometimes called hefeweizen.

American pale ale is similar in color to British pale ale. It is on the heavy side of the spectrum, typically 1.045 to 1.055 in original gravity. It also usually leans to the high side in bitterness; British pales run the gamut from quite moderate to rather high hop rates, but most well-known American pales are definitely in the high range. Typical examples are Anchor Liberty Ale and Sierra Nevada Pale Ale. Other distinguishing features are the use of American malts and American aroma hops, typically Cascades. The malt produces rather subtle differences in the aroma and flavor, but the flowery American hops are quite distinctive from the earthy tones of the East Kent Goldings preferred by British brewers.

American microbrewed porters and stouts are somewhat closer to British examples, though again leaning to the hoppy side. Another distinguishing feature, which also applies to pale ales, is that many of them are fermented with clean, neutral yeasts, and lack the estery, fruity notes of most British beers.

A few regional breweries in the East still make a different type of porter, which is very sweet, light brown in color, with low bitterness. Often these porters are made with lager yeast, and in general they much more closely resemble American lager beer than either British or microbrewed porter.

American brown ale is usually higher in bitterness than its British prototype, and often has some hop aroma as well. Like American pale ale, it is usually brewed from malt alone; unlike British brewers, American microbrewers tend to look askance at the use of sugar and adjuncts except for special cases like oatmeal stout.

American fruit beers are usually based on a clean, neutral beer like wheat ale, but sometimes a darker beer, even a stout. Unlike the Belgian lambic-based fruit beers, hop bitterness as well as fruit tartness is often evident. The combination sometimes produces a clash as they work against each other as well as against the malt sweetness. Other times the fruit aroma is overwhelmed by the malt and hops and the only evidence of fruit is a sour taste. However, when all the elements are well-balanced, a fruit ale can be a pleasant change from "regular" beer, and the variety of fruits available offers an almost unlimited territory for exploration.

# Lager Beers

Lager beer originated in Bavaria, and it has spread throughout the world by virtue of its clean, crisp underlying flavor profile—a result of the lager fermentation method and the *S. Carlsbergensis* yeast strains. The lager brewing tradition is much more narrowly focused in that a clean, simple flavor profile is expected and therefore unusual ingredients like dark sugar are never used. Lager brewing focuses on the essentials— malt and hops—and fermentation character, if evident, is subdued.

The most famous lager style is Pilsner, which originated in Bohemia. This is a pale all-malt beer of normal gravity (1.045 to 1.050), characterized by medium to high bitterness and strong Saaz hop aroma. German Pilsners are brewed to the same general specifications as Czech ones, though they are often less complex in aroma. The old, cold fermentation method still used for Pilsner Urquell, for example, leaves a trace of diacetyl in the finished product. German examples are generally simpler in character. Pilsner Urquell is very highly hopped, but other Bohemian and German beers are not hopped quite as aggressively. The very low mineral content of the Pilsen water (less than 50 ppm total dissolved solids) permits a high hop rate without a harsh clinging bite.

In Northern Germany and the Low Countries Pilsners are often made with adjuncts. In North Germany the usual adjunct is a barley malt that is so undermodified it may as well not be malted at all. It gives a smooth grainy flavor to the beer. In Holland and Belgium, rice or corn are used to lighten the body. Hop aroma remains distinctive in all cases, and Saaz is almost the only choice.

Closely related to Pilsner is the Munich helles or pale lager, of similar color and gravity. The difference is in the balance, both of flavor and aroma. In Helles beer, malt predominates over hops, which is not the case with Pilsner. Commercial examples of Helles include Spaten and Paulaner. They are not labeled as "helles" or anything else—this is the companies' mainline, regular beer.

A stronger type of pale, malty lager is the "export" style associated with Dortmund. Except for gravity, and a slightly darker color, it is very similar to Helles. All the Dortmund breweries also make Pilsners these days, so commercial beers from Dortmund breweries may be either style. Altenmunster, in its green swing-top bottle, is one brand that is easily distinguished without a taste comparison.

The old-time beer of Munich was a dark (by German standards—brown not black) lager of 1.050–1.055 gravity. This beer, often called Dunkel, is richly malty in aroma and flavor, with light hop bitterness. Spaten dark is a good example.

A similar beer, but amber in color, was brewed in Vienna. These beers are almost extinct now, but a stronger version, the Marzen beer brewed originally for the Munich Oktoberfest, is still going strong. It has less caramel sweetness than the dark Munich beers, but a higher gravity and a rich malty flavor and aroma. Spaten, Paulaner, and the other Bavarian breweries all make excellent examples.

Bock beers originated from a dark, top-fermented brew created in Einbeck centuries before lager brewing became popular. However, all modern bocks, except for Weizenbock, are now lagers. Regular, normal Bock is a dark malty beer of 1.064 to 1.068 gravity, very sweet and with only enough hops to avoid cloying. Doppelbock is similar, with just a little more of everything, including gravity (1.073–1.078). Helles bock (sometimes called Maibock because it is typically brewed for release on May Day) is of the same gravity as regular Bock, but is golden in color—hence the name. It may be hopped a bit more aggressively. Finally, there is Ice Bock (Eisbock), which is made by freezing a regular beer until ice crystals form, then decanting the liquid fraction. Because alcohol freezes at a lower temperature than water, this procedure yields a super-concentrated beer, often 13 percent or more alcohol by volume. Note however that the process is technically a form of distillation, and may therefore be illegal for homebrewers (or for commercial brewers unless they obtain a distiller's license).

American lagers are a separate style, light in body, aroma, and bitterness. They are some of the mildest beers in the world, though the alcohol content is actually higher than for typical British draft ales, and on a par with ordinary German beers. They were originally brewed with rice or corn in order to compensate for the high haze potential of American six-row barley; these days, the light body created by adjuncts is a desired aspect of the flavor.

American bock beers are similar to American lagers in general character. Some brands use an almost flavorless malt coloring material for darkness. The better ones use caramel and dark malt, which impart flavor and aroma.

# A Final Word

This discussion of beer styles has cited commercial examples. Please remember that, by the time they reach these shores, many imported beers are months old and heavily oxidized. Some of the greatest beers in the world are nothing more than a pathetic shadow of themselves after enduring weeks or months in cargo containers and hot warehouses. In fact, if you want to learn about oxidation, you hardly need to do more than sample half a dozen import beers with an experienced taster, who will identify the various off flavors in most of them.

The point is, then, that in sampling commercial beers, you often have to ignore the old, oxidized character and try to look backwards in time, through what you can taste now to what the beer must have been like when it was fresh. This is not always easy; but in trying to gain an understanding of various beer styles, it is important to try.

# 37

# Recipe Formulation

**M**ost homebrewers enjoy modifying or creating recipes. In fact, one of the greatest rewards of the hobby is the opportunity to make a beer that tastes exactly the way you want it to. However, before you can exploit this freedom, you have to understand what contribution each ingredient, and each step of the process, makes to the finished product. The quickest way to do this is to undertake some systematic experiments with your brewing materials.

Before beginning any experimentation with recipe formulation, you have to be sure that your results will reflect the changes you make from batch to batch: that is, you have to be able to make a consistent beer free from random variations. Steve Fried, the brewmaster at McGuire's Pub in Pensacola, Florida, recommends following a simple recipe (6 pounds of pale malt, 1 ounce of hops, a packet of yeast) and brewing it until you get the same results time after time. Liquid yeast is preferable because of the varied levels of contamination from packet to packet of dry yeast, but the basic principle is sound. The first goal is to make clean, drinkable beer. Then you can try complicating it in various ways.

The other key to meaningful experiments with ingredients and processes is to change only one variable at a time. If you undertake a series of experiments with various grades of caramel malt, for example, change only the type of caramel malt — not the quantity, the basic pale malt, hops, or anything else.

Experimental beers should all be designed to produce drinkable results. In other words, do not use outrageous proportions or amounts of special malts or hops in an attempt to make the differences clearer. Seven to 12 percent of caramel malt in a 5-gallon batch, for example, is quite enough to show the differences between one grade and another.

Actual design of the experiments depends on what type or types of beer interest you the most. Any brewer should experiment with hops, but which varieties you need to investigate depends very much on the style of beer you want to brew. Similarly, ale brewers will want to start their malt investigations with different types of caramel malt. Lager enthusiasts may wish to start with different Munich and Vienna-type malts.

If you already have a favorite recipe for a favorite style of beer, you do not need to start from ground zero; you can simply make substitutions, one at a time, in whatever ingredient interests you. Keep in mind, though, that the simpler the recipe, the easier it is to pick out the difference your substitution has made. Also, as a general rule, it is easier to taste differences in mildly to moderately hopped beers. High levels of bitterness tend to mask flavors.

## Basic Parameters

The basic parameters of a beer are gravity, bitterness, and color. Gravity reflects the total amount of grain; bitterness reflects the hop rate; and color reflects the amount and type of specialty malts used in the brew. Obviously, these are far from the only aspects of beer that need to be taken into account in trying to describe a beer style; but the others are hard to quantify and must be described in sensory terms, for example, a flowery or spicy hop aroma, light or heavy body, and so on.

Given identical batch sizes, gravity is affected by three factors: the amount of grain (malt and adjuncts) in the grist, the types of grain used, and the efficiency of the process. The first two factors are straightforward, and can be accounted for mathematically from the maltster's specifications. Efficiency, however, is highly variable, and has to be determined by experience. The numbers in the table in this chapter give extract figures close to the maximum obtainable from homebrewing equipment.

| | | | |
|---|---|---|---|
| Barley flakes | 30 | Malt extract syrup | 36 |
| Black malt | 24 | Mild ale malt | 33 |
| Cane sugar (all types) | 45 | Munich malt | 33 |
| Cara-pils | 30 | Pale ale malt | 35 |
| Corn or rice flakes | 40 | Roast barley | 24 |
| Corn sugar | 40 | Six-row lager malt | 33 |
| Crystal malts | 24 | Two-row lager malt | 35 |
| Honey | 35 | Vienna malt (homemade) | 30 |
| Malt extract powder | 45 | Wheat malt | 38 |

*Numbers represent the extract of 1 pound of material in 1 gallon of water.*

You can calculate from these numbers the maximum theoretical extract obtainable from a recipe, then compare that with your actual extract. The difference tells you the efficiency of your operation.

Example: a Kolsch made using 6 lbs. of pale 2-row brewers' malt, 8 oz. of Vienna malt, and 8 oz. of 10 L caramel malt.

$$6 \times 35 = 210$$
$$.5 \times 32 = 16$$
$$.5 \times 24 = \underline{12}$$
$$\text{Total} = 238 \,/\, 5 = 47.6$$

(i.e., OG of 1.047-8 for a 5-gallon batch)

Suppose the actual measured gravity of your batch is 1.045. Dividing that by your theoretical maximum tells you that your mash is about 95 percent efficient — pretty good.

As you use more grain in a batch, efficiency goes down. This is easy to understand: the more grain, the more first runnings you collect, and the less sparge water you will be able to use. With very strong beers, the final spargings might still have a gravity in the 1.030 to 1.040 range. Obviously, a lot of extract is left in the spent grains.

The second parameter — bitterness — is much more difficult to measure than gravity. It requires a laboratory and is, therefore, beyond the scope of most homebrewers. A number of formulas have been published over the past few years to predict the bitterness of beers. Bitterness is measured in International Bitterness Units, or IBU. One IBU equals one part per million of isohumulone in the finished beer.

It is simple to calculate the amount of humulone one is putting in the kettle. The AAU system does this: an AAU or alpha acid unit is exactly .01 ounce of humulone. However, the hop utilization (percentage of humulone isomerized in the kettle) can vary from zero to over 30 percent, depending on many factors. Some of these factors are very difficult to account for, and all formulas have to include a variable term that recognizes the time factor in isomerization. A formula devised by Jackie Rager (see bibliography) is in wide use. These formulas are predictive, and must be tested by comparing an actual lab analysis of your beer with the number given by the formula. If this is not possible, then you have to regard the formula's prediction as a best guess, but rely on taste to determine what sort of adjustments need to be made in order to approach your desired bitterness level.

The simplest formula for attempting to predict IBU is to use a sliding scale (depending on boil time) as a best-guess for utilization, and use a constant to convert AAU into parts per million. This translates into:

IBU = AAU x 74.4 / wort volume (in gallons) x U (utilization percentage)

For example, if we use 5 AAU of hops in a 5-gallon batch, and assume 25 percent utilization, we get

$$IBU = 5 \times 74.4 / 5 \times .25 = 18.6 \text{ IBU}.$$

Again, the problem is coming up with a utilization percentage number. Using whole hops, the percentage will usually run from about 1 for finish hops, to about 20 for hops boiled an hour. For pellets, the percentage will usually run from about 5 to about 25, for the same times. However, there is so much variation from one brewery to another that, without some actual analyses to base your utilization percentages on, your chances are probably less than 50-50 of getting an accurate estimate (within 1 IBU) from this formula.

Color is, in some ways, even harder to deal with than bitterness. The color of malt is measured by making a standard mash, which after conversion is centrifuged and the color of the clear wort is compared with a standardized set of colored glass pieces. This being the case, it ought to be possible to predict wort and beer color fairly closely by multiplying the color of each grain by the amount used, and dividing by the batch size in gallons. Unfortunately, brewery mashes are quite different from standard lab mashes, and the actual color extracted from grain can vary considerably depending on mash method, sparge water (temperature, mineral content, and pH) and numerous other factors. In practice, the more intensive decoction method will usually extract more color from a grist than infusion methods. Therefore, the most practical way to learn about color, and how color specifications of malt relate to what the malt will give in a real brew, is to do some test brews of the kind described earlier. Nonetheless, malt combinations, as used for many amber and dark beers, can yield color results that are surprising.

If you are interested in calculating values, the simplest formula is based on the *color unit,* or CU. One color unit represents 1 pound of malt with a color rating of 1 degree Lovibond, or any equivalent, such as ¹⁄₁₀ of a pound of 10 L malt. To calculate color, you must first multiply the weight (in pounds) of each malt in your recipe by the malt's color rating. Then add up the figures and divide by the number of gallons in the recipe. The following example is a recipe for 5 gallons of pale ale:

| | |
|---|---|
| 6 lbs. pale ale malt (3 L) | = 18 CUs  (6 x 3) |
| .5 lb. British crystal malt (55 L) | = 27.5 CUs (.5 x 55) |
| Total | = 45.5 CUs |
| CUs per gallon | = 9.1  (45.5 / 5) |

To repeat: color units do not correlate very well with degrees Lovibond, and beers which calculate to the same CU figure can have obvious differences in color, both in tint (dark to light) as well as hue.

As a very approximate guide, beers with 2 CUs per gallon are normally yellow; 5 CUs per gallon, golden; 8 CUs per gallon, light amber; 12 CUs per gallon, deep amber; 16 CUs per gallon, light brown or copper, depending on the dark malt used. Crystal malt gives a reddish hue, while black and chocolate malt are brown. Beers of 20 to 25 CUs per gallon are brown, and beers over 30 are dark brown or black. These numbers will usually work for beers made by infusion mashing.

## Basic Guidelines

For purposes of teaching yourself about the flavor and color of different malts, or the flavor of different hops, very simple recipes are best. However, for the most interesting beers, a bit of complexity helps. Some homebrewers follow a rule of never using fewer than 3 (or 4, or 5, depending on the brewer) types of malt, and a similar number of hop varieties. Any rule of this sort is arbitrary, and many exceptions have to be made; nonetheless, the basic principle is a good one. Most beer styles, even the palest, benefit from some complication. However, the only firm rule is that you have to understand what your ingredients will contribute to the beer: in other words, why you are using them.

An example that illustrates both the exception and the rule is the famous Belgian strong ale, Duvel. This is a very strong blonde ale made from a grist of 100 percent Pilsner malt; what is normally referred to in this country as 2-row brewers' malt. This certainly makes it an exceptional ale. However, the yeast used in the fermentation, working on a wort of very high gravity, produces a veritable blizzard of by-products, including diacetyl, phenolic alcohols, and esters. Thus the beer, despite its simple grain bill, is very complex; in this case the complexity comes from the yeast rather than the malt or hops.

Duvel is an extraordinary beer in every way, but the same principle holds true for the more common and drinkable styles of beer. Most are simple in some ways, but complex in others. Many pale ales use only a single hop for aroma, the famous East Kent Golding, but they gain in complexity from the estery yeasts and the malts used.

# 38

# Recipes

**T**he recipes in this chapter are intended as a starting point for your own experimentation. Not every beer style is included. Some of the exotic Belgian ales, for example, require elaborate mixed fermentations that are beyond the scope of a general handbook. Many more detailed recipes and procedural hints can be found in books and articles on the beer styles, some of which are mentioned in the bibliography. The recipes found here can all be made using ordinary brewing and fermentation methods.

The recipes are generic, though in some cases a specific type of malt or yeast is recommended or cited as an example. Be aware that differences in the grade of caramel malt, for example, can have a large effect on the color and flavor of the finished beer. Choice of hops is just as crucial. Also, remember that if you choose to use pellet hops for finish you will have to cut down your bittering hops to compensate. Hop rates are given in AAU but the approximate IBU equivalent for the pellet rate (assuming 30 percent utilization) is also given so that you can use Jackie Rager's or another formula if you prefer.

*All recipes are for 5 gallons of beer.*

## British Bitter

*This recipe is for a low-gravity "session" bitter. Hopping can be varied according to taste. You can experiment with adjuncts or sugars, both of which are frequently used in Great Britain. Cask-conditioning is the preferred form of packaging, though most bitter these days is served as "keg" beer — carbonated and filtered.*

> 5 lbs. British pale ale malt
> 8 oz. British crystal malt
> Bittering hops: 7 AAU pellets or 8.5 AAU whole hops —
> Fuggle, Golding, or Northern Brewer
> Finishing hops: 1 oz. Golding

### Brewer's Specifics

Original gravity: 1.038
31 IBU
Use single infusion mash.
Use British ale yeast strain.
Bottle-conditioning or cask-conditioning preferred; if cask-conditioning,
use dry hopping rather than finish hopping.
Beer should be clear; use isinglass finings or (if not bottle-
or cask-conditioned) filter.
Terminal gravity: 1.006–1.009

## British I.P.A.

*I.P.A. is a strong version of bitter with plenty of hops. It can either be bottle- or cask-conditioned. Some brewers add oak chips to the carboy to get the flavor they think was imparted by the casks used in former days. However, this practice is highly controversial and brewing historians are divided on the question of whether I.P.A. once had a woody flavor. Some of the old-time brewers did add sugar to the kettle, and you may want to experiment with small amounts of various dark sugars when making your own I.P.A.*

8 lbs. British pale ale malt

12 oz. British crystal malt

Bittering hops:  10 AAU pellets or 13 AAU whole hops —
Fuggle, Golding, or Northern Brewer

Finishing hops:  2 oz. Golding

### Brewer's Specifics

Original gravity: 1.050

44 IBU

Use single infusion mash.

Use British ale yeast strain.

Bottle-conditioning preferred.

Use isinglass for clarity.

Terminal gravity: 1.008–1.014

## E.S.B.

*E.S.B. can vary greatly in bitterness; this recipe is moderate in that respect. What distinguishes an E.S.B. from other variations of pale ale is the full malt flavor. High starting gravity is also a requisite.*

7 lbs. British pale ale malt

1 lb. flaked barley

12 oz. British crystal malt

Bittering hops:  7 AAU pellets or 8.5 AAU whole hops —
Fuggle, Golding, or Northern Brewer

Finishing hops:  ½ oz. Golding

### Brewer's Specifics

Original gravity: 1.050

31 IBU

Use single infusion mash.

Use British ale yeast strain.

Cask-conditioning preferred.

Use isinglass for clarity.

Terminal gravity: 1.008–1.014

# *Light Ale*

*Light ale is usually bottled, comparable in gravity to the lighter draft bitters, but often paler in color. Bitterness is restrained to maintain the balance. This recipe calls for flaked maize, which lightens the body. A light colored sugar could also be used for this purpose.*

4.5 lbs. British pale ale malt
4 oz. British crystal malt
½ lb. flaked maize (corn)
Bittering hops:  6 AAU pellets or 7 AAU whole hops — Fuggle, Golding, or Northern Brewer
Finishing hops:  ½ oz. Golding

### Brewer's Specifics

Original gravity: 1.032–1.034
26 IBU
Use single infusion mash.
Use British ale yeast.
Bottle-condition or filter and carbonate.
Terminal gravity: 1.004–1.006

# *Brown Ale*

*Brown ale is dark but not opaque, and lightly hopped. It is a bottled beer with a normal gravity by American standards. Dark sugars are popular for brown ales as they contribute to the flavor as well as color of the beer.*

5.5 lbs. British pale ale malt
8 oz. British crystal malt
4 oz. chocolate malt
1 lb. dark brown sugar (add to boiler)
Bittering hops:  5 AAU pellets or 6 AAU whole hops — Fuggle or Northern Brewer
Finishing hops:  none

### Brewer's Specifics

Orignal gravity: 1.044–1.048
22 IBU
Use infusion mash.
Use British ale yeast.
Bottle-conditioning preferred.
Terminal gravity: 1.010–1.012

## *Mild Ale*

*Mild ale is often described as a draft version of brown ale, but the original gravity is usually lower. Compared to a draft bitter of similar gravity, the hops are restrained and the color (perhaps to compensate) is somewhat darker. The beer should have a smooth finish, with no bite from either the hops or the dark malt.*

                **4 lbs. British pale ale malt**

                **5 oz. British crystal malt; 3 oz. chocolate malt; and 0.5 lb. dark brown sugar (add to boiler)**

**Bittering hops:**  **4 AAU pellets or 5 AAU whole hops — Fuggle or Northern Brewer**

**Finishing hops:**  **none**

### Brewer's Specifics

Original gravity: 1.034–1.038
17 IBU
Use infusion mash.
Use British ale yeast.
Cask-conditioning preferred.
Terminal gravity: 1.007–1.010

## *Scotch Ale*

*Scotch ales vary widely, with several sub-styles recognized with different gravity bands. This recipe is middle-of-the-road. All Scotch ales have a pronounced malty character and sweet finish. Some have a hint of smoke that comes from a small proportion of smoked malt in the grist. You can smoke pale malt at home, but it takes some practice to get the right degree of smokiness.*

> 7 lbs. British pale ale malt
> 1 lb. British crystal malt
> 4 oz. chocolate malt
> 1 lb. dark brown sugar (add to boiler)

Bittering hops:  6 AAU pellets or 7.5 AAU whole hops — Fuggle or Northern Brewer
Finishing hops:  none

### Brewer's Specifics

Original gravity: 1.050–1.055
26 IBU
Use single infusion mash.
Use British ale yeast.
Bottle-conditioning or cask-conditioning preferred.
Terminal gravity: 1.012–1.016

## *Old Ale*

*These days, molasses is* de rigeur *for this style of beer. The recipe calls for a generous measure of molasses, and the flavor is certain to evoke a strong response, one way or the other, from everyone who tastes it.*

> 8 lbs. British pale ale malt
> 1 lb. 60 L crystal malt
> 8 oz. chocolate malt
> 24 oz. light molasses (add to boiler)

Bittering hops:  7 AAU pellets or 8 AAU whole hops — Fuggle or Northern Brewer
Finishing hops:  none

### Brewer's Specifics

Original gravity: 1.060–1.064
31 IBU
Use single infusion mash.
Use British ale yeast.
Bottle-conditioning or cask-conditioning preferred.
Terminal gravity: 1.014–1.018

## Porter

*Porter is a revival beer. It died out in commercial brewing and was brought back to life by homebrewers and microbrewers. Porter was made for two centuries using a variety of ingredients. Obviously there is no way this recipe can be more than a modern interpretation. It attempts to recognize the common origin of stout and porter while avoiding the heavy roasted grain flavor that is such a signature of modern stouts.*

**6.5 lbs. British pale ale malt**

**4 oz. British crystal malt**

**3 oz. black malt**

**4 oz. chocolate malt**

**Bittering hops:  7 AAU pellets or 8.5 AAU whole hops —
Northern Brewer or other high alpha British**

**Finishing hops:  none**

### Brewer's Specifics

Original gravity: 1.044–1.047
31 IBU
Use single infusion mash.
Use British ale yeast.
Bottle-conditioning or cask-conditioning preferred.
Terminal gravity: 1.009–1.012

## Dry Stout

*This recipe is based on one published by the late Dave Line in his* classic Big Book of Brewing. *The dry character comes from both the hops and the grain bill: roasted barley has a sharp, dry edge. Note the absence of crystal malt.*

> 6 lbs. British pale ale malt
> 1 lb. flaked barley and 12 oz. roasted barley
> Bittering hops:  10 AAU pellets or 12 AAU whole hops —
>                  Northern Brewer or other high alpha British
> Finishing hops:  none

### Brewer's Specifics

Original gravity: 1.045–1.048
44 IBU
Use single infusion mash.
Use British ale or stout yeast.
Bottle-conditioning or cask-conditioning preferred.
Terminal gravity: 1.010–1.013

## Sweet Stout

*Some commercial sweet stouts are actually dosed with sugar before being bottled, a practice that is obviously only possible if the beer can be pasteurized. This version gets its sweetness from crystal malt.*

> 6.5 lbs. British pale ale malt
> 8 oz. British crystal malt
> 6 oz. roasted barley
> Bittering hops:  6 AAU pellets or 7 AAU whole hops —
>                  Northern Brewer or other high alpha British
> Finishing hops:  none

### Brewer's Specifics

Original gravity: 1.045–1.048
26 IBU
Use single infusion mash.
Use British ale or stout yeast.
Bottle-conditioning or cask-conditioning preferred.
Terminal gravity: 1.010–1.013

## *Oatmeal Stout*

*Oatmeal stout is another revival style, with a very full body and rich, balanced flavor. Note that the recipe specifies flaked oats made specifically for brewing. Do not substitute rolled oats (oatmeal) if you expect to sparge in a reasonable amount of time.*

<blockquote>

7.5 lbs. British pale ale malt

8 oz. British caramel malt

8 oz. roasted barley

12 oz. flaked oats

Bittering hops:  8 AAU pellets or 10 AAU whole hops — Fuggle or other high alpha British

Finishing hops:  none

</blockquote>

### Brewer's Specifics

Original gravity: 1.054–1.058, T.G. 1.014–1.017. 35 IBU.
Use single infusion mash. Use British ale or stout yeast.
Bottle-conditioning or cask-conditioning preferred.

## *Imperial Stout*

*Unlike other stouts, Imperial stout need not be black. This recipe produces a very dark example. Also notice the use of sugar — another anomaly, as this ingredient is not typical of other stouts. While the bitterness appears to be high, the sweetness of the finished beer will make it seem quite normal.*

<blockquote>

10 lbs. British pale ale malt

1 lb. British crystal malt

8 oz. chocolate malt

4 oz. roasted barley

1 lb. dark brown sugar (add to boiler)

Bittering hops:  10 AAU pellets or 12 AAU whole hops — Northern Brewer or other high alpha British

Finishing hops:  none

</blockquote>

### Brewer's Specifics
Original gravity: 1.080–1.085
44 IBU
Use single-infusion mash.
Use a British ale yeast with high alcohol tolerance.
Bottle-conditioning preferred.
Terminal gravity: 1.016–1.022

## *Barley Wine*

*This recipe is on the low-gravity side of the style. Higher gravity barley wines (OG 1.100 and higher) tend to have fermentation difficulties, and the finished beers are usually dominated by ethyl acetate and other esters. A "light" barley wine like this one is easier to drink, though it is certainly a sipping beer rather than a session beer.*

**10 lbs. British pale ale malt**
**12 oz. British crystal malt**
**1.5 lbs. light brown or raw sugar (add to boiler)**
**Bittering hops:  11 AAU pellets or 13 AAU whole hops —**
**Fuggle, Golding, or Northern Brewer**
**Finishing hops:  none**

### Brewer's Specifics
Original gravity: 1.084–1.088
49 IBU
Use single infusion mash.
Use a British ale yeast with high alcohol tolerance.
Bottle-conditioning preferred.
Terminal gravity: 1.018–1.024

## *Altbier*

*This recipe gives a fairly pale alt — they can be darker. Higher proportions of Munich malt or dark crystal malt will intensify the color and flavor, as will decoction mashing.*

5 lbs. 2-row brewers' malt
1 lb. Munich malt
1 lb. wheat malt
8 oz. 60 L crystal malt
1 oz. black malt (optional)
Bittering hops: 6 AAU pellets or 7.5 AAU whole hops —
Hallertau, Tettnang, Spalt, or Perle
Finishing hops: .5 oz. same type hops

### Brewer's Specifics

Original gravity: 1.045–1.050
26 IBU
Use step or decoction mash.
Use German ale yeast.
Filtration preferred.
Terminal gravity: 1.011–1.014

## Kolsch

*This brew should be light in body and slightly tart. A yeast strain specifically selected for this style will give the most authentic results. Hop bitterness should be low, and hop aroma must not overwhelm the malt.*

6 lbs. pale 2-row malt
8 oz. wheat malt (crush fine)
8 oz. Vienna malt
Bittering hops: 4 AAU pellets or 5 AAU whole hops —
Hallertau, Tettnang, Spalt, or Perle
Finishing hops: 1 oz. same type hops, whole

### Brewer's Specifics

Original gravity: 1.042–1.046
17 IBU
Step or decoction mash preferred.
Use German ale yeast.
Filtration preferred.
Terminal gravity: 1.009–1.012

## *Weizen*

*This recipe calls for the maximum proportion of wheat malt. Be careful and gentle with your initial runoff from the lauter tun. Smaller proportions of wheat malt (some German breweries use as little as 40 percent) may cause less trouble.*

> 2.5 lbs. pale 2-row malt
> 5 lbs. wheat malt
> Bittering hops:  4 AAU pellets or 5 AAU whole hops —
> Hallertau, Tettnang, Spalt, or Perle
> Finishing hops:  none

### Brewer's Specifics

Original gravity: 1.045–1.049
17 IBU
Decoction mash preferred.
Use Weizenbier yeast only.
Bottle-condition for hefeweizen, filter for kristallweizen.
Note: For flavor stability in hefeweizen, filter out the weizen yeast, then add lager yeast at bottling along with primings.
Terminal gravity: 1.010–1.013

## *Belgian Wit*

*As with Weizen, the proper yeast is essential for this brew. Proportions of spices can be adjusted to suit your taste. Wheat malt may be substituted if necessary, but the flaked wheat called for in the recipe is preferable.*

> 5 lbs. pale 2-row malt
> 2 lbs. wheat malt or flaked wheat
> Bittering hops:  3 AAU pellets or 4 AAU whole hops —
> Hallertau, Fuggle, or Golding
> Finishing hops:  none
> Spices:  ½ oz. dried orange peel, I oz. crushed
> coriander (add to kettle like finish hops)

### Brewer's Specifics

Original gravity: 1.045–1.048
13 IBU
Step infusion mash preferred.
Use Belgian wit yeast or other mildly fruity ale yeast.
Bottle-condition.
Terminal gravity: 1.010–1.013

## Trappist Ale (Double)

*This recipe is for a brown "Double" of comparatively low gravity. Some doubles are heavier, as high as 1.081. If you raise the gravity, raise the hop rate as well.*

9.5 lbs. pale 2-row malt
1 lb. 40 L crystal malt
1 lb. dark brown sugar (add to boiler)
Bittering hops:  7 AAU pellets or 8 AAU whole hops —
Hallertau and Fuggle (50-50 blend)
Finishing hops:  none

### Brewer's Specifics

Original gravity: 1.074–1.078
30 IBU
Step or single infusion mash.
Use Belgian Trappist ale yeast.
Bottle-condition.
Terminal gravity: 1.015–1.020

## American Cream Ale

*Some commercial cream ales are made by blending ale and lager, but such complications are not necessary to create a convincing homebrewed version. This recipe will give a light-bodied beer but with more malt character than a typical American lager.*

5 lbs. pale 6-row malt

4 oz. Vienna malt

4 oz. 10 L crystal malt

4 oz. cara-pils malt

1 lb. flaked maize (corn)

Bittering hops: 3.5 AAU pellets or 4.5 AAU whole hops —
Liberty, Mt. Hood, Centennial, or Cascade

Finishing hops: ½ oz. Cascade or other American aroma hop

### Brewer's Specifics

Original gravity: 1.042–1.047

15 IBU

Step or single infusion mash.

Use a neutral American ale yeast such as Wyeast #1056.

Filtration preferred.

Terminal gravity: 1.009–1.012

## ——— *American Pale Ale* ———

*This recipe gives a typical American pale ale with a strong floral aroma from the Cascade finish hops. Unlike British pale ales, strong fermentation characteristics (estery aromas) are not a hallmark of this style.*

7.5 lbs. pale 2-row malt

8 oz. dextrin malt

12 oz. 60 L crystal malt

Bittering hops: 11 AAU pellets or 13.5 AAU whole hops —
Northern Brewer or Cascade

Finishing hops: 1.5 oz. Cascade whole

### Brewer's Specifics

Original gravity: 1.047–1.052

49 IBU

Step or single infusion mash.

Use a neutral American ale yeast such as Wyeast #1056.

Filtration preferred.

Terminal gravity: 1.010–1.014

## American Fruit Ale

*Many American microbreweries use natural fruit concentrates and essences for their fruit beers. If you can find one you like, it will save you a lot of trouble compared with the whole fruit called for in this recipe. The intensity of the fruit flavor in this style of beer can vary from "a hint" to "knock you over." After the first brew, you can adjust it to suit your own taste.*

5 lbs. pale 2-row malt
2 lbs. wheat malt
Bittering hops: 1.5 AAU pellets or 2 AAU whole hops —
any type
Finishing hops: none
Fruit: 10 lbs. cherries, raspberries, or peaches,
washed and crushed

### Brewer's Specifics
Original gravity: 1.042–1.046
6 IBU
Step or single infusion mash. Almost any conventional, non-phenolic ale yeast will do. Add fruit to oversize secondary fermenter and rack green beer over it when primary fermentation has ended. Allow beer to ferment on the fruit at least 14 days. Rack off, let stand another 7 days, then bottle-condition or filter.
Terminal gravity: 1.009–1.012

## American Brown Ale

*This recipe produces a typical American brown ale — hoppy and clean, without the brown-sugar flavor often found in British versions.*

7.5 lbs. pale 2-row malt
8 oz. 40 L crystal malt
4 oz. chocolate malt
Bittering hops: 8 AAU pellets or 10 AAU whole hops —
Northern Brewer, Centennial, or American
high alpha
Finishing hops: 1 oz. Cascade or American aroma variety (opt.)

### Brewer's Specifics

Original gravity: 1.045–1.050
35 IBU
Single or step infusion mash.
Use a neutral ale yeast such as Wyeast #1056.
Filtration preferred.
Terminal gravity: 1.010–1.014

## *American Porter*

*American porter is distinguished from stout mainly by the absence of roast barley. This recipe makes a robust, bitter porter; a softer version can be made by reducing the quantities of chocolate and black malt and cutting back on the hops.*

7.5 lbs. pale 2-row malt
8 oz. 40 L caramel malt
8 oz. chocolate malt
4 oz. black malt
Bittering hops: 10 AAU pellets or 12.5 AAU whole hops —
Cascade, Centennial, or high alpha
American variety
Finishing hops: none

### Brewer's Specifics

Original gravity: 1.047–1.052
44 IBU
Single or step infusion mash.
Use a neutral ale yeast such as Wyeast #1056.
Filtration preferred.
Terminal gravity: 1.011–1.015

## *American Lager*

*This recipe is different from commercial versions of the style. It is the most delicate of all beer styles, and small differences in the process, as well as the ingredients, have a perceptible impact on the flavor. This recipe is generic. Milled rice may be substituted for corn meal. Big American breweries often blend several varieties of hops.*

5.5 lbs. pale 2-row malt

1.5 lb. flaked maize (corn) or corn meal

Bittering hops:  3 AAU pellets or 4 AAU whole hops —
Hallertau, Tettnang, or Cascade

Finishing hops:  ½ oz. Tettnang, Cascade, or other aroma hop

### Brewer's Specifics

Original gravity: 1.041–1.044

13 IBU

Single infusion mash or, if using grits, double mash.

Use an American lager yeast.

Filter the finished beer.

Terminal gravity: 1.007–1.010

## Classic All-Malt Pilsner

*Another generic recipe. The cara-pils and crystal malt may be omitted to lighten the body, color, and sweetness. To get a Czech-style pilsner, use soft water, low fermentation temperatures, and a hop rate on the high end of the range. Average water, lower hop rates and warmer fermentation will approximate the German "pils" variation. Mash schedules are also important because lower attenuation (terminal gravities as high as 1.014) are typical of the Czech sub-style.*

7 lbs. pale 2-row malt

8 oz. dextrin (cara-pils) malt

4 oz. 10 L crystal malt

Bittering hops:  7–9 AAU pellets or 9–11 AAU whole hops —
Hallertau, Tettnang, or other Continental
aroma types

Finishing hops:  1–1.5 oz. Saaz

### Brewer's Specifics

Original gravity: 1.045–1.050

30–40 IBU

(Note: Higher level of bitterness occurs only with very soft water.)

Single, step, and decoction mash all acceptable.

Use a Continental lager yeast — Wyeast #2124 recommended.

Filter the finished beer.

Terminal gravity: 1.008–1.012

## Munich Helles

*This beer is almost as delicate as American lager. It has more malt flavor and aroma and a slightly higher hop rate to balance. Another requirement, imposed by German law since 1516, is that the beer be made from water, hops, yeast, and malt only. No adjuncts are allowed.*

> 6.5 lbs. pale 2-row malt
> 8 oz. Vienna malt
> 8 oz. dextrin (cara-pils) malt

Bittering hops:  4 AAU pellets or 5 AAU whole hops —
> Hallertau, Tettnang, Perle, Liberty,
> or Mt. Hood

Finishing hops:  ½ oz. Tettnang or Hallertau

### Brewer's Specifics

Original gravity: 1.044–1.048
17 IBU
Single, step, and decoction mash all acceptable.
Use a Continental lager yeast — Wyeast #2124 recommended.
Filter the finished beer.
Terminal gravity: 1.008–1.012

## Munich Dunkel

*This recipe requires a decoction mash to extract the color and flavor from the dark malts.*

> 2.5 lbs. pale 2-row malt
> 5 lbs. Continental Munich malt
> 8 oz. dark Continental caramel malt
> (e.g., DeWolf-Cosyns caramunich)
> 2 oz. very dark caramel malt
> (e.g., DWC Special B)

Bittering hops:  4.5 AAU pellets or 5.75 AAU whole hops —
> Hallertau, Tettnang, Perle, or Mt. Hood

Finishing hops:  none

**Brewer's Specifics**

Original gravity: 1.048—1.052
20 IBU
Decoction mash.
Use a German lager yeast.
Filter the finished beer.
Terminal gravity: 1.011–1.014

# Dortmunder Export

*Export is basically a higher-gravity version of Helles. Mash method is not critical for this style, but hop rate is. Overhopping, either in the kettle or the finish, will detract from the malt that should dominate in this beer.*

7.5 lbs. pale 2-row malt

1 lb. Vienna malt

8 oz. cara-pils malt

Bittering hops:  5 AAU pellets or 6.5 AAU whole hops —
Hallertau, Tettnang, Perle, or Mt. Hood

Finishing hops:  ½ oz. Tettnang or Hallertau

**Brewer's Specifics**

Original gravity: 1.052–1.055
22 IBU
Single, step, and decoction mash all acceptable.
Use a Continental lager yeast — Wyeast #2124 recommended.
Filter the finished beer.
Terminal gravity: 1.010–1.014

# Oktoberfest (Marzen)

*This recipe will give a fairly dark result if you use a decoction mash. For a lighter color, reduce the quantities of aromatic and caramel malt.*

>             3 lbs. pale 2-row malt
>             5 lbs. Continental Munich malt
>             8 oz. dark high-kilned malt (e.g., DWC
>                 aromatic)
>             8 oz. medium Continental caramel malt
>                 (e.g., DWC caravienne)
> Bittering hops:  6 AAU pellets or 7 AAU whole hops —
>                 Hallertau, Tettnang, Perle, or Mt. Hood
> Finishing hops:  ½ oz. Tettnang

### Brewer's Specifics

Original gravity: 1.054–1.058
26 IBU
Decoction mash preferred.
Use a Continental lager yeast — Wyeast #2124 recommended. Filter the finished beer.
Terminal gravity: 1.012–1.016

# Maibock (Helles Bock)

*The strongest member of the Helles-Export family. As gravity goes up, yeast selection becomes more critical, as some of the German lager yeasts tend to produce esters when working on a high-gravity wort. Fruity, estery notes are not desirable in this style.*

>             8.5 lbs. pale 2-row malt
>             1 lb. Vienna malt
>             8 oz. dextrin malt
>             8 oz. light caramel malt (e.g., DWC
>                 caramel pils)
> Bittering hops:  7 AAU pellets or 8 AAU whole hops —
>                 Hallertau, Tettnang, Perle, or Mt. Hood
> Finishing hops:  ¼ oz. Tettnang or Hallertau

## Brewer's Specifics

Original gravity: 1.064–1.067
31 IBU
Single, step, and decoction mash all acceptable.
Use a Continental lager yeast — Wyeast #2124 recommended.
Filter the finished beer.
Terminal gravity 1.013–1.017

## *Dunkel Bock*

*Filtration is prescribed in this recipe as in the other lager recipes because yeasty flavors are not welcome in lager beers. However, if you can lager the beer (store it cold) for several months, you may be able to rack it off the yeast without filtering. Chill haze is less of an issue for a darker beer as well.*

> 3.5 lbs. pale 2-row malt
> 6 lbs. Continental Munich malt
> 1.5 lbs. dark Continental crystal malt (e.g., DWC caramunich)

Bittering hops: 7 AAU pellets or 8 AAU whole hops — Hallertau, Tettnang, Perle, or Mt. Hood
Finishing hops: none

## Brewer's Specifics

Original gravity: 1.064–1.068
31 IBU
Decoction mash.
Use a Continental lager yeast — Wyeast #2124 recommended.
Filter the finished beer.
Terminal gravity: 1.014–1.018

## *Doppelbock*

*Like other strong beers, doppelbock can be difficult to brew. If you cannot collect a considerable excess of wort (say 7 gallons for a 5-gallon batch) and boil it down in a reasonable length of time, you may have to resort to pale malt extract to boost the gravity of the wort. This is not usually necessary with strong ales, because most of their excess gravity is contributed by sugar.*

> 4.5 lbs. pale 2-row malt
> 8 lbs. Continental Munich malt
> 2.5 lbs. dark Continental crystal malt (e.g.,
>   DWC caramunich)
> Bittering hops:  8 AAU pellets or 9.5 AAU whole hops —
>   Hallertau, Tettnang, Perle, or Mt. Hood
> Finishing hops:  none

### Brewer's Specifics

Original gravity: 1.073–1.077
35 IBU
Decoction mash.
Use a Continental lager yeast — Wyeast #2124 recommended.
Filter the finished beer.
Terminal gravity: 1.015–1.020

# Appendix

## Metric Conversions

### *Volume*

| U.S. | METRIC | U.S. | METRIC |
|------|--------|------|--------|
| ½ teaspoon | 2.5 ml | 3 cups | 710 ml |
| 1 teaspoon | 5 ml | 4 cups | 946 ml |
| 2 teaspoons | 10 ml | 1 pint | 473 ml |
| 3 teaspoons | 15 ml | 2 pints | 946 ml |
| 1 tablespoon | 15 ml | 1 quart | 946 ml |
| 2 tablespoons | 30 ml | 2 quarts | 1.9 liters |
| 3 tablespoons | 44 ml | 3 quarts | 2.8 liters |
| 4 tablespoons | 59 ml | 4 quarts | 3.785 liters |
| ¼ cup | 59 ml | ½ gallon | 1.9 liters |
| ⅓ cup | 79 ml | 1 gallon | 3.785 liters |
| ½ cup | 118 ml | 2 gallons | 7.6 liters |
| ⅔ cup | 158 ml | 3 gallons | 11.4 liters |
| ¾ cup | 177 ml | 4 gallons | 15.1 liters |
| 1 cup | 237 ml | 5 gallons | 18.9 liters |
| 2 cups | 473 ml | 6 gallons | 22.7 liters |

The volume chart is based on the following:

1. 1 U.S. Gallon = 3.785 Liters

2. 1 Gallon = 8 Pints
   8 Pints = 16 Cups
   16 Cups = 256 Tablespoons
   256 Tablespoons = 768 Teaspoons

3. 1 Gallon = 4 Quarts
   1 Quart = 2 Pints
   1 Pint = 2 Cups
   1 Cup = 16 Tablespoons
   1 Tablespoon = 3 Teaspoons

# Ounces and Pounds

| POUNDS | OUNCES | GRAMS(G) OR KILOGRAMS(KG) | POUNDS | OUNCES | GRAMS(G) OR KILOGRAMS(KG) |
|---|---|---|---|---|---|
| 0 | 0 | 0 | 2 | 1 | 936g |
| 0 | 1/5 | 5.7g | 2 | 2 | 964g |
| 0 | 1/4 | 7.1g | 2 | 3 | 992g |
| 0 | 1/3 | 9.4g | 2 | 4 | 1.02kg |
| 0 | 2/5 | 11.3g | 2 | 5 | 1.05kg |
| 0 | 1/2 | 14.2g | 2 | 6 | 1.08kg |
| 0 | 3/5 | 17.0g | 2 | 7 | 1.11kg |
| 0 | 2/3 | 18.7g | 2 | 8 | 1.13kg |
| 0 | 3/4 | 21.3g | 2 | 9 | 1.16kg |
| 0 | 4/5 | 22.7g | 2 | 10 | 1.19kg |
| 0 | 1 | 28.4g | 2 | 11 | 1.22kg |
| 0 | 2 | 57g | 2 | 12 | 1.25kg |
| 0 | 3 | 85g | 2 | 13 | 1.28kg |
| 0 | 4 | 113g | 2 | 14 | 1.30kg |
| 0 | 5 | 142g | 2 | 15 | 1.33kg |
| 0 | 6 | 170g | 3 | 0 | 1.36kg |
| 0 | 7 | 198g | 3 | 1 | 1.39kg |
| 0 | 8 | 227g | 3 | 2 | 1.42kg |
| 0 | 9 | 255g | 3 | 3 | 1.45kg |
| 0 | 10 | 284g | 3 | 4 | 1.47kg |
| 0 | 11 | 312g | 3 | 5 | 1.50kg |
| 0 | 12 | 340g | 3 | 6 | 1.53kg |
| 0 | 13 | 369g | 3 | 7 | 1.56kg |
| 0 | 14 | 397g | 3 | 8 | 1.59kg |
| 0 | 15 | 425g | 3 | 9 | 1.62kg |
| 1 | 0 | 454g | 3 | 10 | 1.64kg |
| 1 | 1 | 482g | 3 | 11 | 1.67kg |
| 1 | 2 | 510g | 3 | 12 | 1.70kg |
| 1 | 3 | 539g | 3 | 13 | 1.73kg |
| 1 | 4 | 567g | 3 | 14 | 1.76kg |
| 1 | 5 | 595g | 3 | 15 | 1.79kg |
| 1 | 6 | 624g | 4 | 0 | 1.81kg |
| 1 | 7 | 652g | 4 | 1 | 1.84kg |
| 1 | 8 | 680g | 4 | 2 | 1.87kg |
| 1 | 9 | 709g | 4 | 3 | 1.90kg |
| 1 | 10 | 737g | 4 | 4 | 1.93kg |
| 1 | 11 | 765g | 4 | 5 | 1.96kg |
| 1 | 12 | 794g | 4 | 6 | 1.98kg |
| 1 | 13 | 822g | 4 | 7 | 2.01kg |
| 1 | 14 | 851g | 4 | 8 | 2.04kg |
| 1 | 15 | 879g | 4 | 9 | 2.07kg |
| 2 | 0 | 907g | 4 | 10 | 2.10kg |

| POUNDS | OUNCES | GRAMS(G) OR KILOGRAMS(KG) | POUNDS | OUNCES | GRAMS(G) OR KILOGRAMS(KG) |
|---|---|---|---|---|---|
| 4 | 11 | 2.13kg | 6 | 13 | 3.09kg |
| 4 | 12 | 2.15kg | 6 | 14 | 3.12kg |
| 4 | 13 | 2.18kg | 6 | 15 | 3.15kg |
| 4 | 14 | 2.21kg | 7 | 0 | 3.18kg |
| 4 | 15 | 2.24kg | 7 | 1 | 3.20kg |
| 5 | 0 | 2.27kg | 7 | 2 | 3.23kg |
| 5 | 1 | 2.30kg | 7 | 3 | 3.26kg |
| 5 | 2 | 2.32kg | 7 | 4 | 3.29kg |
| 5 | 3 | 2.35kg | 7 | 5 | 3.32kg |
| 5 | 4 | 2.38kg | 7 | 6 | 3.35kg |
| 5 | 5 | 2.41kg | 7 | 7 | 3.37kg |
| 5 | 6 | 2.44kg | 7 | 8 | 3.40kg |
| 5 | 7 | 2.47kg | 7 | 9 | 3.43kg |
| 5 | 8 | 2.49kg | 7 | 10 | 3.46kg |
| 5 | 9 | 2.52kg | 7 | 11 | 3.49kg |
| 5 | 10 | 2.55kg | 7 | 12 | 3.52kg |
| 5 | 11 | 2.58kg | 7 | 13 | 3.54kg |
| 5 | 12 | 2.61kg | 7 | 14 | 3.57kg |
| 5 | 13 | 2.64kg | 7 | 15 | 3.60kg |
| 5 | 14 | 2.66kg | 8 | 0 | 3.63kg |
| 5 | 15 | 2.69kg | 8 | 1 | 3.66kg |
| 6 | 0 | 2.72kg | 8 | 2 | 3.69kg |
| 6 | 1 | 2.75kg | 8 | 3 | 3.71kg |
| 6 | 2 | 2.78kg | 8 | 4 | 3.74kg |
| 6 | 3 | 2.81kg | 8 | 5 | 3.77kg |
| 6 | 4 | 2.84kg | 8 | 6 | 3.80kg |
| 6 | 5 | 2.86kg | 8 | 7 | 3.83kg |
| 6 | 6 | 2.89kg | 8 | 8 | 3.86kg |
| 6 | 7 | 2.92kg | 8 | 9 | 3.88kg |
| 6 | 8 | 2.95kg | 8 | 10 | 3.91kg |
| 6 | 9 | 2.98kg | 8 | 11 | 3.94kg |
| 6 | 10 | 3.01kg | 8 | 12 | 3.97kg |
| 6 | 11 | 3.03kg | 8 | 13 | 4.00kg |
| 6 | 12 | 3.06kg | 8 | 14 | 4.03kg |
|  |  |  | 8 | 15 | 4.05kg |

# *Tenths of a Pound*

| POUNDS | OUNCES | GRAMS(G) OR KILOGRAMS(KG) | POUNDS | OUNCES | GRAMS(G) OR KILOGRAMS(KG) |
|---|---|---|---|---|---|
| 0 | 0 | 0 | 4 | 5 | 2.04kg |
| 0 | 1 | 45.36g | 4 | 6 | 2.09kg |
| 0 | 2 | 91g | 4 | 7 | 2.13kg |
| 0 | 3 | 136g | 4 | 8 | 2.18kg |
| 0 | 4 | 181g | 4 | 9 | 2.22kg |
| 0 | 5 | 227g | 5 | 0 | 2.27kg |
| 0 | 6 | 272g | 5 | 1 | 2.31kg |
| 0 | 7 | 318g | 5 | 2 | 2.36kg |
| 0 | 8 | 363g | 5 | 3 | 2.40kg |
| 0 | 9 | 408g | 5 | 4 | 2.45kg |
| 1 | 0 | 454g | 5 | 5 | 2.49kg |
| 1 | 1 | 499g | 5 | 6 | 2.54kg |
| 1 | 2 | 544g | 5 | 7 | 2.59kg |
| 1 | 3 | 590g | 5 | 8 | 2.63kg |
| 1 | 4 | 635g | 5 | 9 | 2.68kg |
| 1 | 5 | 680g | 6 | 0 | 2.72kg |
| 1 | 6 | 726g | 6 | 1 | 2.77kg |
| 1 | 7 | 771g | 6 | 2 | 2.81kg |
| 1 | 8 | 816g | 6 | 3 | 2.86kg |
| 1 | 9 | 862g | 6 | 4 | 2.90kg |
| 2 | 0 | 907g | 6 | 5 | 2.95kg |
| 2 | 1 | 953g | 6 | 6 | 2.99kg |
| 2 | 2 | 998g | 6 | 7 | 3.04kg |
| 2 | 3 | 1.04kg | 6 | 8 | 3.08kg |
| 2 | 4 | 1.08kg | 6 | 9 | 3.13kg |
| 2 | 5 | 1.13kg | 7 | 0 | 3.18kg |
| 2 | 6 | 1.18kg | 7 | 1 | 3.22kg |
| 2 | 7 | 1.22kg | 7 | 2 | 3.27kg |
| 2 | 8 | 1.27kg | 7 | 3 | 3.31kg |
| 2 | 9 | 1.32kg | 7 | 4 | 3.36kg |
| 3 | 0 | 1.36kg | 7 | 5 | 3.40kg |
| 3 | 1 | 1.41kg | 7 | 6 | 3.45kg |
| 3 | 2 | 1.45kg | 7 | 7 | 3.49kg |
| 3 | 3 | 1.50kg | 7 | 8 | 3.54kg |
| 3 | 4 | 1.54kg | 7 | 9 | 3.58kg |
| 3 | 5 | 1.59kg | 8 | 0 | 3.63kg |
| 3 | 6 | 1.63kg | 8 | 1 | 3.67kg |
| 3 | 7 | 1.68kg | 8 | 2 | 3.72kg |
| 3 | 8 | 1.72kg | 8 | 3 | 3.76kg |
| 3 | 9 | 1.77kg | 8 | 4 | 3.81kg |
| 4 | 0 | 1.81kg | 8 | 5 | 3.86kg |
| 4 | 1 | 1.86kg | 8 | 6 | 3.90kg |
| 4 | 2 | 1.91kg | 8 | 7 | 3.85kg |
| 4 | 3 | 1.95kg | 8 | 8 | 3.99kg |
| 4 | 4 | 2.00kg | 8 | 9 | 4.04kg |

# *Temperature*

| U.S. | METRIC |
|------|--------|
| 212° Farenheit | 100° Celsius |
| 170° Farenheit | 77° Celsius |
| 154° Farenheit | 68° Celsius |
| 122° Farenheit | 50° Celsius |
| 80° Farenheit | 27° Celsius |
| 60° Farenheit | 16° Celsius |
| 32° Farenheit | 0° Celsius |

$$C = \tfrac{5}{9}(F - 32)$$
$$F = (\tfrac{9}{5} \times C) + 32$$

# Carbonation Chart

## POUNDS PER SQUARE INCH

| | 1 | 2 | 3 | 4 | 5 | 6 | 7 | 8 | 9 | 10 | 11 | 12 | 13 | 14 | 15 |
|---|---|---|---|---|---|---|---|---|---|---|---|---|---|---|---|
| 30 | 1.82 | 1.92 | 2.03 | 2.14 | 2.23 | 2.36 | 2.48 | 2.60 | 2.70 | 2.82 | 2.93 | 3.02 | | | |
| 31 | 1.78 | 1.88 | 2.00 | 2.10 | 2.20 | 2.31 | 2.42 | 2.54 | 2.65 | 2.76 | 2.86 | 2.96 | | | |
| 32 | 1.75 | 1.85 | 1.95 | 2.05 | 2.16 | 2.27 | 2.38 | 2.48 | 2.59 | 2.70 | 2.80 | 2.90 | 3.01 | | |
| 33 | | 1.81 | 1.91 | 2.01 | 2.12 | 2.23 | 2.33 | 2.43 | 2.53 | 2.63 | 2.74 | 2.84 | 2.96 | | |
| 34 | | 1.78 | 1.86 | 1.97 | 2.07 | 2.18 | 2.28 | 2.38 | 2.48 | 2.58 | 2.68 | 2.79 | 2.89 | 3.00 | |
| 35 | | | 1.83 | 1.93 | 2.03 | 2.14 | 2.24 | 2.34 | 2.43 | 2.52 | 2.62 | 2.73 | 2.83 | 2.93 | 3.02 |
| 36 | | | 1.79 | 1.88 | 1.99 | 2.09 | 2.20 | 2.29 | 2.39 | 2.47 | 2.57 | 2.67 | 2.77 | 2.86 | 2.96 |
| 37 | | | | 1.84 | 1.94 | 2.04 | 2.15 | 2.24 | 2.34 | 2.42 | 2.52 | 2.62 | 2.72 | 2.80 | 2.90 |
| 38 | | | | 1.80 | 1.90 | 2.00 | 2.10 | 2.20 | 2.29 | 2.38 | 2.47 | 2.57 | 2.67 | 2.75 | 2.85 |
| 39 | | | | | 1.86 | 1.96 | 2.05 | 2.15 | 2.25 | 2.34 | 2.43 | 2.52 | 2.61 | 2.70 | 2.80 |
| 40 | | | | | 1.82 | 1.92 | 2.01 | 2.10 | 2.20 | 2.30 | 2.39 | 2.47 | 2.56 | 2.65 | 2.75 |
| 41 | | | | | | 1.87 | 1.97 | 2.06 | 2.16 | 2.25 | 2.35 | 2.43 | 2.52 | 2.60 | 2.70 |
| 42 | | | | | | 1.83 | 1.93 | 2.02 | 2.12 | 2.21 | 2.30 | 2.39 | 2.47 | 2.56 | 2.65 |
| 43 | | | | | | 1.80 | 1.90 | 1.99 | 2.08 | 2.17 | 2.25 | 2.34 | 2.43 | 2.52 | 2.60 |
| 44 | | | | | | | 1.86 | 1.95 | 2.04 | 2.13 | 2.21 | 2.30 | 2.39 | 2.47 | 2.56 |
| 45 | | | | | | | 1.82 | 1.91 | 2.00 | 2.08 | 2.17 | 2.26 | 2.34 | 2.42 | 2.51 |
| 46 | | | | | | | | 1.88 | 1.96 | 2.04 | 2.13 | 2.22 | 2.30 | 2.38 | 2.47 |
| 47 | | | | | | | | 1.84 | 1.92 | 2.00 | 2.09 | 2.18 | 2.25 | 2.34 | 2.42 |
| 48 | | | | | | | | 1.80 | 1.88 | 1.96 | 2.05 | 2.14 | 2.21 | 2.30 | 2.38 |
| 49 | | | | | | | | | 1.85 | 1.93 | 2.01 | 2.10 | 2.18 | 2.25 | 2.34 |
| 50 | | | | | | | | | 1.82 | 1.90 | 1.98 | 2.06 | 2.14 | 2.21 | 2.30 |
| 51 | | | | | | | | | | 1.87 | 1.95 | 2.02 | 2.10 | 2.18 | 2.25 |
| 52 | | | | | | | | | | 1.84 | 1.91 | 1.99 | 2.06 | 2.14 | 2.22 |
| 53 | | | | | | | | | | 1.80 | 1.88 | 1.96 | 2.03 | 2.10 | 2.18 |
| 54 | | | | | | | | | | | 1.85 | 1.93 | 2.00 | 2.07 | 2.15 |
| 55 | | | | | | | | | | | 1.82 | 1.89 | 1.97 | 2.04 | 2.11 |
| 56 | | | | | | | | | | | | 1.86 | 1.93 | 2.00 | 2.07 |
| 57 | | | | | | | | | | | | 1.83 | 1.90 | 1.97 | 2.04 |
| 58 | | | | | | | | | | | | 1.80 | 1.86 | 1.94 | 2.00 |
| 59 | | | | | | | | | | | | | 1.83 | 1.90 | 1.97 |
| 60 | | | | | | | | | | | | | 1.80 | 1.87 | 1.94 |

TEMPERATURE OF BEER (DEGREES F.)

**To Use This Chart:** First find the temperature of your beer in the outside columns. Look across until you reach the carbonation level desired. Then look up to the top of that column to find the required pressure and set your regulator accordingly.

This chart was adapted from one provided courtesy of Byron Burch, Great Fermentations of Santa Rosa, 840 Piner Road, #14, Santa Rosa, CA 95403. Used with permission.

# Carbonation Chart

## POUNDS PER SQUARE INCH

| 16 | 17 | 18 | 19 | 20 | 21 | 22 | 23 | 24 | 25 | 26 | 27 | 28 | 29 | 30 | Temp (°F) |
|---|---|---|---|---|---|---|---|---|---|---|---|---|---|---|---|
| | | | | | | | | | | | | | | | 30 |
| | | | | | | | | | | | | | | | 31 |
| | | | | | | | | | | | | | | | 32 |
| | | | | | | | | | | | | | | | 33 |
| | | | | | | | | | | | | | | | 34 |
| | | | | | | | | | | | | | | | 35 |
| | | | | | | | | | | | | | | | 36 |
| 3.00 | | | | | | | | | | | | | | | 37 |
| 2.94 | | | | | | | | | | | | | | | 38 |
| 2.89 | 2.98 | | | | | | | | | | | | | | 39 |
| 2.84 | 2.93 | 3.01 | | | | | | | | | | | | | 40 |
| 2.79 | 2.87 | 2.96 | | | | | | | | | | | | | 41 |
| 2.74 | 2.82 | 2.91 | 3.00 | | | | | | | | | | | | 42 |
| 2.69 | 2.78 | 2.86 | 2.95 | | | | | | | | | | | | 43 |
| 2.64 | 2.73 | 2.81 | 2.90 | 2.99 | | | | | | | | | | | 44 |
| 2.60 | 2.68 | 2.77 | 2.85 | 2.94 | 3.02 | | | | | | | | | | 45 |
| 2.55 | 2.63 | 2.72 | 2.80 | 2.89 | 2.98 | | | | | | | | | | 46 |
| 2.50 | 2.59 | 2.67 | 2.75 | 2.84 | 2.93 | 3.02 | | | | | | | | | 47 |
| 2.46 | 2.55 | 2.62 | 2.70 | 2.79 | 2.87 | 2.96 | | | | | | | | | 48 |
| 2.42 | 2.50 | 2.58 | 2.66 | 2.75 | 2.83 | 2.91 | 2.99 | | | | | | | | 49 |
| 2.38 | 2.45 | 2.54 | 2.62 | 2.70 | 2.78 | 2.86 | 2.94 | 3.02 | | | | | | | 50 |
| 2.34 | 2.41 | 2.49 | 2.57 | 2.65 | 2.73 | 2.81 | 2.89 | 2.97 | | | | | | | 51 |
| 2.30 | 2.37 | 2.45 | 2.54 | 2.61 | 2.69 | 2.76 | 2.84 | 2.93 | 3.00 | | | | | | 52 |
| 2.26 | 2.33 | 2.41 | 2.48 | 2.57 | 2.64 | 2.72 | 2.80 | 2.88 | 2.95 | 3.03 | | | | | 53 |
| 2.22 | 2.29 | 2.37 | 2.44 | 2.52 | 2.60 | 2.67 | 2.75 | 2.83 | 2.90 | 2.98 | | | | | 54 |
| 2.19 | 2.25 | 2.33 | 2.40 | 2.47 | 2.55 | 2.63 | 2.70 | 2.78 | 2.85 | 2.93 | 3.01 | | | | 55 |
| 2.15 | 2.21 | 2.29 | 2.36 | 2.43 | 2.50 | 2.58 | 2.65 | 2.73 | 2.80 | 2.88 | 2.96 | | | | 56 |
| 2.11 | 2.18 | 2.25 | 2.33 | 2.40 | 2.47 | 2.54 | 2.61 | 2.69 | 2.76 | 2.84 | 2.91 | 2.99 | | | 57 |
| 2.07 | 2.14 | 2.21 | 2.29 | 2.36 | 2.43 | 2.50 | 2.57 | 2.64 | 2.72 | 2.80 | 2.86 | 2.94 | 3.01 | | 58 |
| 2.04 | 2.11 | 2.18 | 2.25 | 2.32 | 2.39 | 2.46 | 2.53 | 2.60 | 2.67 | 2.75 | 2.81 | 2.89 | 2.96 | 3.03 | 59 |
| 2.01 | 2.08 | 2.14 | 2.21 | 2.28 | 2.35 | 2.42 | 2.49 | 2.56 | 2.63 | 2.70 | 2.77 | 2.84 | 2.91 | 2.98 | 60 |

TEMPERATURE OF BEER (DEGREES F.)

The numbers in the grid express the volumes of carbon dioxide ($CO_2$); a liter of beer containing three liters of $CO_2$ (at standard temperature and pressure) is said to contain 3 volumes of $CO_2$. Suggested carbonation rates for various styles of beer can be found on page 117.

# Sources

**M**y publisher tells me that the number one response to my earlier book, *The Complete Handbook of Home Brewing*, has been, "Where do I get these things?" — meaning, the special brewing equipment and ingredients that homebrewers need. There are a number of ways to track down suppliers for these items.

The best place to start is your local Yellow Pages, which probably has a listing under "Brewing Supplies" or "Winemaking Supplies." Your local shop is the place you should deal with first. These days, most homebrew supply shops are operated by knowledgeable, experienced homebrewers, and they will carry most of the things you need in stock. Some more exotic items — for example, a particular strain of yeast used only for a certain style of Belgian ale — may have to be special ordered.

A good local shop is your best source of equipment and ingredients. They have the most to gain by serving you well. Unfortunately, there are still some shops where the owners seem either to not know or not care about all the strides homebrewing has made in the last ten years. It is easy to identify these places by their obviously old stock, poor storage practices (e.g., unrefrigerated hops), and recipes that still call for three pounds of corn sugar and one can of malt extract. If the only shop in your vicinity fits into this category, you will have to look elsewhere.

One of the best sources of information on shops is a local homebrewing club. Most metropolitan areas now have one or more. These experienced homebrewers will be glad to share their experiences, positive and negative, with different suppliers. One way to find out about a local club is through your local supplier. In addition, the American Homebrewers Association has a list of all the clubs in the country that are registered with them, and they will gladly tell you if there is a registered club in your area. American Homebrewers Association, PO Box 1679, Boulder, CO 80306, 303-447-0816.

One of the unfortunate facts about the homebrew scene is that areas served (or disserved) by a poor shop usually do not have a thriving homebrew club. The two things — shop and club — go together, and each one supplies an impetus for the other. For example, the greater Dallas area boasts several topnotch, progressive, homebrew suppliers, and, not coincidentally, four homebrewing clubs, all active and enthusiastic.

If your area is not fortunate enough to resemble Dallas–Fort Worth, and you cannot find even one good supply shop or club in your area, you will have to summon up an extra measure of old-fashioned American enterprise and track down or scrounge up the things you need for yourself. If this is your fate, don't be bitter. You are a pioneer, and one day you (and your friends, who will increase in number as word gets around about your homebrew) will form the nucleus of the club you cannot find.

You can start your search by subscribing to *Zymurgy*, the magazine of the American Homebrewers Association. Along with lots of information, the magazine has many advertisements for mail-order dealers and manufacturers of special advanced equipment. To subscribe to *Zymurgy*, call the American Homebrewers Association.

There are other magazines that also cater to homebrewers and beer enthusiasts. The advanced, technical side is well covered by *Brewing Techniques*. This magazine often features articles on fabrication of equipment and other topics of great interest to homebrewers. (You can subscribe by calling 800-427-2993. They can also be reached at PO Box 3222, Eugene, OR 97403, or by e-mail: btcirc@aol.com.) *Brewing Techniques* also features ads for equipment and ingredients suppliers.

Magazines aimed at beer enthusiasts, such as *All About Beer* and *Beer: the magazine*, also carry ads for homebrew suppliers.

However, the various craft-beer newsletters, such as *Southern Draft* and *The Celebrator*, though they focus primarily on micro- and pub breweries, also carry ads and articles about home-brewing, and the ads are often more useful because they feature shops in a particular part of the country. These publications have the great advantage of being given away free at many brewpubs, and sometimes at other places such as stores that carry a good selection of microbrewed beer.

Another, relatively new source of information is the beer and wine forums now available on most of the major online computer services. These forums do not carry ads, of course, but a specific question (for example: "I live in Rochester, Minnesota, and I'm just getting started in homebrewing. Any info or advice on shops and/or clubs in my area?") will usually draw a number of replies from experienced people. Especially for those who live in sparsely populated areas, the online services can be an excellent way to connect with the huge and growing homebrewing movement.

As a last resort, you can contact the Home Wine and Beer Trade Association, the national trade association for winemaking and homebrewing supply shops. The secretary of the association, Dee Roberson, maintains a database listing all the member shops. She can provide you with the names, addresses, and phone numbers of several suppliers in your area. Send a self-addressed, stamped envelope to:

> Dee Roberson, Executive Secretary
> Home Wine and Beer Trade Association
> 604 North Miller Road
> Valrico, FL 33594
>
> Phone 813-685-4261
> Fax 813-681-5625

To summarize, then, these are my recommendations for finding good sources for equipment and ingredients:

1. Check your Yellow Pages to see if there is a home wine and beer supplier in your area. If so, try them out.
2. Find out if there is a nearby club. If so, join it.
3. Check the ads in *Zymurgy, Brewing Techniques,* and other beer and brewing-related publications.
4. If you have a computer with a modem, check out the homebrewing forums on the various online services.
5. Contact the Home Wine and Beer Trade Association (HWBTA).

One point to keep in mind when shopping by mail is that malt and malt extract are very heavy. Shipping costs can be a large part of the total bill. A local supplier may be cheaper even if their prices are not as low as a mail-order firm.

# Glossary

*Acidification.* The process of lowering the pH of a solution until it falls below 7.0 pH.

*Acrospire.* The embryonic barley plant that grows inside the husk during germination.

*Adjunct.* Unmalted grain used in making beer; its starch must be converted to sugar by malt enzymes in the mash kettle.

*Adsorb.* To collect a substance on a surface; for example, protein molecules are adsorbed onto the surface of particles of silica gel.

*Aerate.* To dissolve air in a liquid.

*Albumins.* The name for a group of water soluble proteins that coagulate when heated.

*Alpha Acid.* The soft, bitter hop resin that is responsible for the bitterness of beer. Measured as a percentage of the total weight of the hop cone.

*Alpha Acid Content.* The percentage of alpha acid in the hop cone.

*Alpha Acid Units (AAU).* The percentage of alpha acid in a given sample of hops multiplied by the weight in ounces of that sample. One ounce of hops with an alpha content of 1 percent contains 1 AAU, or .01 ounce of alpha acid.

*Alpha Amylase.* A diastatic enzyme produced by malting barley. Attacks the 1-4 links of straight chains.

*Amylase.* Any enzyme that breaks the bonds that hold starch molecules together.

*Amylopectins.* The branched chain fraction of starch. Barley contains approximately 73 percent amylopectin and 27 percent amylose.

*Amylose.* Starch. Starch molecules are made up of long strings of glucose or other sugar molecules.

*Amyloses.* The straight-chain fraction of starch. Barley contains approximately 27 percent amylose and 73 percent amylopectin.

*Aroma Hops.* Hops used primarily to impart aroma, as opposed to bitterness, to beer.

*Aromatic Hops.* Hop varieties known for their fine aroma and flavoring properties; also called "noble hops."

*Attenuation.* The drop in specific gravity that takes place as the wort ferments.

*Autolysis.* A process in which starving yeast cells feed on each other by excreting enzymes; causes a rubbery stench in beer.

*Beta Acid.* A soft, bitter hop resin; harsher in flavor than alpha acid but almost insoluble at normal wort pH values.

*Beta Amylase.* A diastatic enzyme produced by malting barley. Attacks the 1-4 links of straight chains.

*Beta Glucanase.* An enzyme that breaks the 1-3 links that hold branched starch molecules together.

*Bittering Hops.* (1) Hops used to add bitterness, but not aroma, to beer. (2) Hop varieties of high alpha acid content, bred for this purpose.

*Body.* The sensation of fullness or viscosity in the mouth, imparted by malt dextrins and proteins in beer.

*Boiling.* The step in brewing at which hops are added and the wort is bittered.

*Brewing.* The craft and science of making beer.

*Bright Beer Tanks.* Storage tanks for the clarified final beer.

*Calcium.* An ion that lowers mash/wort pH.

*Cane Sugar.* Sucrose obtained from sugar cane.

*Carbon Filtration.* In homebrewing, the dechlorination of a water source by use of a carbon filter.

*Carbonate.* To inject or dissolve carbon dioxide gas in beer.

*Carbonation.* (1) Carbon dioxide gas dissolved in a liquid. 2) The process of dissolving carbon dioxide gas in a liquid.

*Chloride.* An ion that imparts a sweet finish to beer.

*Chlorine.* Can be used as a sterilizing agent in homebrewing. Also used as a gas added to water supplies to kill bacteria.

*Cistern.* A vat in which brewers' grain is soaked.

*Cold Break.* The flocculation of protein and tannin molecules during wort cooling.

*Conditioning.* The process of carbonating beer.

*Copper.* An ion that is a vital yeast nutrient at low levels but that can poison yeast at high levels.

*Couch.* A term that refer to a heap of barley on the malting floor.

*Curing.* The last step in floor malting, when the grain is heated to fully develop flavor and color.

*Decarbonate.* To remove carbonate and bicarbonate ions from water, either by boiling or by adding chemicals.

*Decoction.* A method of mashing that boosts the temperature from one step to the next by removing a portion of the mash, boiling it, and returning it to the main kettle.

*Degrees of Extract.* A measure of *yield* used by homebrewers: the specific gravity of one gallon of wort made from one pound of malt.

*Dextrinase.* An amylolytic enzyme that breaks down the 1-6 bonds that hold dextrins together.

*Diacetyl.* A powerful aromatic compound that imparts the flavor of butter or butterscotch to beer.

*Diastase.* A collective term for all the amylase enzymes in malt.

*Diastatic Power.* A measure of the total amylase content of a given sample of malt; usually expressed in degrees Lintner.

*Dimethyl Sulfide (DMS).* A powerful aromatic compound that imparts a sweet creamed-corn smell to lager mashes. In finished beer it imparts a malty quality or, at higher levels, the taste of cooked vegetables.

*Dissociates.* Ionizes.

*Distillation.* Removes all ions from water.

*Draff.* The solid matter remaining in the mash tun after the malt starch has been converted to sugar.

*Endosperm.* The nonliving part of the barley grain, which contains starch and protein to feed the growing acrospire.

*Enzyme.* A complex protein that has the ability to form or break a particular chemical bond.

*Esters.* A class of compounds formed by joining an alcohol and an acid; many have powerful fruity aromas.

*Extract.* (1) Malt extract. (2) The sugar derived from malt during the mashing process.

*Fatty Acids.* Acids based on a string of carbon atoms; they often have unpleasant flavors.

*Fermentation.* A process in which yeast obtains energy in the absence of oxygen by breaking sugar into carbon dioxide and alcohol.

*Fermenter.* A generic term for any open or closed vessel in which primary and/or secondary fermentation take place.

*Fines.* The finely crushed, flourlike portion of the draff.

*Flocculation.* The clumping together of protein molecules or yeast cells to form relatively large, irregularly shaped particles.

*Flocculence.* The clumping of yeast cells into masses toward the end of the fermentation process. When the yeast flocculates, it contributes to the clarification of the beer.

*Floor Malting.* A traditional germination method that calls for the steeped barley to be spread over a flat surface in order to germinate for approximately 13 days.

*Fluoride.* An ion sometimes added to drinking water in communities across the United States but which has little or no effect on the outcome of beer brewed with that water.

*Fusel Alcohol.* Any alcohol of higher molecular weight than ethanol (drinking alcohol). Fusel alcohols impart a harsh, clinging bitterness.

*Gelatinization.* The process in which particles of starch break up and disperse in hot water to form a thick suspension.

*Globulins.* Large protein molecules that are insoluble.

*Grain Sugars.* Sugar products derived from grain, intended for use as adjunct equivalents for extract-based beers.

*Grist.* The crushed malts and adjuncts that are mixed with hot water to form the mash.

*Heat Exchanger.* A piece of brewing equipment used for heating or cooling the wort or beer rapidly.

*High Alpha Hops.* Hops bred to be high in alpha acid or humulone, the soft resin that is the main contributor in bittering beer. See also *Bittering Hops* (2).

*Hop Oil.* A mixture of volatile aromatic compounds found in the lupulin glands of the hops; imparts hop flavor and aroma to beer.

*Hops.* The flowers (or cones) of the female hop plant, used in brewing.

*Hot Break.* The flocculation of protein and tannin molecules during boiling.

*Hot Side Aeration.* Aerating wort on the hot side of the brewing process; leads to oxidation of the finished beer.

*Humulone.* The soft resin that is largely responsible for the bittering of beer. See also *Alpha Acid.*

*Hydrocarbon.* Any compound made up entirely of carbon and hydrogen atoms.

*Hydrolysis.* The process of breaking peptide or other bonds using a water molecule.

*Infusion.* A mashing method in which grain is mixed with hot water and the mixture is not boiled. See also *Single Infusion, Step Infusion.*

*International Bitterness Units (IBU).* A measure of the actual bitterness level of beer. 1 IBU = 1 part per million of isomerized alpha acid.

*Ion.* An atom or bound group of atoms that carries an electrical charge. Water contains ions that affect enzyme activity in the mash, and others that affect beer flavor.

*Iron.* An ion that causes haze and hampers yeast.

*Isomerize.* To alter the arrangement — but not the kind or number — of atoms in a compound by heating or other means. During boiling, alpha acids are isomerized and these isomers (iso-alpha acids) bitter the finished beer.

*Kettle.* A large vessel, similar in shape to a mash tun, usually made of copper or stainless steel in which the wort is heated. Also called a "brew kettle."

*Kiln.* A large furnace with a perforated floor heated by either fire or heaters through which malt is dried and roasted.

*Kraeusen.* (German, literally "crown.") (1) The large head of foam that forms on the surface of the wort during the early stages of fermentation. (2) A method of carbonation in which green beer in the kraeusen stage is added to finished beer to bring about a second fermentation.

*Lager.* (1) To store beer at low temperatures for a period of weeks or months prior to consumption. (2) Beer that has been lagered.

*Lauter Tun.* A large vessel with a perforated false bottom. It is used to strain the sweet wort off the spent grains after mashing.

*Lead.* An ion that causes haze and is toxic.

*Lovibond.* The scale on which malt, wort, and beer color are usually measured.

*Lupulin Glands.* The tiny yellow sacs found at the base of the petals of the hop cone. They contain the alpha acids, beta acids, and hop oils.

*Lupulone.* See *Beta Acid.*

*Magnesium.* An ion that lowers mash and wort pH but also implants a clinging "bite" to the finished beer.

*Malt.* Barley or other grain that has been malted.

*Malt Extract.* Sweet wort that has been concentrated into a thick syrup or dry powder by removing most or all of the water, and packaged for use by homebrewers.

*Malting.* The process of soaking, sprouting, and then drying barley (or other grain) to develop its enzyme content and render it suitable for mashing.

*Malto-Dextrin.* A general name for unfermentable soluble carbohydrates formed by the diastatic hydrolysis of malt starch.

*Manganese.* An ion important in trace amounts for proper enzyme action in the mash. Large quantities impart a metallic taste to beer.

*Mash.* (1) To mix a grist with hot water, and allow the malt enzymes to convert the grain starch to sugar. (2) The mixture itself.

*Mashing-In.* The initial stage of mashing; the process of mixing grist and water.

*Mealy.* A chewy characteristic of the grain, which is attained only when malt is fully modified. Maltsters use the bite test as means to test malt for full modification. If the grain is mealy, it is considered to be fully modified.

*Mild Ale Malt.* British malts kilned at high temperatures that produce beers of golden and amber colors. Used specifically in the production of mild ales.

*Modification.* The sum of the changes that take place in the barley grain during germination (sprouting). Chief among these are the softening of the endosperm and the development of enzymes.

*Mouthfeel.* See *Body.*

*Naturally Conditioned.* Carbonated by a second fermentation in the bottle or cask.

*Nickel.* An ion that causes foaming in beer.

*Nitrate.* An ion that, while harmless in itself, can be reduced to nitrite by certain "wort spoiler" bacteria.

*Nitrite.* An ion that interferes with yeast metabolism.

*Nitrogen Content.* The percentage of the weight of barley or malt that is nitrogen. Protein content of the grain is about 6.25 times the nitrogen content.

*Noble Hops.* See *Aromatic Hops.*

*Original Gravity.* The specific gravity of a wort prior to fermentation.

*Oxidation.* Any chemical reaction in which oxygen combines with another substance. Oxidation of finished beer produces unpleasant flavors.

*Palate Fullness.* See *Body.*

*Pale Ale Malt.* Considered to be the standard British malts used specifically in the production of pale ales.

*Pelletized Hops.* Hops that have been dried, powdered, and pressed into pellets.

*Peptones.* Soluble proteins of moderate size, intermediate between polypeptides and albumins.

*pH.* The measure of acidity or alkalinity; 7 is the neutral point of the scale, with lower values being acid and higher values alkaline.

*Phenolic.* Any compound based on a ring of six carbon atoms joined by alternating single and double bonds. The tannins contained in grain husks are phenolic in nature, as are the soft hop resins (alpha and beta acids).

*Phytase.* An enzyme common in malt, and most active at 80 to 128 degrees. It breaks down phytin into phytic acid.

*Phytin.* A complex organic phosphate containing both calcium and magnesium. Pale lager malt is rich in phytin.

*Piece.* Refers to the volume of germinating barley.

*Pitch.* To add yeast to a cooled wort.

*Polymerize.* To link together, as in the polymerization of tannins.

*Polypeptides.* Small soluble proteins consisting of a few amino acids linked together.

*Polyphenols.* Complex compounds based on two or more phenolic rings joined together. The malt tannins derived from the husk are more properly termed polyphenols.

*Potassium.* An ion that at high concentrations inhibits certain enzymes in the mash.

*Priming.* Adding sugar to a finished beer in order to produce carbonation by a second fermentation in the bottle or cask.

*Protein Content.* The percentage of the malt grain that is protein. Also see *Nitrogen Content.*

*Proteolysis.* Protein breakdown. The hydrolysis of a protein molecule into amino acids by proteolytic enzymes.

*Proteolytic Enzyme.* An enzyme that hydrolyzes complex proteins into simpler soluble proteins.

*Rack.* To transfer wort or beer from one container to another in order to separate it from the sediment on the bottom of the first container.

*Recirculation.* The action of pumping the wort from the bottom of the mash tun and letting it fall into the surface of the mash. Also called the "Vorlauf."

*Respiration.* The process in which living things oxidize sugar in order to obtain energy.

*Rouse.* To make a yeast starter using sterile wort and ⅓ to ¼ of the normal pitching slurry.

*Saccharomyces Carlsbergensis.* Commonly known as "lager yeast."

*Saccharomyces Cerevisiae.* Commonly known as "ale yeast."

*Salt.* The common name for sodium chloride, or table salt. In brewing terms, any compound produced by the reaction of an acid with an alkali.

*Sanitary.* Clean and practically free of microbes, so that it poses no danger of infecting something that comes into contact with it.

*Silicate.* An ion that causes haze.

*Single Infusion.* More properly, single temperature infusion; the classic British method in which the mash is mixed and held at a single temperature until starch conversion is complete.

*Six-Row Brewers' Malt.* A variety of barley having three rows of fertile spikes at each node, on which six rows of grains are formed. Less developed than 2-row barley, it yields less extract.

*Sodium.* An ion found in water that has little or no chemical effect on beer, although it can create unpleasant flavors.

*Sparging.* (1) Rinsing the draff with hot water in the lauter tun in order to recover the sugar it holds. (2) The entire process of obtaining clear sweet wort from the mash, including runoff, recirculation, and rinsing.

*Specialty Malt.* A term used to describe malts other than the standard brewers' malts. Usually used in very small quantities to impart flavor and sometimes color to the final product.

*Specific Gravity.* The weight of a liquid compared with an equal amount of pure water. The scale is absolute, that is, a specific gravity of 1.050 means the liquid weighs 1.05 times as much as an equal amount of water.

*Standard Mash.* A mash made in a brewer's laboratory using specified amounts of water and malt.

*Starter.* A small volume of wort to which yeast is added, in order to activate it before it is pitched into the main batch.

*Steely.* In malting, a description used for the hard endosperm of the grain at the onset of germination.

*Steeping.* The action of soaking hard dry barley grains in water in order to soften them. Steeping is best accomplished in stages separated by air rests.

*Step Infusion.* A method of mashing in which several temperature rests are attained by directly heating the mash kettle. See also *Decoction.*

*Sterile.* Totally devoid of life. A more rigid term than sanitary.

*Stewing.* A process used by maltsters to create specialty caramelized malts.

*Strike Heat.* The temperature of the mash water before the grist is mixed into it.

*Style.* The whole sum of flavor and other sensory characteristics by which individual beers may be placed in categories for purposes of comparison. Beers of the same style have the same general flavor profile.

*Sulfate.* An ion that imparts a sharp "dry" edge to beers.

*Tannins.* See *Polyphenols.*

*Terminal Gravity.* The specific gravity of a beer after fermentation is complete.

*Tin.* An ion that causes haze.

*Titration.* A measurement that gives brewers the total acid content of a solution.

*Total Acidity.* The measure of the actual amount of acid in a given volume of water. It is found by titration.

*Total Alkalinity.* The measure of the actual amount of alkali in a given volume of water.

*Trub.* The sediment formed by the hot and cold break on the bottom of the kettle (hot trub) or the cooling or fermenting vessel (cold trub).

*Two-Row Brewers' Malt.* A variety of barley on which only the central piece of each triad is fertile, forming two rows of grains each.

*Underletting.* Filling the space beneath the false bottom of the lauter tun with hot water before putting in the mash.

*Vicinal Diketones (VDK).* Pentanedione and diacetyl, two closely related fermentation by-products with strong aromas. See also *Diacetyl.*

*Volatile.* Capable of vaporizing at low temperatures.

*Whirlpool.* A piece of equipment used for the clarification of beer, usually consisting of a large cylindrical tank. The wort is introduced at high speed through a pipe. As the wort comes into the tank, the trub or hot break deposits as a cone at the bottom by a process of sedimentation.

*Whole (Leaf) Hops.* Hops that have been dried and compressed but retain their natural form.

*Wild Yeast.* Any yeast strain that is not deliberately selected and introduced into the beer by the brewer.

*Wort.* The solution of malt sugars, proteins, and other substances that is produced by mashing.

*Wort Chiller.* A piece of equipment used to cool the wort rapidly.

*Yeast.* A single-celled fungus capable of fermentation.

*Yield.* The percentage by weight of the malt that will be converted into soluble substances (chiefly sugars) in the mash kettle. Determined by making a standard mash.

*Zinc.* An ion that is a yeast nutrient but that at high levels gives a metallic taste to beer.

# Annotated Bibliography

## Periodicals

*Brewing Techniques*. Eugene, Oregon: The New Wine Press. Published six times a year, this magazine is aimed at homebrewers and microbrewers, more technical than *Zymurgy* in orientation. Currently features a monthly column on beer styles, plus a Q & A column written by Dave Miller. Contact New Wine Press, PO Box 3222, Eugene, OR 97403-9917; phone 800-427-2993.

*Zymurgy*. Boulder, Colorado: The American Homebrewers Association. This journal is published each season, with a special issue coming out late in the fall devoted to a select topic. These special issues contain many excellent articles on advanced brewing techniques. Back issues are available. A one-year subscription, which includes membership in the AHA, costs $25. Write to: AHA, PO Box 287, Boulder, CO 80306-0287.

## Beer and Beer Styles

*The Beer Styles Series*. Boulder, Colorado: Brewers Publications. An ongoing project that will eventually comprise 15 volumes, each on one of the world's great beer styles. So far, nine volumes have appeared. Contact the AHA at the address given for *Zymurgy*, above.

Eckhardt, Fred. *The Essentials of Beer Style*. Portland, Oregon: Fred Eckhardt Associates, 1989. Eckhardt is one of the founders of the home brewing movement.

Jackson, Michael. *The New World Guide to Beer*. Philadelphia: The Running Press, 1988.

Jackson, Michael. *The 1991 Simon and Schuster Pocket Guide to Beer.* New York: Simon and Schuster, 1991. A British journalist, Jackson is the preeminent authority on the beers and breweries of the world.

# Homebrewing

Burch, Byron. *Brewing Quality Beers.* Fulton, California: Joby Books, 1986. Clear, concise, basic brewing text. Burch is a longtime homebrewing teacher and the driving force behind the Sonoma County Beerocrats, seven-time winners of the club trophy at the national homebrew competition.

Lutzen, Karl F. and Stevens, Mark. *Homebrew Favorites. A Coast-to-Coast Collection of More than 240 Beer and Ale Recipes.* Pownal, Vermont: Storey Publishing, 1994. The most comprehensive homebrewers recipe book available today.

Miller, Dave. *Brewing the World's Great Beers.* Pownal, Vermont: Storey Publishing, 1992. Aimed at beginner and intermediate homebrewers, less technical than this book.

Mosher, Randy. *The Home Brewers Companion.* Seattle, Washington: Alephenalia Press, 1994. A wide-ranging book with information on a host of advanced homebrewing techniques. Especially useful for those seeking to home kiln malts and do other special projects.

Noonan, Greg. *Brewing Lager Beer.* Boulder, Colorado: Brewers Publications, 1986. Focuses on the decoction method of mashing. Excellent for the technically minded. Noonan is an accomplished home- and microbrewer.

Papazian, Charlie. *The Complete Joy of Brewing.* New York: Avon Books, 1983. Papazian is president of the American Homebrewers Association, publisher of *Zymurgy,* and a pioneer of the homebrewing movement.

# Brewing Science

de Clerck, Jean. *A Textbook of Brewing,* 2 vols. Translated by K. Barton-Wright. London: Chapman-Hall Ltd., 1957. Long out of print, this is still a great reference book for home- and microbrewers. The author was probably the greatest brewer of this century. Other textbooks have more up to date scientific information, but this one is still worth seeking out for its author's practical insights.

Fix, George. *Principles of Brewing Science*. Boulder, Colorado: Brewers Publications, 1989. Written by the most respected researcher in the field of small-scale brewing. If you can only read one book on brewing science, this is it.

Hough, Briggs, Stevens, and Young. *Malting and Brewing Science*. 2nd ed., 2 vols. London: Chapman-Hall Ltd., 1981. Very technical; a summation of commercial brewing research from all over the world.

# Yeast

Raines, Maribeth. *Advanced Yeast Culturing for Homebrewers.* Woodland Hills, California: Brewers Resource, 1992. Available as part of the Brewers Resource yeast culturing kit from Brewers Resource, PO Box 507, Woodland Hills, CA 91365. An excellent introduction to yeast-culturing techniques.

# Index

Page references in *italics* refer to illustrations;
those in **bold** refer to charts and tables.

**A**cetaldehyde, 172–73
Acidification, 63
Acidity, 52–53
Acid rest, 85–86
Acrospire, 6, 30–31, *31*
Activated acetic acid, 172, 175
Adenosine triphosphate (ATP), 172
Adjuncts, 45–47
Aeration
    equipment, 156–57, 162–64, *163*
    process, 24, *24*, 180–83
Aerobic bacteria, 280
Agitation, 226
Airlocks, 165
Albumins, 88
Alcohol content, determining, 19
Aldehydes, 178
Alkalinity, 52–53, 54–55, 57–58
Alpha acid content in hops, 115, 120
Alpha acid units (AAUs), 120, 301–2
Alpha amylase, 94
Alpha glucans, 93
Altbier, 314–15
Amber malt, 40
American ales, 293–94
American Brown Ale, 319–20
American Cream Ale, 317–18
American Fruit Ale, 319
American Homebrewers Association,
    274, 289, 335
American Lager, 320–21
American lagers, 13
American Pale Ale, 318
American Porter, 320
Amino acids, 86–88
Amylases, 32, 93–95
Amylopectins, 93, *93*
Amyloses, 93, *93*
Aromas, 270–73
Artificial carbonation
    natural versus, 218–20
    process, 225–27

Attenuation, 143
Autolysis, 159, 177–78, 229, 283–84

**B**acterial infections, 279–81
Barley adjunct, 46
Barley malt, 28
Barley Wine, 314
Barrier filters, 204, 205
Beer Judge Certification Program, 274
Beer styles
    American ales, 293–94
    for beginners, 12–13
    Belgian ales, 291–92
    British ales, 13, 37, 289–90
    German ales, 292–93
    lager beers, 294–96
Belgian ales, 291–92
Belgian Wit, 291, 316–17
Beta acids, 115
Beta amylase, 94
Beta glucanase, 94–95
Beta glucans, 92–93, *93*
Bicarbonate, 57–58
*Big Book of Brewing*, 312
Bitterness
    maintaining levels of, 115, 120
    measuring, 299, 301–2
Black malt/black patent, 41
Bock beers, 296
Body, weak, 286
Boiling/decontamination of water, 60,
    62
Boiling process, 128–33, 135–37
Bottle-conditioned beer, 230–31
    advantages of, 245
Bottles, cleaning, 263–64
Bottling
    dangers associated with, 246
    process, 246–50, *247*, *248*, *249*
Brewcaps, 165
Brewers' malt, 28
Brewing process, description of, *5*, 6–9

Brewing process steps, 10
    adding hops to boiling wort, 20, *20*,
        21, *21*
    aerating the wort, 24, *24*
    allowing fermentation, 24
    allowing solid particles to settle, 23,
        *23*
    boiling the wort, 20–21, *20*
    decanting bottled beer, 27
    filling bottles for fermentation, 27
    making extract wort, 20, *20*
    preparing ingredients, 19
    preparing yeast, 21, 22
    racking beer into the fermenter, 26
    racking fermented beer into the
        carboy, 25–26, *25*
    sanitizing equipment, *22*, 26
    siphoning beer into bottles, 26
*Brewing Techniques*, 335
Bright beer tanks, 9
British ales, 13, 37, 289–90
British Bitter, 306
British I.P.A. (India Pale Ale), 289, 306–7
Brown Ale, 15, 308–9
Brown ales, 13
Brown malt, 40–41
Brown sugar, 48
Buffers, 54
Burton Union system, 158–59
Buying
    hops, 119–20
    malt, 10, 42


Calcium, 56
Cane sugars (sucrose), 47–48
Cara-crystal/cara-pils malt, 40
Caramelization, 133
Caramel malt, 40
Carbonate, 57–58
Carbonation, 211
    artificial, 225–27
    basics of, 214–17, *216*
    in bottled versus draft beer, 217–18
    chart, **332–33**
    defined, 214
    Kraeusening, 224
    natural, 221–25
    natural versus artificial, 218–20
    over-, 223
    priming, 222–23
    spunding, 224

Carbonators
    in-line, 226
    in-tank, 226–27
Carbon filtration/dechlorination, 60, 61
Carboys, 25–26, *25*, 164
    cleaning of, 261–62
Cartridge filters, 206, *206*
Cask breathers, 232
Cask-conditioned beer, 231–33
Caustic soda/potash, 256–57
Chill haze, 197, 199, 284
Chloride, 51, 58
Chlorination, 58–59
Chlorine dioxide, 258, 259
Chlorine sanitizers, 257–58
Chloroform, 59
Chlorophenols, 59
Chocolate malt, 41
Cistern, 29
Clarification
    finings, 192–93, 198, 202–3, 209–10
    flavor stability and, 200
    haze, 36, 88, 90, 131–33, 134, 196–99
Clarifiers, 201–4, 210–11
Clarity, wort, 100, 110
Classic All-Malt Pilsner, 321
Cleaners, types of, 255–57
Cleaning
    bottles, 263–64
    cold-side, 261–63
    equipment, 259
    equipment selection and issues of,
        253–54
    hot-side, 260–61
    kegs, 264–65
    importance of, 251
    versus sanitary, 253
    *See also* Sanitation/sanitizing
Cohumulone, 115
Cold-side cleaning, 261–63
Cold side of brewing process, 251–52
Cold storage, 8, 160–61
Color specification, 33, 36, 299, 302–3
Color unit (CU), 303
Competitions, 274, 289
Conditioning
    bottle-conditioned beer, 230–31
    cask-conditioned beer, 231–33
    defined, 228
    problems in, 228–30
    rest, 194
Coolant sources, 126–27

Coolers
  cleaning, 262–63
  immersion and counterflow, 125–26, 138–39, *138*
Cooling process, 134, 138–39, *138*
  crash, 161, 193
Copper, 57
Corn adjunct, 46
Corn sugar (glucose/dextrose), 47
Couch, 29
Counterflow coolers, 125–26, 138–39, *138*, 262–63
Counterpressure bottle fillers, 246–50, *247, 248, 249*
Crabtree effect, 169, 170–71, 223
Crash cooling, 161, 193
Crushing malt, 101–3
Crystal malts, 39–40
Cubitainers, 233
Curing, 30, 33, 38–39

**D**ecanting bottled beer, 27
Decoction mashing, 71–72, 98, 107–8
Delta rating, 204
Denaturing, 131–32
Depth filters, 204–5
Dextrinase, 94
Dextrin malt, 40
Dextrose, 47
  converting starch to, 90–93
Diacetyl, 142, 173–74
Diacetyl rest, 190–91
Diastatic power, 33
Diatomaceous earth (D.E.) pressure filters, *206*, 207–8, 213
Dimethyl sulfide (DMS), 37, 134, 178
Dipeptide, 87
Dissociates, 51
Distase, 33, 94
Distillation/demineralization, 60–61
Doppelbock, 326
Dortmunder Export, 323
Double mashing, 46, 70–71, 108–9
Draff, 99
  blockage by, 110
Draft beer equipment, 234–39
Draft systems
  design, 241–43
  how they work, 240–41, 243
  troubleshooting, 243–44
Dry priming, 230
Dry Stout, 17, 312

Dunkel Bock, 325

**E**ndosperm, 30–31, *31*
Enzymes
  breaking down of proteins by, 89–90
  pH and temperature conditions, 95–97
  role of, 6, 30, 31–32, 85
Equipment
  for boiling and cooling wort, 123–27
  for cleaning, 259
  cleaning considerations when selecting, 253–54
  for draft beer, 234–39
  for fermentation and lagering, 162–67
  for filtration, 205–8, *206*, 211–13
  kits, 10
  list of basic, 11, *12*
  for measuring and testing, 81–83
  for wort production, 73–83
  yeast kits, 151, 152
Esters, 142, 175–76
European Brewing Convention (EBC) units, 33
Evaluation of beer
  appearance, 273
  aromas, 270–73
  competitions, 274
  flavor, 270–71, 273–74
  taste testing concepts, 268–70, *268*
Evaporation rate, 135–36
Extract, 32
Extract wort, making, 20, *20*
Extra Special Bitter (E.S.B.), 289, 307

**F**atty acids, 142, 175
Fermentation
  aeration and pitching, 156–57
  by-products, 173–76
  defined, 168–69
  filling bottles for, 27
  open versus closed, 157–59
  primary, 188–89
  secondary, 177, 190
  signs of, 24, 186
  single- versus two-stage, 159–60
  steps, 155–56, 172–73
  temperature, 8, 187–88
Fermenters
  defined, 8
  open versus closed, 157–59

Fermenters *(continued)*
racking beer into, 26
types of setups, 164–65
unitanks, 159–60, *158, 160*
Filters
barrier versus depth, 204–5
cartridge, 206, *206*
diatomaceous earth (D.E.) pressure, *206*, 207–8, 213
plate-and-frame, 207
sheet, 207
Filtration
equipment, 205–8, *206, 212*
process, 9, 198–99, 211–13, *212*
Finings
in bottle-conditioned beer, 230–31
defined, 192–93, 198
effectiveness and types of, 202–3
how to use, 209–10
Flakes, 46–47
Flavor, 270–71, 273–74
Flocculation, 131–32, 176–77, 192
Flocculence, 141
Floor malting, 29–30
Flotation tank, 157, 181, 182
Fluoride, 58
Foaming, 210–11, 247
Foundation water, 109
Fried, Steve, 298
Fusel alcohols, 142, 174–75

Gas break-out, 243–44
Gas hoses, 238–39
Gas tanks, 237
Gelatin, 203
Gelatinization, 45, 95
German ales, 292–93
Germination phase of malting, 29
Gibberellic acid, 30
Globulins, 88
Glucose, 47
converting starch to, 90–93
W. W. Grainger, 259
Graininess, 99, 273–74
Grain malt, 28
Grains for brewing, types of, *7*
Grain sugars, 48
Grant, 77, 79, *79*
Gravity-flow method of filling bottles, 247–49, *248*
Gravity measurements
original versus terminal, 19

taking, 24, *24*, 26, 299, 300–301
Grist, 36, 84
Grist case, 7
Gushing, 284–85

*H*afnia protea, 279, 280
Harshness, 286–87
Haze, 36
causes of, 88, 197, 284
chill, 197, 199, 284
how to deal with, 90, 131–33, 134, 198–99, 201–4, 284
Headspace, 27
in bottle-conditioned beer, 230
Heat exchanger, 8
Heat sources, 81
Hemacytometers, 184
High-kilned malts, 37–38
Homebrew bitterness units (HBUs), 120
Homebrewing, growth of, 1–2
Home kilning, 38–39
Home Wine and Beer Trade Association, 336
Hop(s), *114*
adding to boiling wort, 20, *20*, 21, *21*
breeding of, 113–15
buying, 119–20
defined, 8
extraction of, 129–31
extracts, 45
finishing, 121, 122, 129
forms of, 117–18
high alpha, 114
measuring quantities, 18
noble, 114
rates, 120–21
schedules, 121
specifications, 115–17
storage of, 117, 119–20
utilization, 130–31
varieties of, 113–15, 118–19
Hop strainers, 124–25
Hoses, gas and beer, 238–39
Hot break, 90, 132–33
Hot-side cleaning, 260–61
Hot side of brewing process, 251–52
Hot water tank, 76
Humulone, 115
Hydrogen sulfide, 178
Hydrolysis, 89
Hydrometers, 82–83

Immersion coolers, 125–26, 138–39, *138*
Imperial Stout, 313–14
Infusion mashing, 68–69
   step, 69–70
Ingredient kits, 11
Ingredients, preparation of, 19
International Bitterness Units (IBUs), 120, 301–2
Iodine-based acid sanitizers, 258
Iodine test, 106
Ionization, 51
Ion(s)
   needed for brewing, 56–58
   supplements, 61, 62–63
Iron, 57
Isinglass finings, 202
Isohumulone, 269
Isomerization, 129–31

Jackson, Michael, 12, 289, 291
Jacobsen, Jacob Christian, 140–41

Kegs
   cleaning, 264–65
   description of, 164–65, 167, 234–37, *235, 236*
   drawbacks of, 235
   used for cask-conditioned beer, 232–33
Kettles, 8, 75–76, 123–24
Kiln, 6
Kilning, home, 38–39
Kolsch, 292, 315
Kraeusening, 178, 188, 224

Lactic acid bacteria, 280–81
Lager beers, 294–96
Lagering process, 193, 194–95
Lag period, 170–71, 186–87
Lautering, 47
Lauter tuns. *See* Mash/lauter tuns
Lead, 57
Light Ale, 14, 308
Line, Dave, 312
Logbooks, 83
Lupulone, 115

Magnesium, 56
Maibock (Helles Bock), 324–25
Malt(s)
   buying and storing, 42–43

crystal, 39–40
   high-kilned, 37–38
   measuring, 43
   mills, 74–75, *75*, 102–3
   pale, 28, 36–37
   roasted, 40–41
   rye, 41
   specialty, 39–42
   specifications, 32–36
   wheat, 41
Malt extracts
   buying prepared, 10
   pros and cons of, 43–44
   specifications, 45
   types of, 44–45
Maltiness, 274
Malting process
   description of, 4, 6, 29–30
   modification during, 30–32, *31*
Malto-dextrin, 49
Malto-tetraose, 92
Manganese, 57
Mash
   cold-water, 32–33
   defined, 7
   standard, 32
Mash-in, 84–85, 104–5
Mashing methods
   decoction, 71–72, 98, 107–8
   double, 46, 70–71, 108–9
   infusion, 68–69
   selection of, 97–98
   step, 69–70, 105–6
Mashing process
   clarifying wort, 110
   crushing the malt, 101–3
   maintaining and boosting temperature, 105
   mash-in, 84–85, 104–5
   mash-out, 106
   preparation for sparging, 109–10
   running off wort, 110–11
   sparging, 111–12
   testing for conversion, 106
   water preparation, 103–4
   *See also* Mashing methods
Mash/lauter tuns, 7
   types of, 76–77, *78*
Mash-out, 106
Maturation process, 192–94
Measurements
   alpha acid units (AAUs), 120, 301–2

Measurements *(continued)*
  European Brewing Convention
    (EBC) units, 33
  International Bitterness Units
    (IBUs), 120, 301–2
  Lintner, 33
  Lovibond, 33, 40
  metric conversions, 327–31
  titration, 53
  *See also* Gravity measurements
Measuring
  acidity and alkalinity, 52–53
  bitterness, 301–2
  color, 302–3
  equipment, 81–83
  malt, 43
Melanoidins, 133
Mild Ale, 309
Mild ale malt, 37
Mills, malt, 74–75, *75*, 102–3
Modification, 30–32, *31*
Mouthfeel/body, 40
Munich Dunkel, 322–23
Munich Helles, 322
Munich malt, 38

**N**atural carbonation
  process, 221–25
  versus artificial, 218–20
Nickel, 57
Nitrate, 58
Nitrite, 58
Nitrogen content of grain, 33

**O**at adjunct, 46
Oatmeal Stout, 313
Oktoberfest (Marzen), 324
Old Ale, 310–11
Original gravity, 19
Oxidation, 229–30, 282–83
Oxygen, injection of, 157, 176, 182–83

**P**ale Ale, 13–14
Pale ale malt, 37
Pale malts, 28, 36–37
Papain, 203
Pasteur, Louis, 140
Pasteurization, 205
*Pectinatus*, 281
Peptidases, 89
Peptide bond, 87, 89
Peptones, 88

Peroxyacetic acid, 258–59
pH
  basics of, 51–52
  enzyme activity and, 95–97
  isomerization and wort, 130–31
  mash, 104–5
  measuring, 83
  for proteases and peptidases, 89–90
  for sparge water, 109
Phytase, 85–86
Phytin, 85
Piece, 29
Pilsners, 295
Pitching
  equipment, 156–57
  problems with over- and under-, 185
  process, 183–85
  rates, 176, 184
  re-, 185
Plate-and-frame filters, 207
Polyclar, 203, 211
Polymerization, 132
Polypeptides, 88
Polyphenols, 132
Polyvinyl pyrrolidone (PVP), 203–4, 210,
  211
Porter, 16, 290, 311
Potassium, 57
Priming, 222–23
  dry, 230
Proteases, 89
Protein
  coagulation, 131–33
  content of grain, 33
  -degrading enzymes, 203
  deposits, cleaning of, 261
  rest, 86–89
Proteolysis, 88
Pumps, 80, *80*
Pyruvic acid, 172

**R**acking
  beer into the fermenter, 26
  fermented beer into carboy, 25–26,
    *25*
  process, 189
Recipes, 306–26
  for beginners, 13–18
  guidelines, 18–19, 298–99, 303–4
  parameters for creating, 299–303
Recirculation, 8, 110
Refrigerators, 166–67, *166*

Regulators, 237–38
Rice adjunct, 46
Roast barley, 41
Roasted malts, 40–41, 273
Rousing yeast, 154, 185
Rye adjunct, 46–47
Rye malt, 41

Saint Louis Brewery, 6
Salts, 53–54
Sanitation/sanitizing
    equipment, 22, 26
    importance of, 251
    no-rinse, 265
    principles of, 265–66
    of thermometers/spoons, 21
    versus clean, 253
    wort cooling and, 139
    yeast propagation and, 150, 151, 154
    See also Cleaning
Sanitizers, types of, 257–59
Scales, 81
Scotch Ale, 15–16, 310
Sedelmayr, Gabriel, 140
Sheet filters, 207
Silica gel, 203, 210, 211
Silicate, 58
Siphoning equipment, 167
Six-row brewers' malt, 36
Skunky, 285–86
Sodium, 56–57
Sparging, 8, 99–100, 109–10, 111–12
Specialty malts, 39–42
Spunding, 224
Starch conversion, 90–93
    testing for, 106
Steely, 30, 31
Steeping, 29
Step mashing/step infusion, 69–70,
    105–6
Sterile filtration, 205
Stewing, 39
Storage
    of flakes, 47
    of hops, 117, 119–20
    of malt, 42–43
    of yeast, 152, 184
Stout, 290
Strike temperature, 103
Stripping, 205
Sugar
    converting starch to, 90–93

types of brewing, 47–49
Sulfate, 58
Sweet Stout, 17–18, 312

Tannins, 132, 203–4
Taps, types of, 238, 243
Taste testing
    basic concepts, 268–70, 268
    evaluation steps, 271–74
    flavor, 270–71, 273–74
Temperature
    for decoction mashing, 107
    for double mashing, 108
    enzyme activity and, 95–97
    fermentation, 8, 187–88
    maintaining and boosting, 105
    mash, 104
    metric conversions, 331
    for sparging, 100, 109
    for step mashing, 105
    strike, 103
Terminal gravity, 19, 26
Testing for conversion, 106
Thermometers, 81–82
Thermostats, refrigerator, 166–67
Tin, 57
Titration, 53
Trappist Ale (Double), 317
Trisodium phosphate (TSP), 256, 257
Troubleshooting
    chart of common problems, causes,
        and remedies, 276–78
    See also under type of problem
Trub separation, 137, 171, 181
Two-row brewers' malt, 36–37

Unitanks, 158, 159–60, 160

Vacuum evaporators, 43
Varnish deposits, 261
Vicinal diketones (VDK), 173–74
Vienna malt, 37–38
Vinegar odor/taste, 280
Vorlauf (clarifying wort), 100, 110

Water
    alkalinity, 54–55, 57–58
    analysis of, 59–60
    chlorination, 58–59
    foundation, 109
    hard versus soft, 55–56
    importance of, 50–51

Water *(continued)*
   ions in, needed for brewing, 56–58
   measuring acidity and alkalinity, 52–53
   preparation of, for mashing, 103–4
   preparation of, for sparging, 109–10
Water treatment methods
   acidification, 63
   boiling/decontamination, 60, 62
   carbon filtration/dechlorination, 60, 61
   distillation/demineralization, 60–61
   examples of, 64–67
   ion supplements, 61, 62–63
Weizen, 316
Wheat adjunct, 46–47
Wheat malt, 41
Whirlpool, 8
Wort (sugar solution)
   adding hops to boiling, 20, *20*, 21, *21*
   aerating, 24, *24*, 180–83
   boiling, 20–21, *20*
   checking temperature of, 21
   chiller, 8
   clarity, 100, 110
   defined, 8
   equipment for boiling and cooling, 123–27
   equipment for producing, 73–83
   making extract, 20, *20*
   running off, 110–11, 137
   spoilers, 279–80
   taking gravity measurements, 24, *24*

**Y**east
   addition of, 8
   agar, 151
   autolysis, 159, 177–78, 229
   bite, 197, 228
   characteristics, 141–43
   choosing, 145–46
   dry, 13, 143–44, 148
   feeding, 154
   forms of, 143–45, *143, 144*
   growth and respiration, 171–72
   historical background of, 140–41
   lager versus ale, 141–42
   lag period, 170–71
   maintaining, 151–53, *152*
   pitching, 183–85
   preparing, 21, 22
   propagating, 147–51
   rehydrating dry, 148
   repitching, 153–54
   rousing, 154, 185
   storage of, 152, 184
   wet, 145, 149–51
   wild, 282

**Z**inc, 57
*Zymomonas,* 281
*Zymurgy,* 335